365
VEGETARIAN
SOUPS

365 VEGETARIAN SOUPS

Gregg R. Gillespie

STERLING PUBLISHING CO., INC.
New York

Edited by Jeanette Green
Designed by Rhea Braunstein
Illustrated by Charlene Rendeiro
Indexed by Kathy Garcia

Library of Congress Cataloging-in-Publication Data Available

4 6 8 10 9 7 5 3

Published by Sterling Publishing Co., Inc.
387 Park Avenue South, New York, N.Y. 10016
© 2002 Gregg R. Gillespie
Distributed in Canada by Sterling Publishing
^{c}/o Canadian Manda Group, 165 Dufferin Street,
Toronto, Ontario, Canada M6K 3H6
Distributed in the United Kingdom by GMC Distribution Services,
Castle Place, 166 High Street, Lewes, East Sussex, England BN7 1XU
Distributed in Australia by Capricorn Link (Australia) Pty. Ltd.
P.O. Box 704, Windsor, NSW 2756 Australia
Printed in the United States of America

ISBN-13: 978-0-8069-9398-0
ISBN-10: 0-8069-9398-7

For information about custom editions, special sales, premium and
corporate purchases, please contact Sterling Special Sales
Department at 800-805-5489 or specialsales@sterlingpub.com.

CONTENTS

AUTHOR'S NOTE

When preparing and creating recipes, my first thought is: "There's only one expert preparing food in your kitchen, and that's you!" I must admit, although I've eaten soup all my life, I am a "come-lately" about soup. Or, to put it another way, I've enjoyed soup all my life, but I've never gone out of my way to prepare it. To this I must add: I have learned the delight . . . and it is a delight . . . of eating something that didn't make me feel as though I were ready to burst because I ate too much. There's something special about soup. We rarely over-indulge and leave the table feeling well nourished, sated, and quite satisfied.

I've written many cookbooks and invented many recipes. However, none have made me feel better than the soup recipes in this book. And I'm most proud that all these recipes were created in my own kitchen. I've loved every minute I've spent cooking up these soups, and I've loved every spoonful of the soups I've served at my table. I hope you enjoy them, too. Bon appétit.

—GREGG R. GILLESPIE

A SHORT HISTORY OF SOUP

Well, we really weren't around. However, we can speculate that early humans learned to make soup roughly when they learned to burn a piece of raw meat over an open fire. The first soup might have been something created by accident, but our cave-dwelling, tree-sitting, plain-roaming ancestors eventually discovered that meat alone wasn't the answer to good-tasting soup. They began, we suppose, to add vegetables, plants with long or bulbous roots, and soon, herbs. When meat became scarce, we suppose that early humans began to eat or drink hot soup. Little was discarded in the frugal economies of our forebears. Vegetarian soups seem natural. Why not soften tough plant fibers to create a tea to imbibe healthful herbs or to make soup to warm the body in winter?

Melokhia, a soup made with meat, onions, garlic, melokhia leaves, coriander, and a type of pepper, is the earliest soup recipe I've found. Older versions probably had fewer ingredients.

All great ancient civilizations—Egyptian, Greek, Persian, Roman, Indian, Chinese, Aztec, Inca, and more—have prepared soups. The richness of the broth and whether it contained meat, fowl, or fish usually depended on the wealth of the diner. We do know that in the Middle Ages most European peasants had little or no meat in the diet. Their soups were largely vegetable-based. The landed gentry seem to have enjoyed meatier fare.

Today, the variety of cans, jars, and packages of soup seems endless. However, only five basic types dominate the market: clear, cream, thick, hearty, and dessert. The only real variation is stews, and sometimes the distinction between a soup and a stew is arbitrary. To help you find your favorite soup, we've collected recipes under more familiar categories: Stocks, Basic, Fruit, Cream, Hearty, Chilled, and Dessert and suggested what season you might best enjoy the particular soup.

Vegetarian, or vegetable, soups often contain potatoes, rice, pasta, beans, peas, lentils, dairy products, and flour as well as vegetables and fruits. Potatoes make a hearty, filling soup. Milk, cheese, or eggs added to these ingredients help provide the body with needed protein. Any two of these three provide complete protein: dairy, grains, and legumes (beans, peas, and lentils). The egg is an economical source of complete protein, neatly packed in a shell.

Most nutritionists and physicians insist that soup is good for us. That's because soup broth retains many of the vitamins and minerals we pour down the drain when cooking vegetables and other foods on the stove. It's also because cooking helps break down tough plant fibers and therefore makes it easier to digest soup than its raw counterparts. Also, the body depends on water and water-laden food for easy digestion, regularity, washing out toxins, and nourishment.

Soup can be one of the easiest dishes to prepare. However, even the best cooks can make mistakes when ingredients are sautéed too long or dairy products cause soup to curdle.

The recipes in this book attempt to explain each step to preparing a good, nutritious soup. Most don't require fancy cutting or mixing or expensive kitchen gadgets. We offer this simplicity for everyday cooks, not professional gourmet chefs. You'll be able to create these soups in your home and even, if you're so inclined, outdoors.

THE AMAZING VEGETARIAN SOUPER BOWL

My earliest recollection of soup making is from the 1930s when I was small child playing in my mother's kitchen. I remember one day watching her spend most of the afternoon preparing an evening meal. That giant pea-green, four-legged iron stove dominated the room. Its green surfaces were each painted with darker border decorations. Mom was constantly wiping them to keep them clean. I remember the upper shelf where she kept the wooden matches to light the gas burners and the salt and pepper shakers shaped like little barrels with silver tops. My father had a shaker filled with what he called his special blend—simply powdered garlic, powdered onion, salt, and pepper. I also remember the wooden box under the stove where I kept my toys.

The next day, as I was playing, I noticed that my mother hardly appeared in the kitchen at all. Oh, she came in, picked up the long wooden spoon my father had carved, stirred the soup simmering on the stove, and quickly left.

I didn't stay around long enough to observe the whole soup process. However, what I did see caused me to wonder: if soup is so easy to make, why was it necessary for mother to go to all the trouble I saw yesterday? I wish I had asked. Always remember: soup is one of the easiest meals you can prepare.

Then why aren't more people making soup? Soup can be one of the most nutritious additions to the diet; it's good for body and soul.

Cut an orange or lemon in half and squeeze. The juice contains most of the nutrients; while the pulp, nutritious in its own way, doesn't add as much. As for the zest, you could float it in the juice to draw out the flavor and vitamins. This liquid is similar to what happens when you prepare soup. You leave some of the roughage behind, but you gain most of the nutrients. And soup, like juice, goes down easily.

A well-prepared soup is certainly tastier than a handful of vitamins. If soup is good for you and easy to prepare, why don't more people make soup? Maybe it's because, unlike fast food, it takes too long for the soup to simmer, and soup does not have the texture we've come to expect from food. Although we may allow hours for meat to become tender in a marinade, we don't usually think ahead about making soup.

Perhaps we shy away because soup had once been thought the mainstay of poor folk who could not afford the more delicate foods we've all been conditioned to eat. Somehow, it has seemed to be peasant fare. We remember the European medieval tale of stone soup that began with nothing but a stone in a pot and grew into a hearty-soup feast with the addition of a carrot here, a leek there, some peas, and more, added one by one by town folk.

We've allowed exotic flavors, unusual textures, foreign terms, attractive packaging, and convenience to cause us to forget that the primary importance of food is to nourish the body. Today it seems that many people habitually make poor food choices, always seem hungry, sport greater girth, and have little energy. Refilling a snack bowl does not take care of the body's very real nutritional needs. As scientists discover more and more nutritional deficiencies responsible for not just birth defects but disease, we owe it to ourselves and to our own future health to make better food choices.

Many of us are in the habit of eating badly, eating on the run, or eating packaged foods. We fail to add the needed five to ten vegetables and fruits to our diet daily. And while we ourselves eat deficient diets, we also neglect those of our children. It's the parents' duty to be sure that their child is well fed, not with calorie-laden foods, but with healthful foods that help body and mind develop fully.

Many of us do not take the time to cook properly. Some families now exist on fast-food fried chicken one night, hamburgers the next, and pizza the night after that. Further, high school students now also buy fast food for lunch instead of the old cafeteria fare their parents may remember. Yes, steam-table food may not be exciting, but the old cafeteria lunches were far more nutritious than the soda-pop with fries offerings at schools today.

We've allowed ourselves to fall into the habit of not setting time aside to cook properly. What saves us is the slow cooker, or Crock Pot. That little modern device allows us to fill the pot with delectable ingredients, leave the house for a full work day, and come home to a hot dinner that you ladle into a bowl or plate. Imagine the hearty soups you can enjoy on a winter's eve, and think about the no-sweat cooking in summer.

Not Just Rabbit Food

For a few decades, vegetable soup was thought of as bowls of green stuff—ingredients fit for a rabbit, not a human. These are ideas of the past. Many newer vegetarian ideas have been influenced by Asian traditional cooking and haute cuisine, especially Thai and Chinese. We've moved away from traditional European soups—thick liquids filled with meat and potatoes, maybe a few onions, and a little celery. This is also why many of us have been confused about what constitutes a soup and what qualifies as a stew.

The Mirror of Health

Many people believe that if they eat a diet exclusively of vegetables, they will not get all the nutrients the body needs. Many eaters of meat and fat, however, have rather narrow diets and often fail to receive the nutrients available in vegetables and fruits. Of course, the key to any good diet is balance and a variety of healthful foods. Too often, we limit our diet to the same eight foods we eat over and over through the week.

So look at your whole diet. It's important for vegetarians to establish a habit of eating enough protein and to fill the gap for certain nutrients, like vitamin B12. If you're a strict vegetarian, to get complete protein, with all 16 essential amino acids, you'll need to combine two of these three things in a meal: legumes, grain, and dairy. So, you need to eat legumes with dairy, legumes with grains, or dairy with grains.

Legumes (lentils, beans, broad beans, soybeans, peanuts) alone, while healthful, do not contain all essential amino acids. They're rich in folic acid, potassium, iron, and magnesium and supply good dietary fiber. However, legumes lack the essential amino acids methionine, cystine, and tryptophan.

Most unrefined grains contain iron, phosphorus, magnesium, zinc, B-complex vitamins, folic acid, and vitamin E. Hulling and polishing tends to strip away outer layers of the plant and causes them to lose many of these nutrients. Cereals and grains contain 8% to 15% protein and eight of the essential amino acids. The amino acid lysine is usually lacking and must be found in legumes or dairy products.

Dairy products, such as milk, cheese, or yogurt, provide an excellent source of protein, calcium, phosphorus, and potassium. They also contain the essential fatty acid, linoleic acid. For complete protein, combine dairy products with grains or legumes.

But this is all stuff for books on nutrition, and this is a cookbook. Consult a nutrition almanac or government tables (available from the U.S. Department of Agriculture and other sources) on nutrients.

Whether the soup you prepare will be the entrée or a side dish, it will be a healthful addition to your menu. And in the end, it will please you more than the jumbo drinks from fast-food counters and the all-you-can-eat buffets at fancy resorts.

Meals for the Heart

A diet high in vegetables means we're less likely to be overweight or suffer high blood pressure, heart attacks, and cancer. Most people who live on a diet high in vegetables have also chosen a more healthful lifestyle; generally they don't smoke or drink alcohol in excess. A healthful diet, by the way, helps curb such harmful habits and addictions.

This doesn't mean that you must exclude meat from your daily fare. It's just that we need to make vegetables a larger part of the diet. Eating soups is one of the easiest ways to increase vegetable consumption.

Be sure to rotate your diet and include a variety of healthful foods. Remember those five to ten fruits and vegetables each day.

PREPARING GREAT SOUPS

Begin with Fresh Ingredients

When making soup with healthful ingredients, you need to consider taste. As we all know, taste is an individual matter. You know your own taste, but when making soup for family, friends, or an elegant dinner party, you need to be concerned about delicious results. Besides having a great recipe, here are a few general rules to create the best-tasting soup possible.

The most important rule: always use the freshest ingredients possible. Never settle for second best. Remember, the ingredients will directly affect the final taste of your soup. If you use old and wilted vegetables and herbs, their deterioration has already affected how they taste. With them, you simply cannot achieve the end you desire.

In ingredient lists for recipes, we assume that you prepare all fresh vegetables washed and scrubbed as you normally would for cooking with stems and bitter or tough parts removed. Remove both stems and seeds from peppers. Prepare spinach leaves with stems removed. Trim and remove tops and greens and bottom tips from carrots, turnips, parsnips, beets, radishes, rutabagas, and other root vegetables, unless otherwise specified. Discard outer leaves and remove the core of cauliflower, cabbage, lettuce, and celery. Remove the strings and ends of green beans. Peel onions and garlic. Clean mushrooms thoroughly but delicately, and cut off any tough parts. Peel and remove seeds from winter squash (acorn, buttercup, butternut, hubbard, spaghetti, turban) and pumpkin. Summer squash (crookneck or yellow, pattypan, zucchini) does not have to be peeled unless the recipe specifies. Wash and drain fruit, berries, cherries, and grapes, and remove their leaves, stems, and pits, stones, or seeds. (Of course, fruits like strawberries and kiwi are used with their seeds.) Sort out the bad berries and cherries. Core apples and pears. Remove the rind, seeds, and stringy pulp from melons. Check dried fruits, like prunes or apricots, to be sure that all stems and pits or stones have been removed. All nuts, of course, must be shelled. Canned beans, peas, and lentils are rinsed and drained of liquid, unless otherwise specified. Dried beans, peas, and lentils need to be rinsed, sorted, and soaked overnight. Hint: If you wash and drain dried beans several times, they'll produce less intestinal gas.

Experiment

Why do we prefer one dish to another? Usually, it's a matter of taste or flavor. We rarely choose to eat bland, odorless, and tasteless dishes. Texture and appearance also play a role, but we respond most to smell and taste. Good cooks as well as gourmet chefs blend flavors to please discriminating palates.

When making soup, we can experiment with different flavors. Mix onion and water to make an onion flavor. Simple enough? Add oregano to tomato and water to make a definite flavor of tomato soup. Tomato and water by itself may taste good, but the oregano gives the soup more definition.

While thoughts of chocolate make us smile and vinegar makes us turn the head away, vinegar is used more often in flavoring. Both sugar and honey make things sweet, as do many fruit juices.

Thousands of recipes use wine, liqueur, beer, vanilla extract, or other alcohol-containing ingredients. As long as these ingredients are blended with other foods and cooked, no alcohol will remain. The flavor, however, will remain.

As long as we love the flavor of the finished dish, we don't care whether it's spinach or broccoli, strawberries or watermelon, kale or cabbage.

When using herbs, spices, and seasonings, we need to be aware of those that naturally go together and those that do not. Unfortunately, we cannot simply sprinkle fine-smelling ingredients into a pot at random. For example, basil and curry do not really go together. Instead, it's best to blend basil with parsley or rosemary. Curry goes well with cumin and fenugreek. Store spices in a cool, dry place no longer than 6 months.

The herbs garlic and onion, however, seem to go with almost everything (well, except vampires). Also, sweet and sour things, two flavors that are not complete opposites, do blend well.

If you discover a mixture of flavors you like, keep a tightly sealed jar of the herb, spice, or seasonings mixture on your shelf to have on hand.

It's a great idea to have small pots of fresh herbs growing in your kitchen. My kitchen is a virtual greenhouse; the blend of smells makes it a delightful place to work.

Creating a Pleasing Blend

Flavoring is such an elusive subject that few cookbooks attempt to write about it. Because taste is so individual, no book or series of books can cover the whole subject. Nearly every food can act as a flavoring, depending on your individual taste.

Useful flavoring ingredients for soup include: spices and seasonings, beer, cheese, fruits, fruit juices, herbs, liqueur, meats (all varieties), nuts, salt, vegetables and vegetable juices, vinegar, and wine. This is only a small list of the cornucopia of ingredients that can create fantastic soups.

When a guest tasting soup at my table can tell me what ingredients I used, then I've made a mistake. No matter whether it's called Potato Celery Soup or Thai Peanut Soup, a good cook's objective should be to blend the flavorings in the dish in such a way that the soup's primary ingredients cannot be tasted.

How many vegetables does it take to make vegetable soup? Actually just one. One vegetable, a sprinkling of herbs, and water. With a combination this thin, I doubt that many people would want to eat the soup. That would be little more than boiling a vegetable, draining it off, and eating it. Of course, depending on the vegetable, say broccoli, the resulting liquid could have a lot of flavor.

HINTS

Quick Problem Solving

To heighten the color of a brown soup: Add 1 tablespoon of a commercial gravy booster. For a more delicate color and flavor, add caramelized sugar, and no, it does not make the soup taste sweeter.

To caramelize sugar: Over a very low heat, melt 1 cup sugar, stirring, in a heavy non-iron saucepan. When darkened to a deep color, remove from heat, and cool to room temperature. Add 1 cup boiling water, a little at a time, and blend, stirring constantly, until incorporated. Return to a very low heat, and cook, stirring frequently, until the sugar is completely dissolved.

To color bland-looking soups: Add 1 or 2 drops of food color.

To degrease soup: The simplest way is to remove the soup from the heat, cool to room temperature, and place in the refrigerator. Remove the grease floating on top after it has solidified. Or carefully spoon off the grease floating on top of the warm or hot soup. Then use a paper towel to blot up what cannot be easily removed from the soup.

To dilute soups: Chilled soups are usually served thin. If the soup appears too thick, thin it with cream, milk, soy milk, wine, or broth. If the soup contains tomatoes, a tomato juice or vegetable juice does the job.

For Great Taste

- Most soups will offer more taste and flavor if used one or two days after they are made. Keep the prepared soup refrigerated.
- When using a canned consommé or broth, use vegetable cooking water as a thinning liquid instead of water. Remember that they can add salt to the recipe, so adjust it accordingly.
- Bouillon cubes or powder can be used to strengthen weak soups.
- Always try to cool soups as quickly as possible, uncovered, unless otherwise directed. To speed cooling, place the hot pot of soup in a large pan of cold water.

- When using wine or beer in a soup recipe, reduce the salt at least by half. Add wine to the soup just before serving.
- When using wine in a soup, a little goes a long way. Rarely will more than ¼ cup be needed.
- To give tomato-based soups a more mellow taste, add 1 tablespoon of granulated or light brown sugar.
- To give cream soups more taste, purée any vegetables used in preparation.

VEGGIES' HERB, SEASONING & SPICE COMPLEMENTS

When making a soup from scratch, you might stop to consider what ingredient, herb, seasoning, or spice goes with what. Here are some suggestions. Be sure to use fresh herbs; their flavor will be stronger and give the soup a better taste than herbs past their prime. When using these vegetables, add a little of these herbs, spices, or seasonings:

Asparagus tarragon, lemon, dill
Beets allspice, ginger, orange, lemon, lime
Broccoli dill, tarragon, lemon, orange, lime
Cabbage caraway, tarragon, savory, dill
Carrots ginger, mace, nutmeg, caraway, cinnamon, dill, mint, orange, lemon, lime
Cauliflower caraway, dill mace, nutmeg, tarragon
Eggplant marjoram, sage, oregano, basil, lemon thyme
Green Peas mint, chervil, marjoram, rosemary, garlic, onion, tarragon, butter
Greens *(like spinach, Swiss chard, kale, or watercress)* basil, chives, oregano, dill, tarragon, mace, nutmeg, rosemary, lemon, orange
Potatoes lemon, parsley, chives, dill, basil, thyme
Squash basil, garlic, rosemary, dill, thyme, oregano
String Beans *(haricots verts)* basil, dill, thyme, mint, oregano, savory, tarragon

ABOUT SALT, PEPPER & SEASONINGS

Always taste soups for seasoning just before serving. In most cases, only add salt and pepper to soup preparation during the last few minutes of cooking time. Never add salt to a soup that has to be reduced. Add the salt after the soup has been reduced, and then only after tasting it. If a soup is too salty to taste, add half of a peeled raw potato.

Clarifying Soup

Here's how to clarify broths and other thin basic soups.

1. For each quart of soup, you will need 1 large egg white and 1 crushed eggshell. In a bowl, beat the egg white until it's stiff but not dry.

2. Stir the egg white into the hot soup along with the eggshell and cook over a very low heat, stirring until the mixture begins to foam. Remove from heat, stirring only once; cover and set aside for at least 1 hour.

3. When ready, line a strainer with a fine piece of clean cloth, and place over a clean bowl. Carefully ladle the soup into the strainer, being careful not to disturb any sediment on the bottom of the soup pan.

To clarify most broths or soups without an egg or egg white, simply remove the soup from the heat, set aside for about 30 minutes, and then strain through a strainer lined with a fine cloth.

Ways to Thicken Soup

Here are four ways to thicken soup.

- Blend 1 tablespoon of flour with 2 tablespoons of liquid, such as milk, cold water, or broth, and stir into the hot soup.
- Blend 2 tablespoons rice, mashed potatoes, soy flour, peanut butter, or wheat germ flour with ¼ cup cold water or milk. Stir into the hot soup.
- Potato flakes are a fine thickening agent for most soups. When used, only add 2 or 3 tablespoons at a time, and allow the flakes to thicken the soup before adding any more flakes.
- Many grains, such as barley, rice and oatmeal, naturally thicken when added to a thin soup.

Storing Soup

You can save leftover soup in a zippered freezer-weight plastic bag and store it flat in the freezer. The process is simple: chill the soup in the refrigerator or put the soup in a pot or bowl and put this in a large pot surrounded with ice water or ice cubes until well chilled. Pour the chilled soup into a plastic bag and freeze as desired. As a rule of thumb, soup can be kept in the refrigerator for no more than 4 to 5 days; reheat thoroughly before serving. It will keep in the freezer for up to 6 months. Be sure to write, using a permanent marker, the soup's name and date on the plastic bag before filling it with the chilled soup. You'll be able to have a quick meal straight from the freezer. Simply heat the soup in a microwave or on the stove.

Microwave Caution

Observe caution in cooking plain water or broth in a smooth container in the microwave. If surface tension isn't broken and the container is too smooth, the hot liquid may fly out of the container and burn you. This won't be a problem with a chunky soup, for instance.

GARNISHES

Popular garnishes sprinkled on top of a hot or cold soup are croutons; chopped, hard-cooked eggs; lemon slices; whipped sour cream; grated cheese; sliced nuts; and meatballs. Here are more.

For Hot Clear Soups

sliced or diced avocado
sautéed shreds of lettuce
French-fried onions, rings or crumbled
diced, peeled, and seeded tomatoes
dumplings
Matzo balls
minced fresh herbs, such as chives, dill, mint, or parsley
sliced green olives

For Chilled Clear Soups

sliced or diced avocado
sliced or diced, peeled, and seeded cucumbers
minced fresh herbs, such as chives, dill, mint, or parsley
diced, peeled, and seeded tomatoes
whipped sour cream

For Cream Soups, Hot or Cold

crumbled bacon or bacon bits
herb or cheese croutons
grated cheese
thinly sliced lemons or limes
minced fresh herbs, such as chives, dill, mint, or parsley
chili or curry powder
nutmeg or mace powder
sliced ripe or green olives

For Thick Hearty Soups

crumbled bacon or bacon bits
croutons
grated cheese
sliced pepperoni or other sausage
finely minced olives
finely minced garlic
coarsely crushed cracker crumbs

ACCOMPANIMENTS

Bread & Anything Goes

Some soups can be ladled over bread; others go well with bread sticks or crackers, and still others demand a salad or sandwich to make the meal just right. Some recipes suggest how to serve your soup at your own private table or for a house full of guests.

There's no set list of accompaniments for soup. When preparing soup, any soup, the only standard that exists is yours. If you want nothing more than a plate of shredded carrots next to your soup bowl, that's fine. Here are some suggestions, but remember that they're merely suggestions. There are no hard, fast rules.

The first suggestion is bread—any kind of bread! Focaccia, breadsticks, olive breads, or even biscuits of any and all descriptions. Also try fried vegetable chips, even potato chips. Of course, you can choose from a large variety of dumplings, bread balls, and potatoes. Even stale bread that has been sitting around in the breadbox can be eaten as is, dipped into the soup. Or use the stale bread to soak up the soup in the bottom of the bowl, made into croutons, or prepared as rusks. Find recipes below.

CROUTONS
Yield: about 2 cups

3 to 4 slices stale white or whole wheat bread
1½ tablespoons melted butter or margarine
salt to taste

1. Position the rack in the center of the oven and preheat to 350°F.
2. Using a sharp knife, cut the crust away from the bread, and then cut the bread into small cube shapes. Then put the cubes in a bowl, sprinkle with melted butter and salt to taste.
3. Toss gently, and then spread out in a single layer on a cookie baking sheet, and bake, turning occasionally, for about 7 to 10 minutes, or until the cubes are just beginning to toast. Remove from the oven and serve in a bowl as an accompaniment to soup.

Hint: Fresh bread may be used for the cubed croutons. Place them on a cookie sheet in a 200–250°F. oven for about 5 to 7 minutes.

Crouton Variations
Garlic-Flavored Blend ¼ teaspoon of garlic powder into the butter before sprinkling on the bread cubes.

Onion-Flavored Blend ½ teaspoon of onion powder into the butter before sprinkling on the bread cubes.

Savory-Flavored Blend about 2 tablespoons of dried herbs or mixed herbs with the butter before sprinkling on the bread cubes.

Cheese-Flavored After tossing the cubes, sprinkle lightly with a dried grated Parmesan or Romano cheese.

CHEESE RUSKS

Yield: about 4 to 8 rusks

8 slices French bread, each ½ inch thick
1 cup grated cheddar cheese

1. Position the rack 6 inches from the broiler heat source and preheat.
2. Arrange the slices of bread on a lightly greased cookie or baking sheet, and toast, turning, until lightly browned on both sides. Then sprinkle the cheese over the toasted bread, and put it back under the broiler until the cheese melts and begins to bubble. Remove from the oven, and serve as whole, half, or quarter slices with soup.

Hint: You can create variations by choosing another cheese. If you use goat cheese, do not to allow it to brown. Add flavor by lightly sprinkling an herb on top. Also try Italian or another bread to add another flavor.

A SOUP GLOSSARY

Bisque A cream soup, usually made from puréed seafood or shellfish.

Borscht (or borsch) Originally from Russia or Poland, a soup made with fresh beets. It can be prepared using assorted vegetables and or meat and meat stock. Served hot or cold, usually with a dollop of sour cream. However, to others in Russia and Poland, *borscht* simply means "soup."

Bouillabaisse This seafood stew or chowder from Provence in France is served ladled over thick bread. Ingredients include fish and shellfish, onions, tomatoes, white wine, olive oil, garlic, saffron, and herbs.

Bouillon (or broth) A rich liquid made by simmering meat with vegetables and seasonings in water. For a lighter bouillon, the vegetable matter usually only consists of onion or garlic with a few herbs. Bouillon (or broth) is frequently served as is, as a thin soup, or it can be jelled to create a consommé.

Broth See Bouillon.

Chowder Usually refers to a fish or shellfish soup; also refers to soups made with dairy products and vegetables.

Clear These soups are also called *potage clair*, and are usually simple white consommé or grand marmite.

Consommé A thin broth made by clarifying meat or poultry broth. Varieties may be served hot or cold.

Cream Béchamel sauce, made by pouring boiling milk on white roux (a blend of butter and flour), is added to shellfish, fish, meat, or vegetable(s). Some sauces use thick cream and egg yolks.

Madrilène A thin, clear soup, ruby in color. It's usually a blend of beef or chicken consommé blended with tomatoes.

Gumbo A thick stew or soup with vegetables such as okra, tomatoes, onions, and meats such as chicken, sausage, ham, shrimp, crab, or oysters. Popular in New Orleans, Creole gumbos begin with dark roux. The word *gumbo* is derived from an African word for "okra."

Potage In the 17th century, this meant big dishes of meat or fish boiled with vegetables. This French word for "soup" is often used to refer to a creamed vegetable soup. *Potage clair* is a clear soup or consommé.

Purée While purée is not a soup category, it's important to know that a puréed ingredient can become a vital part of any soup. Usually the puréed ingredient is made from starchy vegetables processed at high speed in a food processor or mashed through a fine sieve. A purée can also apply to fish, some shellfish, or combinations of meats and vegetables. Usually a puréed mixture is very thick and can be added to a stock or broth to heighten flavor or taste. If the puréed ingredient is used as a soup base, then a liquid, such as water, stock, broth, fruit juice, or vegetable juice should be added to obtain the desired thickness.

Stock Stock results from boiling together ingredients such as vegetables, meat, fish, and seasonings; the resulting liquid is then strained through a fine sieve and used as a soup base. For brown stock, meat bones and vegetables are browned in a saucepan before they are boiled in water. Most soup recipes begin with a stock or a reduced stock as a primary ingredient. Remember that the idea of using stock is to flavor soup, not overpower it with the stock's flavor.

There are four types of basic stock: meat, fish, poultry (usually chicken), and vegetable. While stock can be made from vegetables or fruits, these have only recently become classified as stock. Rarely do people serve a stock as a soup. Often people confuse the terms *stock* and *bouillon*, as though they were interchangeable. You would not offer stock to a guest, you would serve bouillon as part of a meal.

Thick The French call these soups *potages liés*. These include cream, purée, and velouté soups.

Velouté This soup is enriched with egg yolks and cream.

Vichyssoise This rich, creamy potato-and-leek soup is usually served chilled with chopped chives.

METRIC EQUIVALENTS

Liquid Measures

1 quart = 4 cups = 960 milliliters = 32 fluid ounces
1 pint = 2 cups = 480 milliliters = 16 fluid ounces
1¾ cups = 420 milliliters = 14 fluid ounces
1½ cups = 360 milliliters = 12 fluid ounces
1¼ cups = 300 milliliters = 10 fluid ounces
1 cup = 240 milliliters = ½ pint = 8 fluid ounces
¾ cup = 180 milliliters = 6 fluid ounces
½ cup = 120 milliliters = 4 fluid ounces
⅓ cup = 80 milliliters = 2.6 fluid ounces
¼ cup = 60 milliliters = 2 fluid ounces
⅛ cup = 30 milliliters = 1 fluid ounce

Tablespoons & Teaspoons

2 tablespoons = ⅛ cup = 30 milliliters = 1 fluid ounce
1 tablespoon = 3 teaspoons = 15 milliliters
1 teaspoon = 5 milliliters
¾ teaspoon = 4 milliliters (3.75 milliliters)
½ teaspoon = 2.5 milliliters
¼ teaspoon = 1.25 milliliters
⅛ teaspoon = 0.5 milliliter = pinch
dash = less than a pinch or ¹⁄₁₆ teaspoon

Weight

2.2 pounds = 1 kilogram
2 pounds = 900 grams or 0.9 kilograms (908 grams)
1½ pounds = 675 grams (681 grams)
1 pound = 16 ounces = 450 grams (454 grams)
8 ounces = ½ pound = 225 grams (227 grams)
4 ounces = ¼ pound = 110 grams (112 grams)
1 ounce = 30 grams (28 grams)
½ ounce = 15 grams (14 grams)

Length

1 inch = 2.54 centimeters

½ inch = 1.25 centimeters

Temperature

To convert Centigrade (Celsius) to Fahrenheit degrees

$(\frac{9}{5} \times C) + 32 = F$

To convert Fahrenheit to Centigrade (Celsius) degrees:

$(F - 32) \times \frac{5}{9} = C$

Degrees Fahrenheit	Degrees Centigrade (Celsius)
32	0 (water freezes)
60	15.6
65	18.3
70	21.1
75	26.7
80	26.7
85	29.4
90	32.2
95	35.0
100	37.8
110	43.3
125	51.7
150	65.6
175	79.4
200	93.3
212	100.0 (water boils)
225	107.2
250	121.1
275	135.0
300	148.9
325	176.7
375	190.6
400	204.4
425	218.3
450	232.2
475	246.1
500	250.0

VEGETABLE STOCKS

Stock can be as simple as boiling one or two vegetables in a little water or as complicated as you want to make it. Like all good things, stock will develop its own attributes with age. Seal it tightly and set it in the coldest part of the refrigerator for a few days before using it. You can put stock in zippered freezer bags and store it in the freezer for up to 3 months.

VEGETABLE STOCK FROM ONE VEGETABLE

If you don't have a soup stock or broth, here's how to make a quick vegetable broth as a substitute. Asparagus, beets, broccoli, cauliflower, carrots, celery, garlic, mushrooms, onions, parsnips, peas, potatoes, tomatoes, and turnips can become a broth. Simply put the chosen vegetable in a saucepan, cover with water (remember the more water, the weaker the stock), bring to a boil, and cook, using the normal cooking time for that vegetable or until fork tender. As a general rule of thumb, the longer you boil a vegetable or combination of vegetables, the stronger the broth. Be very careful not to over boil; if you do, the vegetable can have a bitter taste. Some vegetable stocks work best in combination with other vegetables; and yet a single vegetable broth can be used to heighten soup with the same vegetable.

Asparagus Boil. Use this broth only to make asparagus soup.

Beets First trim away the roots; boil and use. You may find another use for the green leaves.

Broccoli Boil and use with other vegetables.

Carrots Trim off the leaves; boil and use the carrot. Both outer peelings and inner carrot are great in soup and add sweetness.

Cauliflower Boil and use with other vegetables.

Celery Use the stalk and leaves; boil. For a sweet soup, you can also chop and boil the heel.

Garlic Boil and use. For a smooth, mellow taste, press the garlic meat into the broth.

Mushrooms Use whole mushrooms. First sauté in butter; then boil gently.

Onions Boil and use.

Parsnips Boil and use sparingly.

Peas Boil and use.

Potatoes Boil and use. Potato broth is excellent for body and texture but adds little flavor.

Tomatoes Boil and use. Tomato broth adds a little flavor, but be aware of its acidity.

Turnips Boil and use. Turnip broth adds a sweet flavor to soups.

BASIC
VEGETABLE
STOCK
Year-Round
Yield: about 4½
pints

3 medium yellow onions, chopped
5 medium carrots, trimmed, peeled, and chopped
3 medium leeks, trimmed and sliced
3 medium stalks celery, sliced
1 medium head lettuce, sliced
3 tablespoons chopped fresh parsley
2 teaspoons crushed dried French thyme
1 bay leaf, crushed
cold water to cover
salt and pepper to taste

1. In a large saucepan, combine the onions, carrots, leeks, celery, lettuce, parsley, thyme, bay leaf, and add enough water to cover by 1 inch. Place over medium heat, cover, and bring to a slow boil. Reduce to a simmer, and cook, skimming any scum that may accumulate, for about 40 minutes.
2. Remove from heat, cool slightly, strain through a fine sieve, and discard the vegetable matter. Place in a container, and refrigerate or freeze until ready to use.

Hint: Be careful not to push any of the vegetable matter through the sieve. This might cloud the stock.

HEARTY
VEGETABLE
STOCK
Year-Round
Yield: about 4 to 6
servings

5 quarts water
2 large yellow onions, quartered
4 medium cloves garlic, peeled
4 celery stalks, sliced thick
4 large carrots, trimmed, peeled, and sliced
2 large potatoes, peeled and diced
2 leeks, white parts only, chopped
several large sprigs fresh parsley
10 whole peppercorns
4 tablespoons soy sauce

1. In a soup kettle or Dutch oven, combine the water, onion, garlic, celery, carrots, potatoes, leeks, parsley, peppercorns, and soy sauce. Bring to a boil, then reduce to a simmer, cover tightly, and simmer over a low heat for about 2 hours.
2. Strain through a fine sieve, discarding the vegetable matter, and use the stock as desired.

Hint: Prepare this stock, let it cool, and pour it into zippered freezer bags and freeze. It will keep for about 3 to 4 months in the freezer, and you'll have it on hand when you need it.

AROMATIC STOCK WITH VEGETABLES

Year-Round
Yield: about 4 to 5 servings

3 cups vegetable stock
½ cup chopped fresh cilantro or parsley
1 serrano or jalapeño chili, stemmed, seeded, and chopped
½ teaspoon grated lime zest
lime juice to taste
1 stalk lemongrass, cut into 2-inch strips
4 cups cubed crookneck squash
3 ounces fresh snow peas, trimmed and cut into 2-inch strips
1 medium carrot, peeled and chopped
4 medium radishes, trimmed, sliced, and halved
salt and pepper to taste
2 tablespoons whole cilantro leaves for garnish
2 tablespoons chopped lemon chives for garnish

1. In the container of a blender or food processor, combine 1 cup stock, cilantro, chilies, and lime zest. Process on HIGH until smooth.
2. In a soup kettle or Dutch oven, combine the mixture from the blender, lemongrass, and remaining stock. Bring to a boil, then reduce to a simmer, cover lightly, and cook for about 15 minutes.
3. Remove from heat, strain through a fine sieve, returning the liquid to the pot and discarding the vegetable matter. Add the squash and lime juice. Return to a boil, then reduce to a simmer, cover lightly, and cook for about 10 minutes. Add the peas and carrot. Return to a boil, reduce to a slow boil, and add the radishes. Cook for 2 to 3 minutes.
4. Remove from heat; adjust the salt and pepper to taste. Garnish as desired and serve immediately if you're not saving it as a stock.

Hint: You may serve this thin soup by itself. Or strain it and use it as a stock in recipes for soups without a definite aroma.

6½ quarts water

2 cups white wine or unsweetened apple juice

6 celery stalks, sliced thick

6 large carrots, peeled and chopped

2 large potatoes, peeled and diced

3 medium zucchini, sliced thick

2 large yellow onions, chopped

1 leek (white part), thickly sliced

6 medium cloves garlic, peeled and crushed

½ pound mushrooms, trimmed

large fresh sprigs parsley

large sprigs fresh thyme

2 bay leaves

LIGHT VEGETABLE STOCK

Year-Round

Yield: about 6 to 8 servings

1. In a soup kettle or Dutch oven, combine the water, wine, celery, carrots, potatoes, zucchini, onions, leek, garlic, mushrooms, parsley, thyme, and bay leaves. Bring to a boil, then reduce to a simmer, cover lightly, and cook for about 2 hours, or until the potatoes are very soft.

2. Turn off the heat, strain through a fine sieve, discarding all the vegetable matter. Adjust the seasoning to taste.

Hint: This stock is great for a soup that only has one or two vegetables. If there are many vegetables, use another stock.

WINTER VEGETABLE STOCK

Winter

Yield: about 4 servings

2 tablespoons margarine
1 large yellow onion, diced
1 cup leek greens, roughly chopped
2 medium carrots, peeled and diced
4 stalks celery with leaves, diced
1 cup cubed winter squash
1 cup chard stems, cut into 1-inch lengths
1 medium potato, peeled and diced
½ celery root, diced
¼ cup rinsed lentils
1 teaspoon crushed dried thyme
2 bay leaves
10 parsley sprigs, roughly chopped
4 medium gloves garlic, peeled and chopped
2 teaspoons nutritional yeast (optional)
8½ cups cold water

1. Heat the margarine in a soup kettle or Dutch oven and combine the onion, leeks, carrots, celery, squash, chard stems, potatoes, celery root, lentils, thyme, bay leaves, parsley, garlic, yeast, and ½ cup water. Bring to a boil. Then reduce to a simmer, cover tightly, and simmer for about 15 minutes. Add the remaining water, bring to a boil. Reduce to a simmer, cover lightly, and continue to cook for about 30 minutes.
2. In the container of a blender or food processor, purée the mixture in batches, until smooth. Strain through a sieve, pressing out the liquid using the back of a spoon. Adjust the salt and pepper to taste, and use as desired.

Hint: This soup takes advantage of end-of-season garden vegetables. It makes a great stock. Prepare it, cool, and pour into zipper freezer bags. Freeze and use in the cold winter months.

12 cups potato skins, chopped
12 cups water
14 medium cloves garlic, peeled and crushed
2 medium yellow onions, sliced
1 stalk celery, sliced
3 sprigs parsley or cilantro
1 bay leaf

1. In a soup kettle or Dutch oven, combine the potato peel, water, garlic, onions, celery, parsley, and bay leaf. Bring to a boil, cover lightly, and cook, stirring frequently, and skimming scum as it accumulates, for about 60 minutes.
2. Turn off the heat, and in the container of a blender or food processor, purée the mixture in batches until smooth. Then strain the mixture through a fine sieve, pressing with the back of a spoon to remove all liquid. Discard the vegetable matter.
3. Cover tightly and refrigerate or freeze until needed.

Hint: Most people throw away potato skins or peels. Here's how you can make use of a healthful nutrient.

¼ cup extra virgin olive oil
2 large cloves garlic, peeled and chopped
4 cups hot water
⅔ cup stale bread crumbs, toasted
2 large eggs, beaten
salt and pepper to taste

1. Heat the oil in a saucepan, and sauté the garlic until tender and lightly colored. Then discard the garlic.
2. Turn off the heat, and pouring in a narrow stream, stirring constantly, add the water to the oil, and return to the heat. Stir in the bread crumbs, bring to a boil, and remove from heat.
3. Using a wire whisk, beat the eggs into the hot mixture, one at a time, until incorporated. Adjust the salt and pepper to taste, and ladle into heated bowls. Serve immediately with a crusty bread or roll on the side. Or save this stock to be the base of another soup.

DASHI

Year-Round

Yield: about 6 servings

This good, thin stock is used in many Japanese soups. Enjoy it as a simple soup or as a base for many soup creations.

5 cups water
3 square inches kombu seaweed
½ cup katsuobushi
¼ teaspoon gourmet powders

1. In a soup kettle or Dutch oven, bring water to a boil, add the kombu and katsuobushi. Remove from heat, and set aside for 10 minutes.
2. Strain through a fine sieve, discarding the ingredients, and use as desired.

Hint: The kombu seaweed and katsuobushi (dried, flaked tuna) can be found in Asian grocery stores. Choose from gourmet powders at your grocer's or specialty food store.

JAPANESE STOCK

Year-Round

Yield: about 6 cups

2 tablespoons extra virgin olive oil
4 medium white onions, sliced
9 medium cloves garlic, peeled and chopped
3 medium carrots, peeled and chopped
2 sprigs fresh thyme
¼ teaspoon ground cumin
4 teaspoons tamari sauce
6 cups water

1. Heat the oil in a saucepan or soup kettle, and sauté the onion and garlic until translucent. Add the carrots, thyme, cumin, tamari sauce, and water. Bring to a boil, then reduce to a simmer, cover tightly, and cook for about 30 minutes.
2. Remove from heat, and use a blender or food processor to purée the mixture in batches until smooth. Strain through a very fine sieve into the saucepan, discarding the vegetable matter, and use as desired.

Hint: Make this stock ahead of time and keep it in the freezer until needed.

BASIC SOUPS

To me, a basic soup is easy to make, has few ingredients, and by adding other ingredients, it can be made into an entirely different soup. Soup stock, like those on pages 21–28, may also be considered basic soups that can serve as the beginning of a soup with many layers of flavor.

ACORN SQUASH & APPLE SOUP

Autumn

Yield: about 4 to 6 servings

2 pounds acorn squash, peeled and chopped
3 cups vegetable stock
2 cups finely chopped apples
1 medium yellow onion, chopped
1 cup unsweetened apple juice
3-inch piece fresh ginger root, peeled and grated
1 tablespoon fresh lemon or lime juice
salt and pepper to taste
1 cup unflavored low-fat yogurt

1. In a soup kettle or Dutch oven, combine ¼ cup vegetable stock, apples, and onion. Cover and simmer for about 10 minutes.

2. Add the squash, remaining vegetable stock, apple juice, ginger, and salt and pepper to taste. Bring to a boil, then reduce to a simmer, cover, and cook for about 20 minutes.

3. Remove from heat, and blend in a food processor or blender until quite smooth. Strain through a sieve into a clean saucepan and press all liquid from the purée. Reheat, add lemon juice, and readjust the salt and pepper to taste. Serve immediately with sour cream, yogurt, and chives on the side.

Hint: If ginger root is soft to the touch, get rid of it. Although acorn squash is called a winter squash, we can find it year-round. It has a thick skin, doesn't have to be refrigerated, and is a good source of iron, riboflavin, and vitamins A and C.

ASPARAGUS POTATO SOUP

Autumn

Yield: about 6 servings

1 pound fresh asparagus, cut into 1-inch lengths
1 large baking potato, peeled and cubed
1 medium yellow onion, cut in wedges
3½ cups vegetable stock
¼ teaspoon ground cinnamon
⅛ teaspoon ground nutmeg
salt and pepper to taste
6 tablespoons grated fresh Parmesan cheese for garnish

1. In a soup kettle or Dutch oven, combine the asparagus, potato, onion, stock, cinnamon, and nutmeg. Bring to a boil. Then reduce to a simmer, cover lightly, and cook for about 30 minutes, or until the vegetables are tender. Remove from heat and cool slightly.

2. In the container of a blender or food processor, purée the soup in batches, and then return it to the pot. Return to boil, remove from heat, adjust the salt and pepper to taste. Serve immediately. Garnish with Parmesan cheese.

2 tablespoons margarine
¼ cup chopped onion
8 cups water
½ cup chopped celery
2 tablespoons minced parsley
1 cup diced parsnips
¼ cup quick-cooking barley
1 cup cubed carrot
28-ounce can diced tomatoes
1 cup frozen peas, thawed
salt and pepper to taste

**BARLEY &
VEGETABLE
SOUP**

Autumn
Yield: about 6
servings

1. Melt the margarine in a soup kettle or Dutch oven, and sauté the onions until tender. Add the water, celery, parsley, and parsnips. Bring to a boil, then reduce to a simmer, cover tightly, and cook for about 30 minutes.
2. Add the barley, carrot, tomatoes, and peas. Cook for about 30 minutes or until the barley is tender and the peas are soft. Remove from heat, adjust the salt and pepper to taste, and serve immediately.

¼ pound dried white beans, sorted, rinsed, and soaked in water overnight
5 cups vegetable stock
2 tablespoons olive oil
2 tablespoons minced garlic
1 small white onion, minced
2 cups chopped escarole
salt and pepper to taste

1. In a soup kettle or Dutch oven, combine the bean and stock. Bring to a boil, then reduce to a simmer, cover lightly, and cook for about 30 minutes, or until the beans are tender.
2. Meanwhile, heat the oil in a saucepan, and sauté the garlic and onion until the onions are translucent. Add the escarole, and continue to cook, stirring frequently, for about 10 minutes, or until the escarole is well wilted. Add to the beans, recover, and continue to cook for about 20 minutes.
3. Turn off the heat, and adjust the salt and pepper to taste. Serve immediately.

Hint: The secret of making this soup is to see that the escarole does not become mushy. After adding it, always watch carefully, and pull it off the heat just before it becomes wilted.

BUDDHIST SOUP

Autumn

Yield: about 12 to 16 servings

½ cup unsalted raw peanuts

⅓ cup dried mung beans

½ ounce cellophane noodles

8 cups water

1 medium (1 pound) pumpkin or winter squash, peeled and cubed

1 medium sweet potato, peeled and cubed

3 tablespoons canola or saffron oil

1 small square bean curd

8 cups coconut milk

1. Place the peanuts in a bowl, cover with water and set aside. In a second bowl, combine the mung beans with water and set aside. In a third bowl, cover the noodles with water and set aside.
2. In a saucepan or soup kettle, bring the water to a boil and drop in the pumpkin, potato, peanuts, and beans. Return to a boil, reduce to slow boil, and cook for about 30 to 35 minutes, or until the mung beans are soft.
3. Meanwhile, heat the oil in a skillet, and sauté the bean curd, turning, until lightly browned on both sides. Remove from heat, and slice into ¼-inch pieces, and set aside.
4. Add the coconut milk to the soup, return to a boil, add the noodles and bean curd. Remove from heat and serve in heated bowls, with fresh cooked jasmine rice on the side.

The purity of the Buddhist monk's way of life is reflected in this recipe.

CALABRIAN ASPARAGUS SOUP

Summer

Yield: about 6 servings

2 tablespoons virgin olive oil

2 medium cloves garlic, peeled and minced

2 pounds fresh asparagus, cut into 1-inch pieces

4 cups vegetable stock

4 large eggs, beaten

½ cup freshly grated Romano or Parmesan cheese

6 slices Italian bread, toasted for serving

1. Heat the oil in a soup kettle or Dutch oven, and sauté the garlic until a golden color. Add the asparagus, and cook, stirring constantly, until tender. Add the stock, and bring to a boil. Reduce to a simmer and cook for about 15 minutes.
2. Meanwhile in a bowl, beat the egg foamy, and then beat in ½ cup of cheese. Beating constantly and adding a few spoonfuls at a time, add about 2 cups of the hot liquid.
3. Stir the egg mixture into the soup, stirring constantly. Continue to cook, stirring frequently, until liquid is just thickened. Remove from heat.
4. In each serving bowl, place one slice of bread and ladle the soup over the top. Serve immediately.

Calabria is a region in northern Italy renowned for culinary achievements.

1 large potato, peeled and diced
2 cups vegetable stock
1 large yellow onion, diced
¼ cup diced celery
¼ cup diced carrots
½ cup light cream
1 cup unsweetened apple juice
hot pepper sauce to taste
1 cup grated sharp cheddar cheese
2 tablespoons chopped parsley (optional)
salt and pepper to taste.

CANADIAN-STYLE CHEDDAR CHEESE SOUP

Autumn
Yield: about 4 to 6 servings

1. In a soup kettle or Dutch oven, combine the potato, stock, onion, celery, and carrot. Bring to a boil, then reduce to a simmer, cover lightly, and simmer until the potatoes are tender. Stir in the cream, apple juice, pepper sauce, and cheese, stirring only until the cheese has melted.
2. Remove from heat, stir in the parsley, and adjust the salt and pepper to taste. Serve immediately.

1 tablespoon butter or margarine
1 medium yellow onion, chopped
1 medium clove garlic, peeled and chopped
3 cups chopped carrots
½ cup shredded carrots
3¾ cups vegetable stock
⅛ teaspoon fresh grated nutmeg
1 tablespoon minced fresh coriander
½ cup soy milk or light cream
salt and pepper to taste

CARROT & CORIANDER SOUP

Spring
Yield: about 4 to 6 servings

1. Melt the butter in a saucepan, and sauté the onion and garlic together until the onion is translucent. Add the chopped carrots, stock, and nutmeg. Bring to a boil, then reduce to a simmer, cover and cook until the carrots are very tender.
2. Remove from heat, cool slightly, and purée in batches, using a blender or food processor. Return to the saucepan, and add the shredded carrots, coriander, and soy milk. Adjust the salt and pepper to taste, and garnish with creamed coriander.

Hint: Use fresh coriander for the best flavor.

Creamed Coriander
⅔ cup unflavored yogurt
2 tablespoons minced coriander

In a bowl, using a wire whisk, whip the yogurt and coriander together until smooth.

CARROT & GINGER SOUP

Spring
Yield: about 4 servings

1 tablespoon margarine
1 medium yellow onion, chopped
1½ pounds carrots, trimmed, peeled, and sliced thin
1 teaspoon freshly grated ginger
4½ cups unsweetened apple juice
2 cups chopped Granny Smith apples
3 tablespoons sherry or white wine
black pepper to taste

1. Melt the margarine in a soup kettle or Dutch oven, and sauté the onion until tender. Add the carrots and ginger, cover lightly, and cook over a very low heat for about 10 minutes.
2. Add the apple juice and apples, bring to a boil, then reduce to a simmer, cover lightly, and cook, stirring occasionally, until the carrots are tender.
3. In the container of a blender or food processor, purée the soup in batches until smooth. Return it to the pot, add the sherry, heat through, and adjust the salt and pepper to taste. Serve immediately.

This soup combines the snap of ginger, sweet flavor of fresh carrots, and the delight of apples.

CARROT THYME SOUP

Summer
Yield: about 6 servings

3 tablespoons margarine
½ cup heavy cream
1½ tablespoons freshly minced lemon thyme
1 medium white onion, minced
nutmeg to taste
6 cups vegetable stock or water
1½ pounds baby carrots, quartered
salt and pepper to taste

1. Melt margarine in a skillet and combine the cream, lemon thyme, and onion. Sauté over low heat until the onions are tender. Add nutmeg to taste and set aside.
2. In a soup kettle or Dutch oven, combine the stock and the carrots. Bring to a boil, then reduce to a simmer, cover lightly. Cook for about 15 minutes or until the carrots are tender.
3. In a blender or food processor, purée in batches the hot carrots and stock until smooth. Return to the pot.
4. Add the onion mixture. Bring to a boil, then reduce to a simmer, and cook for about 5 minutes. Remove from heat, adjust the salt and pepper to taste, cover lightly, and set aside for about 10 minutes.
5. When ready, serve immediately with a fresh loaf of crusty bread on the side.

2 tablespoons butter or margarine
2 small (7-ounce) heads of celeriac (celery root)
2½ cups diced potatoes
1 small clove garlic, peeled and minced
2 cups vegetable stock
1 tablespoon fresh lemon juice
1 cup milk
salt and pepper to taste

1. Melt the butter in a saucepan or soup kettle, and sauté the celeriac, potatoes, and garlic, stirring frequently, until heated through. Add the stock and lemon juice, and bring to a boil. Then reduce to a simmer, cover, and cook for about 40 minutes, or until the celeriac is very tender.
2. Remove from heat and add the milk. In a blender or food processor, purée the vegetables in batches until smooth. Return to the pan, adjust the salt and pepper to taste, and serve hot or cold as desired.

4-ounce can chanterelles, drained
1 small leek, trimmed and cut into rings
2¼ cups water or vegetable stock
¾ cup dry white wine
2 tablespoons snipped fresh parsley
5 juniper berries, crushed
1½ tablespoons all-purpose flour
½ cup milk
½ cup plus 1 tablespoon light cream or evaporated milk
salt and pepper to taste
2 tablespoons white port wine or dry sherry
chopped parsley for garnish

1. Measure the drained liquid from the mushrooms, and add enough water to make ¼ cup.
2. In a saucepan, combine the mushroom liquid and water. Bring to a boil, add the leeks, dry white wine, parsley, and juniper berries. Reduce to a simmer, cover lightly, and cook, stirring occasionally, for about 15 minutes. Blend the flour with ½ cup milk.
3. Add the chanterelles and continue to simmer for about 5 minutes. Then add the flour blend and cream. Cook, stirring frequently, for about 5 minutes or until thickened. Remove from heat, adjust the salt and pepper to taste, stir in the white port wine, and ladle into warm soup bowls. Sprinkle with garnish and serve as desired.

Hint: Chanterelle mushrooms usually require longer cooking time than most mushrooms. Chanterelle mushrooms smell like apricots while cooking. This soup has a peppery taste.

CHEDDAR CHEESE SOUP

Autumn

Yield: about 4 servings

5 tablespoons margarine, at room temperature
4 tablespoons all-purpose flour
4 cups vegetable stock or unsweetened apple juice
2 medium carrots, peeled and diced
4 green onions, diced
½ cup grated cheddar or colby cheese
2 snipped sprigs fresh parsley
hot pepper sauce to taste
salt and pepper to taste
imitation bacon bits for garnish

1. In cup, blend 2 tablespoons of margarine and the flour. Set aside.
2. Melt the remaining margarine in a soup kettle or Dutch oven, and sauté the carrots and onions together until the onions are tender. Add the stock and bring to a boil. Then reduce to a simmer, and stir in the flour mixture, stirring constantly, until incorporated.
3. Stir in the cheddar cheese, parsley, and pepper sauce to taste. Continue to cook, stirring constantly, until the cheese has melted. Adjust the salt and pepper to taste, and serve immediately, alone or as part of a menu, with bacon bits on the side as garnish.

CHEESE BROCCOLI SOUP

Spring

Yield: about 14 to 18 servings

2 tablespoons margarine
1 medium clove garlic, peeled and mashed
2 small white onions, chopped
½ cup chopped celery
1 quart vegetable stock
1½ quarts prepared cheese sauce
½ teaspoon white pepper
2½ cups cooked chopped broccoli florets

1. Melt the margarine in soup kettle or Dutch oven, and sauté garlic, onions, and celery until the onion is tender.
2. Add stock and bring to a boil. Then reduce to a simmer, and stir in the cheese sauce and white pepper.
3. Add broccoli and mix well. Remove from heat, adjust the salt and pepper to taste, and serve immediately.

Hint: Adding the broccoli at the last minute means you'll get just a hint of its flavor.

2 large carrots, peeled and diced

2 parsnips, peeled and finely chopped

1 small white onion, finely chopped

1 medium clove garlic, peeled and finely chopped

2 to 3 scallions, finely chopped

3 celery stalks, finely chopped

4 tablespoons margarine

2 pounds fresh chestnuts, peeled and diced

5 cups vegetable stock or unsweetened apple juice

½ teaspoon crushed bay leaf

½ teaspoon lemon thyme

½ teaspoon parsley

¼ cup amaretto

1 cup heavy cream

cayenne pepper to taste

ground nutmeg to taste

salt and pepper to taste

1. Melt the margarine in a soup kettle or Dutch oven, and sauté the carrots, parsnips, onion, garlic, scallions, and celery until tender, but not browned. Add the chestnuts, stock, bay leaf, lemon thyme, and parsley. Bring to a boil, then reduce to a simmer, and cook for about 40 minutes, or until the chestnuts are tender.

2. In a blender or food processor, purée the soup in batches until smooth, and then return to the pot.

3. Stir in the amaretto, ⅔ cup of the cream, cayenne pepper, and nutmeg. Heat through. (Do not allow it to boil.)

4. Turn off the heat; adjust the salt and pepper to taste. To serve, ladle the hot soup into warmed bowls with a little of the remaining cream on top. Using a spoon or fork, lightly swirl the cream through the soup. Serve immediately.

How to Peel a Chestnut

1. Put the chestnut, flat side up, on a flat surface, and using the point of a very sharp knife, cut an "X" across the chestnut's skin.

2. Put the chestnuts in a saucepan, cover with cold water, bring to a boil. Cover and cook for about 2 to 3 minutes.

3. Remove from heat; do not drain.

4. Using a slotted spoon, remove the chestnuts from the hot water, one at a time, and peel off the hard outer shell and the brown inner skin.

Hint: Be sure to keep the chestnuts in the hot water until you are ready to work with them. If the outer skin does not come off easily, return the chestnuts to hot water for a second. If the "X" cut made in the chestnuts is not deep enough, the skin will not come off easily.

CHESTNUT SOUP

Autumn

Yield: about 6 servings

2 teaspoons canola oil
½ white onion, chopped
4 baby carrots, diced
1 stalk celery, diced
4 cups vegetable stock or unsweetened apple juice
1 teaspoon granulated sugar
¼ teaspoon crushed dried basil
⅛ teaspoon crushed dried tarragon
½ pound chestnuts, peeled and diced
½ cup evaporated milk
¾ cup Marsala wine
salt and pepper to taste

1. Heat the oil in a soup kettle or Dutch oven, and sauté the onion, carrot, and celery until tender, but not browned. Add the stock, sugar, basil, tarragon, and chestnuts. Bring to a boil, reduce to a simmer and cook, stirring occasionally, until the chestnuts are tender.
2. In a blender or food processor, purée the soup in batches until smooth, and then return it to the pot.
3. Stir in the milk and bring to a boil. Remove from heat, stir in the Marsala, and adjust the salt and pepper to taste. Serve hot or cold as desired.

Hint: In the Chesapeake Valley of the eastern United States, chestnuts were once used in many recipes.

COLD SPRINGS' COCKTAIL SOUP

Autumn

Yield: about 4 to 6 servings

2½ cups unsweetened apple juice
3 large stalks fresh rhubarb, shaved and chopped
2 to 3 tablespoons packed light brown sugar

1. Pour the apple juice into a saucepan, and bring to a boil. Add the rhubarb, reduce to a simmer, cover, and cook until the rhubarb is very tender. Remove from heat, and purée in a blender or food processor.
2. Strain through a fine sieve, back into the saucepan. Return to heat, add the sugar, and cook, stirring constantly, until dissolved. Remove from heat and serve with a sweet cracker on the side.

Hint: Rhubarb grows abundantly in Cold Springs, a small valley 20 miles north of Reno, Nevada.

two 3.5-ounce packages dried shiitake mushrooms
2 cups boiling water
10 cups water
¼ cup tamari sauce
¼ cup sherry or white port wine
1 tablespoon grated fresh ginger root
3 small cloves garlic, peeled and crushed
1 medium white onion, cut into wedges
1 bunch fresh green onions, cut into 1-inch pieces
3 stalks celery, sliced
2 cups sliced Chinese cabbage
½ pound soba noodles
salt and pepper to taste

CHINESE VEGETABLE SOUP

Summer
Yield: about 4 servings

1. In a bowl, pour 2 cups boiling water over the mushrooms, and set aside for about 15 minutes.
2. In a soup kettle or Dutch oven, combine the 10 cups water, tamari sauce, sherry, ginger, and garlic. Bring to a boil, then reduce to a simmer, and add the onion wedges.
3. Strain the mushrooms through a fine sieve, pressing to squeeze out excess water. Then, to the strained water, add enough water to make 1½ cups. Mince the mushroom pulp and add to the hot stock along with the reserved liquid.
4. Bring the soup to a boil, and add the green onions, celery, and cabbage. Return to a boil, then reduce to a simmer, and cover lightly. Continue to cook for about 10 minutes. Add the noodles, and continue to cook, stirring occasionally, for about 10 minutes, until the noodles are al dente.
5. Turn off the heat, and adjust the salt and pepper to taste. Serve immediately.

CLEAR BEET SOUP

Year-Round

Yield: about 4 servings

1 pound fresh beets
boiling water sufficient for processing
1 vegetable stock cube
1 tablespoon fresh lemon juice
¼ cup dry sherry
salt and pepper to taste
¼ cup sour cream or unflavored yogurt for garnish
chopped fresh chives for garnish

1. Trim and pare the beets. Then, finely grate them, reserving half for garnish.
2. In a soup kettle, combine half the grated beets and enough water to just cover. Bring to a boil. Then reduce to a simmer, cover tightly, and simmer for about 1 hour.
3. Strain the mixture through a sieve and reserve the liquid. Discard the beets. Add enough water to the reserved beet liquid to make up 2⅔ cups. Return to the soup kettle.
4. Add the stock cube, return to boil, and cook stirring until the cubes are dissolved. Reduce to a simmer, add the lemon juice, sherry, and remaining beets, and cook for about 5 minutes.
5. Turn off the heat. Adjust the salt and pepper to taste, and ladle into warmed soup bowls. Serve immediately, alone or as part of a menu with a garnish of sour cream, chives, and bread on the side.

CLEAR JAPANESE-STYLE SOUP

Summer

Yield: about 6 servings

1½ quarts fresh vegetable stock
⅓ cup dry sherry
4½ teaspoons soy sauce
1 lemon, sliced thin
6 fresh mushrooms, sliced for garnish
2 green onions with tops, sliced diagonally for garnish
1 medium carrot, peeled and sliced paper-thin for garnish

1. Strain the vegetable stock through cheesecloth. In a soup kettle or Dutch oven, bring the stock to a boil. Reduce to a simmer, and then add the sherry and soy sauce. Cover lightly and continue to cook, without disturbing, for about 3 minutes.
2. Ladle into deep bowls, float a lemon slice on each bowl of soup, and arrange the mushrooms, onions, and carrots in a decorative manner around the bowl. Serve immediately.

Hint: This soup can also be used as a stock for many other types of soup.

CLEAR
MUSHROOM
SOUP

Year-Round
**Yield: about 6
servings**

2 tablespoons margarine
1 cup carrots, peeled and thinly sliced
1 cup sliced yellow onions
1 cup sliced leeks
½ cup sliced celery
1 teaspoon fresh thyme leaves
2 pounds white mushrooms, trimmed and sliced
6 cups vegetable stock
½ teaspoon minced chives
salt and pepper to taste

1. Melt the margarine in a soup kettle or Dutch oven, and sauté the carrots, onions, leeks, and celery together until tender. Add the thyme and mushrooms and cook for about 5 minutes until the mushrooms are soft. Stir in the stock, cover lightly, and simmer for about 30 minutes.

2. Remove from heat, and in the container of a blender or food processor, purée the soup in batches until smooth. Return it to the pot, heat through, and adjust the salt and pepper to taste. Serve immediately in warm bowls, garnish with chives, and warm fresh bread on the side.

Hint: Freeze this soup and use it as a stock.

Dumplings for Clear Soup

3½ cups all-purpose flour
1 teaspoon salt
2 large eggs
about ⅓ cup water

1. Mix all ingredients together to form a stiff dough and knead.
2. Pinch off pieces about the size of large olives and roll into tiny balls.
3. Drop into a pot of boiling water, cook for about 5 minutes, and then transfer into the pot of soup.

CONSOMMÉ MADRILÈNE VARIATION

Year-Round
Yield: 6 to 8 servings

two 16-ounce cans crushed tomatoes
2 green bell peppers, stemmed, seeded, and quartered
1 leek, trimmed and cut into chunks
4 egg whites, lightly beaten
8 cups vegetable stock
2 medium tomatoes, peeled, seeded, and diced
1 small bunch chives, chopped
2 ounces chopped pimento
salt and pepper to taste

1. In a soup kettle or Dutch oven, combine the canned tomatoes, peppers, leek, and egg whites, mixing well. Add the stock and bring to a slow boil. Cover lightly, and cook, stirring frequently, for about 10 minutes.
2. Strain through a triple thickness of cheesecloth, discarding the vegetable matter, and transfer the liquid into a bowl. Cover tightly and refrigerate.
3. When ready, combine the fresh tomatoes, chives, and pimento in a bowl. Adjust the salt and pepper to taste.
4. Spoon 1 to 2 tablespoons of the chive mixture into soup bowls, and ladle the chilled consommé over the top. Serve immediately.

Hint: This is a variation on a standard soup used in more upscale restaurants than one can imagine. Surprisingly enough, you may need to make it a few times before you get it just right.

CROCK POT FRENCH ONION SOUP

Year-Round
Yield: about 6 servings

4 medium yellow onions, thinly sliced
½ cup margarine
2 tablespoons instant vegetable bouillon granules
4 cups hot water
1 teaspoon Worcestershire sauce
salt and pepper to taste
4 slices French bread, toasted
¼ cup grated Parmesan cheese

1. Melt the margarine in a skillet and sauté the onions until lightly colored.
2. In a Crock Pot, combine the onions, bouillon granules, water, and Worcestershire sauce. Cover and cook on low for 4 to 6 hours.
3. When ready, adjust the salt and pepper to taste. Ladle into bowls, float a slice of bread on top of each bowl, and sprinkle with cheese. Serve immediately.

2 tablespoons olive oil
1 small red onion, diced
1 medium clove garlic, peeled and crushed
1 celery stalk, chopped
4 cups vegetable stock
14.5-ounce can diced tomatoes
3 medium potatoes, peeled and diced
2 medium carrots, peeled and diced
3 peppercorns
1 bay leaf
salt and pepper to taste
½ teaspoon crushed dried thyme
1 teaspoon chopped parsley
1 tablespoon Worcestershire sauce
1 tablespoon honey soy sauce
2 cups frozen mixed vegetables, thawed

{ TOMATO
} VEGETABLE
} SOUP

Summer

Yield: about 4
servings

1. Heat the oil in a soup kettle or Dutch oven, and sauté the onion until translucent. Add the stock, tomatoes, potatoes, carrots, garlic, peppercorn, bay leaf, celery, thyme, parsley, Worcestershire sauce, and honey soy sauce. Bring to a boil, then reduce to a simmer, cover lightly, and cook, stirring occasionally, for about 60 minutes.
2. Remove and discard the bay leaf, adjust the salt and pepper to taste, and stir in the mixed vegetables. Continue to cook for about 10 minutes. Remove from heat and serve immediately.

Hint: A little robust red wine or rum can enhance the flavor.

CURRIED VEGETABLE SOUP

Autumn

Yield: about 4 servings

1 tablespoon canola oil
1 cup chopped leeks, including tops
1 medium clove garlic, peeled and minced
½ teaspoon turmeric powder
½ teaspoon cumin powder
½ teaspoon coriander powder
½ teaspoon ginger powder
½ teaspoon saffron threads
pinch cayenne pepper
3½ cups vegetable stock
1 medium tomato, finely diced
2 small zucchini, cut into julienne strips
2 tablespoons minced fresh parsley

1. Heat the oil in a soup kettle or Dutch oven and sauté the leeks and garlic together until the leeks are tender. Add the turmeric, cumin, coriander, ginger, saffron, and pepper. Cook, stirring constantly, for about 2 minutes.
2. Add the stock and bring it to a boil. Reduce to a simmer, cover, and cook for about 3 minutes.
3. Add half the tomato and zucchini, and cook, stirring occasionally, until the vegetables are tender.
4. Turn off the heat, adjust the salt and pepper to taste, ladle into soup bowls, and garnish with the remaining tomato, zucchini, and parsley.

CLEAR SPINACH SOUP

Year-Round

Yield: about 4 servings

½ pound fresh spinach, trimmed
1 scallion, chopped
1 clove garlic, peeled and minced
4 cups water
1 teaspoon soy sauce
salt and pepper to taste

1. In a pot combine the spinach, scallion, garlic, and water. Bring to a boil, then reduce to a simmer, and cook for about 30 minutes.
2. Turn off the heat. Add the soy sauce, adjust the salt and pepper to taste, and use as desired.

Hint: When you boil vegetables for meals, save the water. This makes a good vegetable stock.

1 medium clove garlic, peeled and minced
1 medium yellow onion, chopped
1 leek (white part only), sliced
1 medium green bell pepper, stemmed, seeded, and chopped
1 small zucchini, trimmed and sliced
8 ounces fresh mushrooms, trimmed and sliced
10-ounce package frozen chopped spinach, thawed
14-ounce can stewed tomatoes
2 cups vegetable stock
1½ cups V-8 juice
1 tablespoon chili powder
1 teaspoon paprika
5½ teaspoons crushed dried oregano
2 bay leaves, crushed
cayenne pepper to taste
4 ounces blue cheese, crumbled

DIET SOUP

Year-Round

Yield: about 8 servings

1. In a nonstick soup kettle or Dutch oven, sauté the garlic, onion, leek, zucchini, pepper, and mushrooms, stirring frequently until the onion is lightly colored. Add the spinach, tomatoes, stock, juice, chili powder, paprika, oregano, and bay leaf. Bring to a boil. Then reduce to a simmer, cover lightly, and cook, stirring occasionally, for about 20 minutes.
2. Turn off the heat and adjust the cayenne pepper to taste.
3. Spoon about 1 tablespoon of cheese into each soup bowl, and ladle the hot soup over the top. Serve immediately.

Hint: This soup is packed with nutrition.

4 cups vegetable stock
1 teaspoon dill weed
1½ cups diced potatoes
½ cup diced yellow onion
3 small carrots, peeled and sliced ¼ inch thick
2 cups sliced zucchini
2 fresh ripe tomatoes, chopped
salt and pepper to taste

DILL VEGETABLE SOUP

Summer

Yield: about 6 servings

1. In a soup kettle or Dutch oven, combine the stock, dill weed, potatoes, onion, and carrots. Bring to a boil. Then reduce to a simmer, cover lightly, and cook, stirring occasionally, for about 20 minutes. Add the zucchini and tomatoes, cover again, and continue to cook for about 10 minutes, or until the vegetables are tender.
2. Turn off the heat, and adjust the salt and pepper to taste. Serve immediately.

DUTCH-STYLE CHEESE SOUP

Autumn

Yield: about 4 to 6 servings

2 teaspoons margarine
¼ cup diced yellow onion
1 cup cauliflower florets
2 cups diced potatoes
¼ cup diced or shredded carrots
¼ cup diced celeriac
2 cups water or vegetable stock
2 teaspoons Herb Ox instant vegetable stock granules
salt and pepper to taste
2 thin slices white bread, halved diagonally
1½ ounce Gouda cheese, shredded

1. Have oven-proof bowls ready.
2. Melt 1 teaspoon of the margarine in a soup kettle or Dutch oven, and sauté the onions until tender. Add the cauliflower, potatoes, carrots, celeriac, and continue to cook, stirring frequently, for about 5 minutes. Add the water and the stock granules. Bring to a boil. Reduce to a simmer, cover lightly, and cook for about 15 to 20 minutes.
3. Remove from heat, and adjust the salt and pepper to taste
4. Melt the remaining margarine in a skillet and toast the bread, turning it until browned on both sides.
5. Put a piece of bread in each oven-proof bowl, sprinkle with cheese, and quickly heat under the broiler until the cheese melts.
6. Remove the bowls from the broiler and ladle the hot soup over the top. Serve immediately.

1 tablespoon margarine
1 medium onion, chopped
3 celery stalks and leaves, chopped
2 medium carrots, peeled and chopped
1 cup diced turnip
3 cups vegetable stock
¼ teaspoon crushed dried bay leaf
½ teaspoon crushed dried thyme
15-ounce can red kidney beans, drained
salt and pepper to taste

EASY BEAN SOUP

Winter

Yield: about 6 to 8 servings

1. Heat the margarine in a soup kettle or Dutch oven. Sauté the onion and celery together until the onion is tender.
2. Add the carrots, turnip, stock, bay leaf, and thyme. Bring to a boil. Then reduce to a simmer, cover lightly, and cook, stirring occasionally, for about 15 minutes or until the vegetables are tender.
3. Add the beans and cook for an additional 5 minutes.
4. Remove from heat, adjust the salt and pepper to taste, and serve immediately.

1 tablespoon margarine
1 shallot, peeled and thinly sliced
1 small fennel bulb, peeled and chopped
1 pound potatoes, peeled and sliced
4 cups vegetable stock
1 teaspoon chopped parsley
½ teaspoon crushed dried lemon thyme
½ cup heavy cream
salt and pepper to taste
4 chopped sprigs watercress for garnish

FENNEL & WATERCRESS SOUP

Spring

Yield: about 4 servings

1. Melt margarine in a soup kettle or Dutch oven, and sauté the fennel and shallot together until fork tender. Add potatoes, stock, parsley, and lemon thyme. Bring to a boil. Then reduce to a simmer, cover lightly, and cook, stirring occasionally, for about 30 minutes.
2. In the container of a blender or food processor, purée the soup in batches until smooth. Return to the pot, bring to a boil, and then remove from heat.
3. Turn off the heat, stir in the cream, and adjust the salt and pepper to taste. Serve immediately, alone or as part of a menu, with chopped watercress as a garnish or on the side.

Hint: This is a very good soup, but I wanted a finishing touch. So I added ¼ cup of chopped watercress leaves just before I took it off the heat.

EGGPLANT SOUP

Autumn

Yield: about 4 to 6 servings

2 tablespoons virgin olive oil
1 small (about 1 pound) eggplant, peeled and chopped
2 shallots, peeled and minced
1 large clove garlic, peeled and minced
2½ cups vegetable or chicken stock
salt and pepper to taste
pepper cream for garnish

1. Heat the oil in a saucepan, and sauté the eggplant and shallots together, over a low heat, stirring frequently, for about 15 to 20 minutes. (Do not allow the eggplant to brown.) Add the stock, and adjust the salt and pepper to taste.
2. Remove from heat, stir in the pepper cream, and serve immediately.

Hint: Eggplant is not commonly used for soup. I don't know whether that's because of the color or the taste. This recipe seems a little different, but most of the taste and appearance comes from the garnish and not from the eggplant. Other recipes use eggplant with the peel, which can boil down to a paste.

Pepper Cream Garnish

　1 medium red pepper, stemmed, seeded, and quartered
　2 tablespoons light cream or evaporated milk
　salt and pepper to taste

1. Place the pepper pieces under a broiler, and heat, turning until the skin starts to change color. Remove from the broiler and cool.
2. In the container of a blender combine the pepper, cream, and salt and pepper to taste. Process on LOW until the pepper is just chopped fine. Remove from the blender and use as desired.

¾ cup uncooked pasta spirals
1½ cups vegetable stock
1 cup finely chopped broccoli florets
1 cup finely chopped cauliflower florets
½ cup chopped tomato
1 cup hot water
¼ teaspoon crushed, dried marjoram
¼ teaspoon crushed, dried thyme
grated Romano cheese (optional)

FRESH
MINESTRONE
SOUP

Year-Round

Yield: about 6
servings

1. In a 2-quart microwave casserole bowl, combine the pasta, stock, broccoli, cauliflower, tomato, water, marjoram, and thyme. Cover and microwave on HIGH, stirring once, for about 11 to 13 minutes or until pasta is al dente.
2. Remove from the microwave. Ladle into soup bowls, sprinkle with cheese, and serve immediately, alone or as part of a menu.

2 tablespoons butter or margarine
2 heads chicory, sliced
1 medium yellow onion, sliced
½ cup diced parsnips or turnips
1½ cups diced potatoes
2 cups vegetable stock
lemon juice to taste
½ teaspoon mace or nutmeg
1 teaspoon crushed dried basil
1 cup milk
½ cup heavy cream

NEW
ENGLAND
CHICORY
SOUP

Summer

Yield: about 4 to 6
servings

1. Melt the butter in a saucepan or soup kettle, and sauté the chicory, onion, parsnips, and potatoes together until the chicory is wilted. Add the stock and lemon juice to taste. Bring to a boil. Then reduce to a simmer, cover lightly, and cook, stirring occasionally, for about 20 minutes. Add the mace and basil, and cook for an additional 10 minutes, or until the vegetables are fork tender.
2. Remove from heat, purée in batches, in the container of a blender or food processor, until coarsely blended.
3. Return to the pan, bring to a boil, remove from heat, and stir in the milk and cream. Adjust the salt and pepper to taste, and serve with a garnish of watercress.

Hint: Chicory is considered a bitter-tasting green that is used primarily for salads. It's available in winter and spring. This soup smells wonderful.

GERMAN BEER SOUP

Year-Round

Yield: about 4 servings

1½ heaping tablespoons all-purpose flour
3½ tablespoons margarine
12-ounce can beer or ale
½ teaspoon ground cinnamon
granulated sugar to taste
2 egg yolks, beaten
½ cup plus ½ tablespoon light cream
French bread, sliced and toasted

1. Melt the margarine in a soup kettle or Dutch oven, and sprinkle in the flour, stirring to make a roux. Pouring in a narrow stream and, stirring constantly, add the beer. Add the cinnamon and sugar. Bring to a boil, then reduce to a simmer, cover lightly, and cook for about 5 minutes.
2. Meanwhile, in a bowl, use a wire whisk to beat the egg yolks and light cream together until smooth. Then stir into the hot beer. Cover again and cook, stirring occasionally, for about 5 minutes.
3. Turn off the heat, discard the cinnamon stick, and adjust the salt and pepper to taste. Put a slice of bread in each soup bowl, and ladle the soup over the top. Serve immediately.

GINGER CARROT BISQUE

Summer

Yield: about 8 to 10 servings

¼ cup plus 2 tablespoons margarine
2 large yellow onions, chopped
2 pounds carrots, peeled and thinly sliced
1 tablespoon peeled and minced ginger root
2 teaspoons orange zest
½ teaspoon ground coriander
5 cups vegetable stock
1 cup half-and-half
salt and pepper to taste
½ cup freshly minced watercress for garnish

1. Melt the margarine in a soup kettle or Dutch oven, and sauté the onions and carrots together until the onions are translucent.
2. In a bowl, combine the ginger, orange zest, coriander, and 2 cups of stock. Stir into the pot with the onions. Cover lightly and continue to cook for about 15 minutes.
3. Turn off the heat. In the container of a blender or food processor, purée the hot mixture until smooth. Return to the pot, and add the remaining stock and half-and-half. Heat through, but do not boil.
4. Turn off the heat, and adjust the salt and pepper to taste. Ladle into soup bowls, garnish with minced watercress, and serve immediately.

2 tablespoons butter or margarine
1 large red onion, sliced
4 tablespoons minced garlic
1 large (about 1½ pounds) potato, thinly sliced
1 teaspoon Hungarian paprika
16-ounce can diced tomatoes
1 teaspoon snipped fresh basil
3¾ cups fresh vegetable stock
1 teaspoon whole wheat flour
1 tablespoon red port wine
seasoning to taste

GREGORIO'S POTATO & GARLIC SOUP

Winter
Yield: about 4 to 6 servings

1. Melt the butter in a saucepan, and sauté the onion and garlic together until the onion is tender. Add the potato and sprinkle with paprika. Cook, stirring and turning the potatoes until fork tender but not brown. Add the tomatoes, basil, and stock. Bring to a boil, then reduce to a simmer, and cook uncovered until the tomatoes are tender.
2. In a cup, blend together the flour and wine until smooth, and stir into the soup. Return to boil and cook, stirring frequently, until thickened.
3. Break the potato slices into pieces, adjust the seasoning to taste, and serve immediately with a sprinkle of watercress sprigs for garnish.

1 tablespoon margarine
2 tablespoons chopped yellow onion
8-ounce can tomato sauce
¼ teaspoon dried, crushed basil
⅛ teaspoon dried, crushed thyme
ground pepper to taste
1 cup vegetable stock
Parmesan-flavored croutons

HERBED TOMATO SOUP

Year-Round
Yield: about 2 servings

1. In a microwave casserole, combine the onion and margarine, and cook on HIGH for about 2 minutes. Add the tomato sauce, dried basil, dried thyme, pepper, and stock. Cover lightly, and cook on HIGH for about 4 to 6 minutes or until the mixture just begins to boil.
2. Remove from the microwave, set aside for about 3 minutes, and then serve immediately.

Hint: Parmesan-flavored croutons are available in many supermarkets.

INDIAN DAHL SOUP

Year-Round

Yield: about 4 to 6 servings

2 tablespoons butter or margarine
2 small cloves garlic, peeled and crushed
1 medium white onion, chopped
½ teaspoon turmeric
1 teaspoon garam masala
¼ teaspoon chili powder
1 teaspoon ground cumin
two 16-ounce cans chopped tomatoes
1 cup red lentils
2 teaspoons fresh lemon or lime juice
2½ cups fresh vegetable stock
1¼ cup coconut milk
seasoning to taste
lemon slice for garnish

1. Melt the butter in a saucepan and sauté the garlic and onion together until the onion is transparent. Add the turmeric, garam masala, chili powder, and cumin. Heat through.
2. Add the tomatoes, lentils, lemon juice, and stock. Bring to a boil, then reduce to a simmer, and cook for about 30 minutes, or until the lentils are fork tender.
3. Remove from the heat and adjust the seasoning to taste. Ladle into warmed soup bowls and garnish with thin slices of fresh lemon.

Hint: Garam masala is an Indian blend of dry-roasted, ground spices that add warmth to the palate. (Garam means "warm" or "hot.") Variations may contain up to twelve spices. As with all spices, store it in a cool, dry place for no more than 6 months.

2 cups diced carrots
½ cup vegetable stock
½ teaspoon granulated sugar
1 tablespoon canola oil
¼ cup minced yellow onion
1 tablespoon all-purpose flour
2½ cups soy milk
3-ounce package cream cheese, diced
seasoning to taste
¼ cup fresh mint

1. Put the carrots and stock in a saucepan. Bring to a boil. Then reduce to a simmer, add the sugar and mint, and cook until the carrots are very tender.
2. Meanwhile, heat the oil in a skillet and sauté the onions until tender. Sprinkle on the flour, stirring to make a roux before adding the soy milk. Cook, stirring constantly, until thickened.
3. In a cup, combine about ½ cup of the hot milk mixture with the cream cheese, and blend back into the hot mixture.
4. In the container of a blender or food processor, purée the carrots with their cooking liquids, until smooth. Stir this into the hot milk mixture, bring to a boil, remove from the heat, adjust the seasoning to taste, and add the mint leaves. Serve immediately.

1 tablespoon virgin olive oil
¼ cup chopped yellow onion
4 cups fresh vegetable stock
¼ cup long grain rice
¼ cup tomato purée
pinch chili powder
10-ounce package frozen mixed vegetables, thawed
seasoning to taste

1. Heat the oil in a saucepan, and sauté the onion until tender. Add the stock, rice, tomato purée, and chili powder. Bring to a boil. Then reduce to a simmer, cover lightly, and cook for about 20 minutes, or until the rice is very tender.
2. Stir in the mixed vegetables, and heat through. Adjust the seasoning to taste and serve immediately with fresh tortillas on the side.

SOPA DE AJO (GARLIC SOUP)

Year-Round

Yield: about 4 to 6 servings

1 tablespoon canola oil
1½ tablespoons minced garlic
5 cups vegetable stock
2 sprigs fresh cilantro
2 large egg yolks, beaten foamy

1. Heat the oil in a saucepan, and sauté the garlic until tender. Add the stock and cilantro. Bring to a boil, then reduce to a simmer, cover lightly, and cook for about 20 minutes.

2. Remove the soup from the heat, strain and discard the vegetable matter, and return to the pan.

3. In a bowl, blend ½ cup of the hot liquid with the beaten egg yolks, and stir into the hot soup. Reheat, stirring constantly, until thickened. Remove from the heat, and serve at once with buttered croutons on the side.

SOPA DE FIDEOS

Year-Round

Yield: about 6 to 8 servings

4-ounce package vermicelli
water
1 tablespoon canola oil
1 medium yellow onion, minced
1 tablespoon minced garlic
6 cups vegetable stock
10.5-ounce can tomato purée
2 tablespoons dried parsley
grated Parmesan or Romano cheese for garnish

1. Break the vermicelli into small pieces. Heat the oil in saucepan, and sauté the vermicelli until a golden brown color. Remove from the heat and drain and reserve the oil. Set the vermicelli aside.

2. Return the oil to the saucepan, and sauté the onion and garlic together until the onion is tender. Add the stock, tomato purée, and vermicelli. Cook, stirring occasionally, for about 20 minutes or until the vermicelli is al dente. Add the parsley, and adjust the seasoning to taste. Transfer to a soup bowl or soup tureen, sprinkle with cheese, and serve.

2 tablespoons virgin olive oil
1 cup finely diced potatoes
1 large yellow onion, chopped
2 tablespoons minced garlic
1 teaspoon garam masala
1 teaspoon crushed coriander
1 teaspoon ground cumin
¼ teaspoon dried pepper flakes
3½ cup vegetable stock
1 cup frozen green peas, thawed
4 tablespoons unflavored yogurt
seasoning to taste
snipped fresh cilantro for garnish

POTATO-PEA SOUP

Year-Round

Yield: about 4 to 6 servings

1. Heat the oil in a skillet. Sauté the potatoes, onion, and garlic until the potatoes are fork tender and the onion is just beginning to turn color. Add the garam masala, coriander, cumin, and pepper flakes. Heat through and stir in the stock. Bring to a boil, then reduce to a simmer. Cover tightly and cook, stirring occasionally, for about 20 minutes, or until the potatoes are very soft.
2. Add the peas and continue to cook for an additional 5 minutes before stirring in the yogurt and seasoning to taste.
3. Ladle into warmed soup bowls, garnish, and serve with hot, freshly baked bread.

1 tablespoon butter or margarine
1 shallot, peeled and chopped
1 leek stalk, sliced
3 cups vegetable stock
1 teaspoon fresh lemon juice
¼ cup fresh orange juice
⅓ cup milk
¼ cup light cream or evaporated milk
salt and pepper to taste

LEEK & ORANGE CREAM SOUP

Summer

Yield: about 5 to 6 servings

1. Melt the butter in a soup kettle or Dutch oven, and sauté the shallot until tender. Add the leek and cook for about 5 minutes longer. Add the stock, lemon juice, and orange juice. Bring to a boil. Then reduce to a simmer, cover tightly, and cook, stirring occasionally, for about 10 to 12 minutes, or until the vegetables are very tender. Remove from heat and cool slightly.
2. When ready, in a blender or food processor, purée the mixture in batches until smooth. Return to the pan, add the milk and cream, and adjust the salt and pepper to taste. Heat through, but do not boil. Remove from heat. Chill thoroughly for at least 3 hours before serving in well-chilled bowls with a sprinkling of chopped chives as a garnish.

HOT & SOUR TOFU SOUP

Autumn

Yield: about 8 servings

3 tablespoons vegetable oil
¾ cup red bell peppers, cut into julienne strips
1½ cups chopped green onions
2 cups vegetable stock
2 cups water
2 tablespoons soy sauce
2 teaspoons red wine vinegar
½ teaspoon crushed red pepper flakes
2 tablespoons cornstarch
3 tablespoons water
1 teaspoon sesame oil
½ pound snow peas, fresh or frozen (optional)
1 pound firm tofu, drained and cut into ½-inch cubes
8-ounce can sliced water chestnuts, drained
salt and pepper to taste

1. Heat the oil in a soup kettle or Dutch oven, and sauté the green onions and bell peppers together until tender. Add water, vegetable stock, and soy sauce. Bring to a boil, then reduce to a simmer, cover lightly, and cook for about 5 minutes.
2. Blend the cornstarch with 3 tablespoons of water. In a bowl, blend the vinegar, pepper flakes, cornstarch blend, and sesame oil. Stir into the hot soup until incorporated, and then add the tofu, snow peas, and water chestnuts. Again cover, and cook for about 5 minutes or until thick and bubbly.
3. Turn off the heat. Adjust the salt and pepper to taste, and serve immediately.

Hint: Tofu is considered a bland ingredient that usually takes on the flavor of anything it's cooked with. In this case, it's the bitter taste of soy and vinegar and the hot taste of pepper flakes.

4 tablespoons extra virgin olive oil
2 large yellow onions, chopped
3 to 4 medium cloves garlic, peeled and minced
1½ cups diced potatoes or turnips
¾ cup diced carrots
1 small green bell pepper, stemmed, seeded, and chopped
16-ounce can crushed tomatoes
4 cups vegetable stock
1 tablespoon tomato paste
4 tablespoons chopped fresh basil
½ cup sliced fresh mushrooms

ITALIAN PEASANT SOUP

Year-Round

Yield: about 4 to 6 servings

1. Heat the oil in a saucepan or soup kettle, and sauté the onions and garlic until the onions are translucent. Add the potatoes, carrots, pepper, and tomatoes. Cook, stirring constantly, for about 3 to 4 minutes, and then stir in the tomato paste. Add the stock and tomato paste. Bring to a boil, then reduce to a simmer, cover lightly, and cook for about 20 minutes, or until the vegetables are tender.
2. Remove from heat. Cool slightly, and then purée in batches, using a blender or food processor, until coarsely smooth. Return the mixture to the pan.
3. Add the basil and mushrooms, adjust the salt and pepper to taste, and serve with grated fresh Parmesan or fresh Romano cheese on the side.

Hint: I tried oregano in place of the basil, and it made this soup taste more like a thin spaghetti sauce.

1 egg yolk
1 teaspoon heavy cream
3½ tablespoons melted margarine
½ cup less 1 tablespoon all-purpose flour
7 ounces Emmenthaler cheese, sliced
4 cups vegetable stock
salt and pepper to taste
pinch of granulated sugar
1½ cups toasted bread croutons

KAESSUPPE (CHEESE SOUP)

Autumn

Yield: about 4 servings

1. In a small bowl, beat the egg yolk until it is foamy, and then beat in the cream.
2. In a cup, blend the margarine and flour.
3. In a soup kettle or Dutch oven, blend the stock and flour mixture until smooth. Bring to a boil, and add the cheese, stirring until melted.
4. Turn off the heat, add the egg mixture, stirring until incorporated. Add the sugar, and adjust the salt and pepper to taste. Serve immediately. Garnish with the croutons as soon as served.

KRAUTLSUPPE (BAVARIAN HERB SOUP)

Autumn

Yield: about 4 servings

4 tablespoons margarine
1 large white onion, chopped
3 sprigs chervil, chopped
3 sprigs of watercress, chopped
2 whole leaves spinach, chopped
4 cups water or vegetable stock
1 large potato, peeled and diced
salt and pepper to taste
croutons

1. Melt the margarine in a soup kettle or Dutch oven, and sauté the onion until translucent. Add the chervil, watercress, and spinach, stirring briefly before adding the water, and potato. Bring to a boil. Then reduce to a simmer, cover lightly, and cook, stirring occasionally, for about 20 minutes.
2. Turn off the heat, and using a potato masher, mash the potato, adjust the salt and pepper to taste, reheat to boiling, and serve immediately. Garnish as desired.

Hint: This soup has enough variety in greens to make it a lovely-looking soup and just enough potato to thicken it to taste.

LIGHT SUMMER SOUP

Summer

Yield: about 4 servings

8-ounce can unsweetened apple juice concentrate
three 8-ounce juice cans water
2½ cups coarsely chopped celery
1 medium onion, halved
¼ teaspoon minced garlic
¼ cup pearl barley

1. In a soup kettle or Dutch oven, combine the juice, water, celery, onion, and garlic. Bring to boil, then reduce to a simmer, and cover tightly. Cook, stirring occasionally, for about 1 hour or until the vegetable matter is very limp.
2. Then using a slotted spoon, remove and discard the vegetable matter, and add the barley. Continue to cook on low heat, for about 1 hour, or until the barley is very soft.
3. Ladle into soup bowls, and serve with angel-hair shredded lettuce and tomato salad on the side.

Hint: This soup may be served hot or cold.

12-ounce can orange juice concentrate, thawed
12-ounce (orange-juice-concentrate) can water
16-ounce jar picante sauce

In a saucepan or Crock Pot, combine the orange juice concentrate, water, and picante sauce. Heat though and serve with thinly sliced oranges as a garnish.

Hint: This soup may be served hot or cold. If cold, heat through first, and then cool to serving temperature. For those who want a nice-tasting bite to the soup, add 2 tablespoons triple sec liqueur.

1 large head (2 pounds) cauliflower, separated into florets
2 tablespoons white wine vinegar or cider vinegar
2 quarts ice cold water
2 quarts water
¼ cup olive oil
4 cloves garlic, peeled and minced
½ teaspoon crushed hot red pepper
4 cups hot vegetable stock
⅓ cup flat leaf, freshly chopped parsley
salt and pepper to taste
Pecorino cheese, freshly grated

1. In a bowl, combine the ice cold water, vinegar, and cauliflower. Set aside for at least 60 minutes.
2. In a large saucepan, bring 2 quarts of water to a boil. Drain the cauliflower and immediately drop into the boiling water. Return to a boil, and simmer for about 15 to 20 minutes or until crisp and tender. Drain.
3. Heat the oil in a soup kettle or Dutch oven, and sauté the garlic and pepper together until the garlic is lightly colored. Stir in the hot vegetable stock and parsley. Add the cauliflower, and cook for about 10 minutes.
4. Using a slotted spoon, remove 1 cup of the cooked cauliflower from the soup and in the container of a blender or food processor, purée until smooth. Then stir it back into the soup and heat through.
5. Turn off the heat, and adjust the salt and pepper to taste. Serve immediately with a fresh loaf of crusty Italian bread.

NETTLE SOUP

Spring

Yield: about 6 to 8 servings

1 tablespoon butter or margarine
1 medium yellow onion, minced
2 medium cloves garlic, peeled and minced
1½ cups finely diced potatoes
2 cups freshly picked nettle tops
2½ cups vegetable stock
½ cup heavy cream
pinch nutmeg or mace to taste

1. Melt the butter in a saucepan or soup kettle, and sauté the onion and garlic together until translucent. Add the potatoes and nettle tops, and stirring, heat through. Add the stock and bring to a boil. Reduce to a simmer, cover lightly, and cook for about 15 minutes.

2. Remove from heat, and purée in batches, using a blender or food processor.

3. Return to the saucepan, stir in the cream, without boiling. Remove from heat, stir in the nutmeg, adjust the salt and pepper to taste, and serve as desired.

Hint: In past centuries, northern Europeans and frontier Americans once commonly made nettle soup in the spring. This soup cleanses the body of excess salt used in curing foods eaten in winter. Fresh nettle is available in the spring in specialty food stores. The plant is quite prickly.

NEW YORK'S CLASSIC ONION SOUP

Year-Round

Yield: about 6 servings

¼ cup margarine
2 large sweet onions, thinly sliced
four 14.5-ounce cans vegetable broth
1 cup water
¼ cup dry red wine
1 teaspoon Worcestershire sauce
3 sprigs parsley
salt and pepper to taste
toasted French bread
½ cup grated Parmesan cheese

1. Melt the margarine in a soup kettle or Dutch oven, and sauté the onion until tender. Add broth, water, wine, Worcestershire sauce, and parsley. Bring to a boil, then reduce to a simmer, and cook, stirring occasionally, for about 20 minutes.

2. Position the rack in the center of the oven and preheat to 450°F. Have oven-proof soup bowls ready.

3. Turn off the heat, adjust the salt and pepper to taste, discard the parsley, and pour into oven-proof soup bowls. Top each bowl with a slice of toasted bread, sprinkle with cheese, and bake until the cheese is melted.

4. Remove from heat and serve immediately.

3 tablespoons margarine
8 cups sliced white onions
2 cups water
4½ cups unsweetened apple juice
½ cup white port wine
½ teaspoon grated orange peel
1 medium apple, pared and grated

1. Melt the margarine in a soup kettle or Dutch oven, and sauté the onions until lightly browned.

2. Add the water, apple juice, wine, and orange peel. Bring to a boil. Stir in the apple, reduce to a simmer, cover, and continue to cook for about 30 minutes.

3. Remove the soup from the heat. Serve immediately with croutons on the side.

Hint: American Indians often combined apples and onions in recipes. They're a great combination.

Parmesan-Garlic Croutons

¼ cup melted margarine

2 tablespoons grated Parmesan cheese

2 tablespoons chopped fine parsley

1 clove garlic, peeled and minced

six 1-inch thick slices French bread

To make the croutons, in a bowl, combine the margarine, cheese, parsley, and garlic. Spread evenly on one side of the bread slices, arrange on the baking sheet, and bake for about 8 minutes in a 350°F. oven or until lightly browned. Then dice into small pieces.

6 ounces pecans, toasted
4 cups vegetable stock
½ cup heavy cream
1 large clove garlic
salt and freshly ground pepper to taste

1. In a blender or food processor, combine the pecans, garlic, and about ½ cup of the stock. With the motor running on LOW speed, add the remaining stock until you create a creamy consistency.

2. Press the mixture through a sieve, and transfer it to a saucepan. Bring to a boil, remove from heat, and stir in the cream. Adjust the salt and pepper to taste and serve immediately.

Hint: Nuts add great flavor to soups.

PORCINI MUSHROOM SOUP

Spring

Yield: about 6 to 8 servings

6 ounces fresh porcini mushrooms
1¼ cups water
2 tablespoons butter or margarine
2 medium yellow onions, chopped
2 medium cloves garlic, peeled and minced
8 ounces sliced cap mushrooms
2 tablespoons all-purpose flour
3 cups vegetable stock
½ cup white port wine
2 tablespoons parsley or cilantro
1 cup light cream
salt and pepper to taste
whipped unflavored yogurt for garnish

1. Thoroughly wash the porcini mushrooms, place in a bowl, cover with water, and set aside for about 20 minutes. Drain and save the soaking liquid.
2. Melt the butter in a small saucepan, add the onion and garlic, cover, and simmer gently for about 10 minutes. Add the porcini and cap mushrooms and cook for about 2 to 3 minutes.
3. Sprinkle on the flour and cook, stirring for about 12 minutes. Then pouring in a narrow stream, and stirring constantly, add the stock and soaking liquid. Bring to a boil, then reduce to a simmer. Cover and cook, stirring occasionally, for about 15 minutes. Add the wine, and continue to cook, undisturbed for about 5 minutes. Remove from heat, stir in the parsley and cool slightly.
4. In the container of a blender or food processor, purée the mixture in batches until smooth. Return to the saucepan, stir in the cream, and reheat. (Do not allow to boil.)
5. Remove from heat, and adjust the salt and pepper to taste. Serve immediately with yogurt on the side or dropped into each bowl and swirled with a spoon once or twice.

Hint: When I make this, I like to use a brandy instead of wine. Wait until the soup has been reheated and removed from the stove to add the brandy.

You'll find porcini mushrooms in specialty food shops and large supermarkets.

½ cup vegetable oil
2 cups diced carrots
1½ cups diced celery
2 cups chopped yellow onions
4 pounds potatoes, peeled and diced
#10 can (6 pounds, 3 ounces) cheddar cheese sauce
2 quarts hot vegetable stock
¾ teaspoon white pepper
2 teaspoons Worcestershire sauce
½ teaspoon garlic powder
1 tablespoon parsley flakes
salt to taste

POTATO-CHEDDAR SOUP

Autumn

Yield: about 30 servings

1. Heat the oil in a large soup kettle or Dutch oven, and sauté the carrots, celery, and onions together until the onions are lightly colored. Add the potatoes, and continue to cook for about 5 minutes. Add the cheese sauce, stock, pepper, Worcestershire sauce, garlic powder, and parsley, stirring constantly. Heat through; do not allow to boil.
2. Turn off the heat, and adjust the salt and pepper to taste. Serve immediately.

Hint: After you add the cheese sauce, you need to stir constantly to prevent scorching.

2 tablespoons butter or margarine
1 medium white onion, chopped
1 head fresh lettuce, chopped
1½ cups diced potatoes
2½ cups vegetable stock
½ cup enriched soy milk
½ cup cheddar cheese for garnish

POTATO-CHEESE SOUP

Year-Round

Yield: about 6 to 8 servings

1. Melt the butter in a saucepan or soup kettle, and sauté the onion until translucent. Add the lettuce and potatoes. Cover lightly, and cook, stirring over a very low heat for about 10 minutes, being careful not to burn the vegetables. Add the stock, and bring to a boil. Then reduce to a simmer, cover tightly, and cook, stirring occasionally, for about 20 minutes, or until the potatoes are fork tender.
2. Remove from heat, and purée in batches, using a blender or food processor.
3. Return to the pan, add the soy milk, and heat through, without boiling. Adjust the salt and pepper to taste, and serve hot with a sprinkling of cheddar cheese.

Hint: Any type of hard or semi-hard cheese can be used.

POTATO-SORREL SOUP

Autumn

Yield: about 6 servings

4 tablespoons margarine
7 cups water
3 medium leeks (whites only), chopped
6 cups chopped sorrel leaves
1½ pounds red potatoes, quartered and thinly sliced
salt and pepper to taste
crème fraîche for garnish
1 tablespoon snipped fresh chives

1. Melt the margarine in a soup kettle or Dutch oven. Add ½ cup water, leeks, and sorrel. Bring to a boil, then reduce to a simmer, and cook gently for about 5 minutes. Add the potatoes and continue to cook for about 10 minutes. Add the remaining water, and bring to a boil. Then reduce to a simmer, and continue to cook, stirring occasionally, until the potatoes are tender.
2. Using a masher, mash the potatoes into smaller pieces.
3. Turn off the heat, and adjust the salt and pepper to taste. Ladle into individual bowls. Drop a spoonful of crème fraîche into each bowl, swirl gently, and sprinkle the chives on top. Serve immediately.

Hint: Remember that there are two varieties of sorrel, wild and French. Wild sorrel is more acidic than French sorrel.

QUICK SPINACH SOUP

Year-Round

Yield: about 3 to 4 servings

1 tablespoon margarine
two 10-ounce packages frozen chopped spinach, thawed
10.75-fluid-ounce can cream-of-potato soup
10.75-fluid-ounce soup can of milk
2 tablespoons white port wine
pinch ground nutmeg
salt and pepper to taste

1. In a microwave casserole dish, combine the margarine and spinach, cover lightly, and cook in the microwave on HIGH for about 1 minute.
2. Add the soup, milk, wine, and nutmeg. Stir to incorporate, cover, and cook in the microwave on HIGH for about 6 minutes or until the soup is bubbly.
3. Turn off the microwave. Adjust the salt and pepper to taste, and serve immediately.

32-ounce can diced beets
3 cups water or vegetable stock
1 celery stalk, chopped
1 medium carrot, quartered
1 bay leaf
1 medium clove garlic, peeled and chopped
¼ teaspoon whole peppercorns
1 tablespoon lemon juice
1 teaspoon granulated sugar
salt and pepper to taste
whipped sour cream for garnish
chopped fresh dill weed for garnish

1. Drain the beets, reserve the liquid, and set aside.
2. In a soup kettle or Dutch oven, combine the beet liquid, water, celery, carrot, bay leaf, garlic, and peppercorns. Bring to a boil, then reduce to a simmer, cover lightly, and cook for about 10 minutes.
3. Turn off the heat, strain the through a fine sieve, discarding the vegetable matter, and return the liquid to the pot. Add the beets, lemon juice, and sugar before returning to a boil.
4. Turn off the heat, and adjust the salt and pepper to taste. Serve immediately, alone or as part of a menu, with whipped sour cream and chopped dill weed on the side.

1 tablespoon extra virgin olive oil
10-ounce package frozen mixed vegetables
4 cups V-8 cocktail juice
4 cups water
2 tablespoons instant vegetable bouillon granules
1 teaspoon chopped fresh basil
1 teaspoon crushed dried marjoram
½ teaspoon onion salt
¼ teaspoon garlic powder
½ pound spaghetti, broken into thirds and cooked al dente
salt and pepper to taste
grated Parmesan cheese (optional)

1. Heat the oil in a soup kettle or Dutch oven, add the vegetables, juice, water, bouillon granules, basil, marjoram, onion salt, and garlic powder. Bring to a boil, then reduce to a simmer, cover lightly, and cook, stirring occasionally, for about 20 minutes. Add the spaghetti and heat through.
2. Turn off the heat, and adjust the salt and pepper to taste. Serve immediately, alone or as part of a menu, with the cheese on the side.

Hint: The slow simmer helps bring out the flavor of the frozen vegetables.

RED BELL PEPPER SOUP

Autumn

Yield: about 8 to 10 servings

1 cup margarine
2 tablespoons vegetable oil
4 cups chopped leeks
6 large red bell peppers, stemmed, seeded, and sliced
3 cups vegetable stock
6 cups buttermilk
2 tablespoons honey, or to taste
salt and pepper to taste
thin lemon slices
caviar (optional)

1. Heat the margarine and oil in a soup kettle or Dutch oven, and add the leeks and red pepper. Reduce heat to a low setting, cover tightly, and cook, stirring occasionally, for about 20 minutes or until vegetables are soft. Add vegetable stock, bring to a boil, then reduce to a simmer, cover, and continue to cook for about 30 minutes.
2. In the container of a blender or food processor, purée the soup until smooth. Stir in the buttermilk, and adjust the salt and pepper to taste. Serve immediately. Place a daub of caviar on a slice of lemon and float it on each bowl of soup.

Hint: Serve in very large pepper shells, with stem and seeds removed, placed in bowls. Ladle the soup into them. By themselves, red bell peppers may have a bitter acidic taste. Adding honey to this soup creates a sweet-and-sour flavor.

ROSE HIP SOUP

Winter

Yield: about 6 servings

8 ounces dried rose hips, soaked 4 hours
6 cups vegetable stock or water
¾ cup dried potato flakes
4 tablespoons Madeira wine
12 blanched almonds, shredded
1 teaspoon lemon juice
1 tablespoon granulated sugar

1. The rose hips should be soaked in just enough water to cover them for 4 hours. In a soup kettle or Dutch oven, combine the rose hips and soaking water. Simmer over a low heat until the hips are soft.
2. Press through a fine sieve, discard the vegetable matter, and return the liquid to the pot. Add the stock, potato flakes, wine, almonds, juice and sugar.
3. Bring to a boil. Then reduce to a simmer and cook, stirring occasionally, for about 30 minutes. Remove from heat, and serve immediately.

Hint: Rose hips are found primarily in health or natural food stores.

2 tablespoons virgin olive oil
4 medium yellow onions, finely minced
2 large cloves garlic, peeled and minced
1½ cups finely diced potatoes
½ cup diced carrots
1 teaspoon ground cumin
1 tablespoon tamari or soy sauce
4 cups Japanese Stock (see page 28)
1 heaping tablespoon dark brown miso

RICH MISO SOUP

Spring
Yield: about 6 to 8 servings

1. Melt the oil in a saucepan or soup kettle, and sauté the onion and garlic together until translucent. Add the potatoes and carrots, heat through, and then add the cumin, tamari, and stock. Bring to a boil. Then reduce to a simmer, cover tightly, and cook, stirring occasionally, for about 30 minutes, or until the vegetables are fork tender.
2. Remove from heat, add the miso, and using a blender or food processor, purée in batches until smooth. Return to the heat, heat through, and serve immediately, with a salt-free cracker on the side.

Hint: Miso, a soybean paste popular in Japan, is available in Asian markets and in very large supermarkets. It can usually be found in three varieties. Yellow is the saltiest and dark brown is the most palatable.

10-ounce package frozen snow peas, thawed
2½ cups vegetable stock
1 tablespoon white port wine
salt and pepper to taste
¼ cup sour cream
1 tablespoon grated horseradish
watercress sprigs for garnish

SNOW PEA SOUP

Spring
Yield: about 4 to 6 servings

1. Place the stock in a saucepan, bring to a boil, add the peas, and boil, stirring occasionally, for about 5 minutes.
2. Meanwhile, in a cup, blend the sour cream and horseradish.
3. Remove the peas from the heat, cool slightly, and then in the container of a blender or food processor, purée the peas and liquid, until smooth. Pour back into the saucepan.
4. Bring to a boil, and remove from heat. Adjust the salt and pepper to taste. Serve in heated bowls, with a daub of the sour cream mixture on top and a garnish of watercress.

Hint: Snow peas are cultivated for their sweet seed pods.

ROASTED TOMATO SOUP

Summer

Yield: about 5 to 6 servings

4 to 4½ pounds ripe tomatoes, halved
¾ cup extra virgin olive oil
6 medium cloves garlic, peeled and mashed
1 teaspoon crushed dried thyme
1 teaspoon crushed dried rosemary
4 medium white onions, thinly sliced
4 stalks celery, sliced
1 medium head of fennel, sliced
4 bay leaves
1 small red chili pepper, trimmed and seeded
2 teaspoons tomato paste
2 teaspoons granulated sugar
salt and pepper to taste

1. Position the barbecue or grill rack 4 inches from the heat source and preheat.
2. When ready, place the tomatoes on the rack, cut side up, and grill until soft, and the skin begins to blacken. Remove from the grill and keep warm.
3. In a large saucepan, heat the oil, and sauté the garlic, thyme, and rosemary until the garlic is translucent. Add the onion, celery, fennel, pepper, and bay leaves, and cook, stirring until the onion is translucent. Add the tomatoes, heat through, and remove from heat. Stir in the tomato paste and sugar, and purée the mixture in a blender or food processor until smooth. Pass the mixture through a fine sieve into a clean saucepan, and discard the vegetable matter. Reheat the soup and serve with basil pesto on the side. Garnish with croutons.

Hint: Vine-ripened tomatoes are recommended. Hot-house tomatoes lack the flavor and taste required for this soup. Because the tomatoes are individually grilled, preparation may seem lengthy, but it's worth it.

Basil Pesto

1½ cups fresh basil leaves
4 tablespoons virgin olive oil
2 teaspoons balsamic vinegar

In the container of a blender, combine the basil leaves, olive oil, and vinegar. Process on LOW until the leaves are just chopped and the mixture is flaky.

3½ tablespoons margarine
3 tablespoons all-purpose flour
1½ quarts vegetable stock
1 bunch fresh French sorrel
1 bunch fresh chervil
1 egg yolk
½ teaspoon granulated sugar
salt and pepper to taste
4 to 5 tablespoons sour cream or unflavored yogurt
finely minced garlic for garnish

SORREL SOUP

Winter

Yield: about 4 servings

1. Melt the margarine in a soup kettle or Dutch oven and sprinkle on the flour, stirring to make a roux. Stir in the stock, sorrel, and chervil, and bring to a boil.
2. Meanwhile, in a bowl, use a wire whisk to beat the egg yolk foamy before beating in ¼ cup of hot soup. Then stir this mixture back into the soup. Cook, stirring constantly, until thickened. Do not allow it to boil.
3. Turn off the heat, stir in the sugar, adjust the salt and pepper to taste, and stir in the sour cream. Serve immediately, with a sprinkling of minced garlic on top.

Hint: This recipe calls for French sorrel, which has less acid content than wild sorrel.

1 large beefsteak tomato, peeled
1 small green bell pepper, stemmed, seeded, and chopped
2 tablespoons extra virgin olive oil
1 clove garlic, peeled and crushed
1½ cups ice-cold water
1 tablespoon very fine bread crumbs
salt and pepper to taste
chopped chives for garnish

SPEEDY GAZPACHO

Year-Round

Yield: about 3 to 4 servings

1. In the container of a blender, combine the tomato, pepper, oil, garlic, water, and bread crumbs. Process on low until just smooth.
2. Pour into a chilled bowl and sprinkle with chives. Serve immediately with sliced dark bread and cheese on the side.

SUMMER VEGETABLE SOUP

Summer

Yield: about 6 servings

4 tablespoons margarine

1 medium yellow onion, chopped fine

2 small zucchini, chopped

½ small cucumber, peeled and chopped

½ cup fresh peas

2 fresh medium tomatoes, peeled, seeded, and chopped

12 scallions, trimmed and sliced

2 tablespoons minced fresh parsley

½ teaspoon crushed dried mint leaves

½ teaspoon crushed dried basil

8 cups boiling vegetable stock

½ teaspoon granulated sugar

½ head lettuce, chopped

salt and pepper to taste

1. Melt the margarine in a soup kettle or Dutch oven, and sauté the onion until tender. Add the zucchini, cucumber, peas, tomatoes, and scallions. Sauté for about 1 minute. Add the parsley, mint, basil, stock, and sugar.

2. Bring to boil, reduce to a simmer, and then cover lightly. Continue to cook, stirring occasionally, for about 10 minutes. Remove from heat, stir in the lettuce, adjust the salt and pepper to taste, and serve immediately, with a variety of crackers on the side.

SWEDISH-STYLE BREAD SOUP

Winter

Yield: about 6 servings

6 slices freshly baked bread

2 large yellow onions, chopped

1 tablespoon all-purpose flour

2 tablespoons margarine

6 cups vegetable stock

salt, pepper, and nutmeg to taste

grated cheese for garnish

1. Melt the margarine in a soup kettle or Dutch oven and sauté the onion until a golden brown color. Sprinkle on the flour, stirring until incorporated.

2. Pouring in a narrow stream, add the stock, and cook, stirring constantly, until thickened. Adjust the salt and pepper to taste. Bring to a boil, then reduce to a simmer, cover lightly, and cook, stirring occasionally, for about 20 minutes.

3. Turn off the heat, and strain through a sieve. Return to the pot, bring to a boil, and adjust the seasonings to taste. Serve immediately, with a slice of bread floated on each bowl. Garnish with cheese as desired.

2 tablespoons canola oil
1 small white onion, chopped
2 medium cloves garlic, peeled and crushed
1 tablespoon minced parsley
1 tablespoon minced green bell pepper
1 small carrot, peeled and diced
½ tablespoon uncooked wild rice
1 plum tomato, finely chopped
2½ cups vegetable stock
¼ cup minced celery stalk including leaves
¼ cup tomato juice or tomato vegetable juice
1 vegetable bouillon cube
½ teaspoon bottled hot sauce or to taste
salt and pepper to taste

1. Heat the oil in a soup kettle or Dutch oven, and sauté the onion, garlic, celery, parsley, green pepper, carrot, and rice together until heated through. Add the tomato, stock, juice, and bouillon cube.
2. Bring to a boil. Then reduce to a simmer, cover lightly, and cook, stirring occasionally, for about 30 minutes, or until the rice is tender.
3. Add the hot sauce and adjust the salt and pepper to taste. Serve immediately.

Hint: The tang comes from the bottled hot sauce. Just remember, you don't want so much tang that it overpowers other ingredients.

1 large fresh, ripe tomato, skinned, seeded, and diced
3 tablespoons vegetable oil
6 cups vegetable stock
3 cups shredded cabbage
2 medium carrots, peeled and cut into julienne strips
1 cup red onion, thinly sliced
2 stalks celery, trimmed and cut into julienne strips
1 teaspoon sesame oil
½ teaspoon Tabasco Sauce
salt and pepper to taste

1. Heat the oil in a soup kettle or Dutch oven, and sauté the tomato until heated through. Add the stock, cabbage, carrots, onion, and celery.
2. Bring to a boil. Then reduce to a simmer, cover lightly, and cook, stirring occasionally, for about 3 to 4 minutes.
3. Add the sesame oil and Tabasco; adjust the salt and pepper to taste. Serve immediately, with bread sticks on the side.

THAI-STYLE CHOCOLATE SOUP

Summer

Yield: about 4 to 6 servings

This great chocolate soup has a special twist that only a Thai cook could add.

2 cups soy milk
3-inch stick cinnamon
1 star anise
2 whole cloves
pinch ground allspice
1 teaspoon grated orange zest
½ cup unsalted, dry-roasted peanuts
1½ cups water
1 tablespoon Dutch cocoa powder
1 tablespoon canola oil
1 medium white onion, diced
2 stalks celery, diced
1 small clove garlic, peeled and mashed
1 large ripe tomato, diced
1 tablespoon bottled ginger syrup or juice
pinch cayenne pepper (optional)
2 tablespoons fresh lime juice
salt and pepper to taste
garnish of roasted peanuts to taste

1. In a saucepan, combine the soy milk, cinnamon, anise, cloves, allspice, and orange zest. Bring to a slow boil, remove from heat, and set aside for about 1 hour.
2. Put the peanuts in the container of a blender with just enough of the water to cover. Process on HIGH until smooth. Add the cocoa powder and remaining water, and process on HIGH until smooth.
3. Using a fine strainer, strain the peanut mixture into a bowl, discarding any material in the strainer. Repeat with the soy mixture.
4. In a skillet or saucepan, heat the oil, and sauté the onion and celery together until the onion is translucent. Add the garlic, and tomato, and cook until the garlic is lightly colored. Remove from heat.
5. In the container of a blender, purée the onion mixture until smooth. Add ½ cup of the cocoa mixture, and process on HIGH until smooth.
6. In a large saucepan or soup kettle, combine the remaining cocoa mixture, the soy mixture, and the onion mixture. Stir in the ginger juice, cayenne pepper, and lime juice. Remove from heat and adjust the salt and pepper to taste. Serve immediately in heated bowls with a garnish of chopped peanuts.

4 tablespoons margarine
2 medium yellow onions, diced
1 large green bell pepper, stemmed, seeded, and diced
2 medium cloves garlic, peeled and crushed
1 small head cabbage, cut into chunks
6 cups vegetable stock
2 large beets, trimmed, peeled, and sliced
3 potatoes, peeled and diced
3 fresh tomatoes, peeled, seeded, and quartered
1 tablespoon lemon or lime juice
2 bay leaves
⅛ teaspoon dill seeds, crushed
⅛ teaspoon cumin seeds, crushed
1 chili pepper, seeded and mashed
2 tablespoons coarsely chopped celery leaves
1 cup sour cream or unflavored yogurt
2 tablespoons chopped parsley

TURKISH BORSCHT

Autumn

Yield: about 6 servings

1. Heat the margarine in a soup kettle or Dutch oven, and sauté the onions and green peppers together until the onion is tender. Add the garlic and cabbage; continue to sauté for about 2 additional minutes. Add the stock, beets, potatoes, tomatoes, lemon juice, bay leaves, dill seeds, cumin seeds, chili pepper, and celery leaves. Bring to a boil. Then reduce to a simmer, cover lightly, and cook, stirring occasionally, for about 40 minutes, or until the vegetables are fork tender.
2. Turn off the heat, remove and discard the bay leaves, and adjust the salt and pepper to taste. Serve immediately, with the sour cream and chopped parsley on the side.

Hint: Although this beet soup recipe originated in Turkey, you can taste its strong Russian influences.

SOUTHWEST ONION PICANTE SOUP

Summer
Yield: about 6 servings

3 cups thinly sliced onions
1 clove garlic, peeled and minced
¼ cup margarine
2 cups tomato juice
10.5-ounce can condensed vegetable stock
10.5-ounce soup can water
½ cup picante sauce
salt and pepper to taste
1 cup unseasoned croutons (optional)
1 cup shredded Monterey Jack cheese (optional)
additional picante sauce

1. Melt the margarine in a soup kettle or Dutch oven, and sauté the onions and garlic until the onion turns a golden color. Add the tomato juice, stock, water, and ½ cup picante sauce. Bring to a boil, reduce to simmer, and cook uncovered, stirring occasionally, for about 20 minutes.

2. Turn off the heat, adjust the salt and pepper to taste, and sprinkle with croutons and shredded cheese. Serve immediately with picante sauce on the side.

WATERCRESS SOUP WITH PEARS

Summer
Yield: about 6 servings

1 bunch fresh watercress
4 Bartlett pears, pared and diced
3¾ cups unsweetened apple juice
½ cup heavy cream
1 tablespoon fresh lime juice
salt and pepper to taste (optional)
3 Comice or dessert pears, pared and halved
sliced almonds for garnish

1. In a large saucepan, combine the watercress leaves (stems removed), Bartlett pears, and apple juice. Bring to a boil. Then reduce to a gentle simmer, cover, and cook, stirring occasionally, for about 15 minutes. Remove from heat.

2. In the container of a blender or food processor, purée the mixture in batches until smooth. Return to the pan; add the cream and lime juice. Heat through, but do not allow to boil. Ladle into heated bowls, float a half a dessert pear on top, cut side down, and sprinkle with almonds. Serve at once with a crusty bread on the side.

Hint: Seasoning to taste could mean a sprinkling of nutmeg or cinnamon. This soup comes from Japan.

1 cup chopped yellow onion
1 cup chopped green bell pepper
6 green onions, sliced
½ cup vegetable oil
½ cup all-purpose flour
3 cups water
14.5-ounce can Cajun-style stewed tomatoes
28-ounce can diced tomatoes
6-ounce can tomato paste
two 10-ounce packages frozen whole-kernel corn
cayenne pepper to taste
hot pepper sauce to taste
salt and pepper to taste

1. Heat the oil in a soup kettle or Dutch oven, and sauté the onion, green pepper, and green onions until tender, for about 5 minutes. Sprinkle on the flour, and cook, stirring constantly, until smooth. Add water, stewed tomatoes, diced tomatoes, and tomato paste.
2. Bring to a boil, then reduce to a simmer, and stir in the corn, cayenne pepper, and pepper sauce. Continue to cook, stirring occasionally, uncovered for about 50 minutes. Remove from heat, adjust the salt and pepper to taste, and serve immediately.

Hint: With the heavy tomato ingredients in this soup, one could almost call it a tomato soup. However, remember that this soup has five flavoring ingredients, and you don't want any one of them to predominate.

WATERCRESS SOUP

Spring
Yield: about 4 servings

2 bunches watercress
1 tablespoon butter or margarine
2 cups vegetable stock or water
1 tablespoon cornstarch
½ cup milk, at room temperature
salt and pepper to taste
3 tablespoons light cream or evaporated milk

1. Thoroughly wash the watercress; cut off and discard the stems. Reserve several sprigs for garnish.
2. Melt the butter in a saucepan, and sauté the watercress for about 2 minutes. Add the stock, bring to a boil, then reduce to a simmer, and cook for about 10 minutes. (Do not overcook.)
3. In a cup, blend the cornstarch and milk until smooth, and stir into the soup, stirring for about 5 minutes, or until thickened.
4. Remove from heat, and in the container of a blender, process in batches on low speed until the watercress is just chopped. (Do not purée the watercress.)
5. Add the salt and pepper to taste and the cream, and pour into heated bowls. Serve immediately, with cubed fruits or vegetables on the side.

Hint: The secret of this soup is to not overcook it at any time. If you boil it too long it will loose all its taste.

FRUIT SOUPS

The jury is still out on fruit soups. Some cooks declare that the so-called fruit soup is little more than warmed fruit juice, or that it's a different way to serve fruit juice. Others consider it a smoothie in a bowl. Fruit soups make good appetizers, and they're great for children when they come home from school.

APPLE SOUP

Summer

Yield: about 4 to 6
servings

16 Granny Smith apples, cored and chopped
5 cups water, unsweetened apple juice or cider
2½ teaspoons grated lemon peel
½ teaspoon English mixture spice
¼ cup maple syrup
1 tablespoon cornstarch
1 tablespoon fresh lemon juice
¼ cup white port wine
½ cup sour cream or unflavored yogurt

1. In a soup kettle or Dutch oven, combine the apples, water, lemon peel, English mixture spice, and maple syrup. Bring to a boil, then reduce to a simmer, and cook, stirring frequently, for about 20 minutes, or until the apples are fork tender.
2. Transfer to the container of a blender or food processor, and process on HIGH until smooth. Blend the cornstarch with the lemon juice.
3. Return to the kettle, bring to a boil, and then stir in the cornstarch mixture. Continue to cook, stirring constantly, until thickened.
4. Turn off the heat and stir in the wine. To serve, place a spoonful of sour cream in each bowl, and spoon the hot soup over the top.

For English mixture spice, you can substitute ½ teaspoon apple-pie spice or a pinch (⅛ teaspoon) each of cinnamon, cloves, and allspice.

Hint: This apple soup is also good cold with whipped heavy cream on the side. Or, if you prefer, try whipped berry yogurt.

APRICOT CELERY SOUP

Autumn

Yield: about 4 to 6
servings

4-ounce package dried apricots
2 small shallots, peeled and minced
6 stalks celery, sliced
1½ teaspoons canola oil
6 cups vegetable stock
salt and pepper to taste

1. Put the dried apricots in a saucepan, cover with boiling water, and set aside for about 5 minutes.
2. Meanwhile, heat the oil in a large saucepan or soup kettle, and sauté the shallots and celery together until the shallots are just tender. Add the stock, bring to a boil, and reduce to a simmer.
3. Drain the apricots and discard the water. Chop the apricots into fine pieces and add them to the simmering water. Cover and continue to simmer, stirring occasionally, for about 40 minutes. Remove from heat.
4. In the container of a blender or food processor, purée the soup in batches until smooth. Adjust the salt and pepper to taste, and serve in heated bowls.

2 ripe avocados, diced
2½ cups unsweetened apple juice or vegetable stock
1 teaspoon curry powder
¼ teaspoon turmeric powder
salt and white pepper to taste
½ cup heavy cream
finely diced avocado for garnish

AVOCADO CURRY SOUP

Autumn

Yield: about 4 to 6 servings

1. Using a blender or food processor, combine the avocado and 1 cup of apple juice. Process on HIGH until smooth. Pour into a soup kettle or large saucepan. Add the remaining juice, curry powder, and turmeric. Bring to a boil, and immediately remove from heat.
2. Adjust the salt and pepper to taste, cool slightly. Then refrigerate for at least 2 hours before serving cold with whipped cream and diced avocado on the side.

1½ pounds fresh blackberries
4 tablespoons granulated sugar
1 tablespoon dark brown sugar
1½ cups red port wine
1 stick cinnamon
1 tablespoon grated orange zest
ice cream

BLACKBERRY SOUP

Summer

Yield: about 4 to 6 servings

1. In a large saucepan or soup kettle, combine the berries, sugar, wine, cinnamon, and orange zest. Bring to a boil, then reduce to a simmer, and cook for about 10 minutes.
2. Remove from heat and ladle into heated bowls. Add a small scoop of ice cream.

Hint: This soup can also be chilled and served in a chilled bowl.

⅔ cup sour cream
two 10-ounce packages frozen blueberries, partially thawed
¼ cup granulated sugar
lemon or lime slices for garnish

BLENDER BLUEBERRY SOUP

Autumn

Yield: about 4 servings

1. In the container of a blender, combine the sour cream, blueberries, and sugar. Process on SLOW until just smooth.
2. Pour into chilled soup bowls. Garnish with citrus slices and serve immediately, with a vanilla wafer on the side.

BRANDIED STRAWBERRY SOUP

Spring

Yield: about 6 servings

2¾ cup fresh strawberries, sliced lengthwise
3 tablespoons brandy
1 cup sour cream
1 cup half-and-half
½ teaspoon almond or hazelnut extract
chopped mint leaves for garnish

1. The day before, combine the ¾ cup of sliced strawberries and brandy. Cover tightly and refrigerate overnight.
2. In the container of a blender or food processor, combine until smooth the remaining 2 cups sliced strawberries, sour cream, half-and-half, and almond extract. Pour into a container, cover tightly, and refrigerate for about 4 hours.
3. When ready, stir the brandied strawberries into the cold soup mix, and serve immediately. Garnish with mint sprigs.

Hint: Serve this as a dessert soup or an elegant appetizer.

CANTALOUPE COOLER

Summer

Yield: about 8 servings

2 pounds fresh cantaloupe, cubed
1½ cups fresh orange juice or unsweetened apple juice
¼ teaspoon ground ginger
1 tablespoon fresh lime juice
5.3-fluid-ounce can sweetened condensed milk
mint springs for garnish
1 lime, thinly sliced

1. In the container of a food processor or blender, combine the cantaloupe, orange juice, ginger, lime juice, and condensed milk.
2. Process on HIGH until smooth. Refrigerate until chilled through. Pour into bowls, garnish with mint and slices of lime. Serve immediately.

1 tablespoon honey
3 tablespoons melted margarine
2 tablespoons prepared mustard
2 to 4 tablespoons snipped fresh parsley
1 to 2 tablespoons freshly chopped tarragon leaves
2 tablespoons orange zest
1 pound small baby carrots, peeled and halved lengthwise
2 small turnips, trimmed, peeled, and diced
2 cups fresh unsweetened orange juice
4 cups vegetable stock or unsweetened apple juice
salt and pepper to taste
6 to 8 pitted plums, sliced thin
4 tablespoons fresh orange juice

CARROT SOUP WITH PLUMS

Summer

Yield: about 6 servings

1. In a small bowl or cup, blend the honey, margarine, mustard, parsley, tarragon leaves, and orange zest. Set aside; do not refrigerate.
2. In a soup kettle or Dutch oven, combine the carrots, turnips, and orange juice. Bring to a boil, then reduce to a simmer, cover tightly, and cook about 10 minutes.
3. Add the vegetable stock, and continue to cook, stirring occasionally, for about 10 to 15 minutes or until the carrots and turnips are tender.
4. In the container of a blender or food processor, purée the carrot mixture in batches until smooth. Return to the pot, heat through, and adjust the salt and pepper to taste.
5. Ladle the soup into bowls, and garnish with a small piece of the honey-margarine mix and sliced plums. Serve immediately.

4 cups fresh strawberries, sliced
15-ounce carton strawberry-flavored yogurt or unflavored sour cream
2 teaspoons almond or vanilla extract
⅓ cup powdered sugar
½ cup light cream or half-and-half
6 slices stale pound cake, cut and toasted like croutons

CREAM-OF-STRAWBERRY SOUP

Spring

Yield: about 4 to 6 servings

1. In a bowl, blend the strawberries, yogurt, extract, and sugar.
2. In the container of a blender or food processor, purée the mixture in batches until smooth, and then pour the mixture back into the bowl.
3. Stir in the cream, cover tightly, and refrigerate for at least 4 hours or overnight.
4. When ready, ladle into well-chilled bowls, sprinkle with pound-cake croutons, and serve with an after-dinner drink.

CELERY-ROOT SOUP WITH APPLES

Autumn

Yield: 8 to 10 servings

2 tablespoons vegetable oil
2 medium yellow onions, coarsely chopped
2 large red potatoes, peeled and diced
3 large Granny Smith apples, pared and chopped
1 medium celery root, peeled and diced
1 gallon unsweetened apple juice or vegetable stock
salt and pepper to taste
chopped chives for garnish (optional)

1. Heat the oil in a soup kettle or Dutch oven, and sauté the onions, potatoes, apples, and celery root until the onions are tender. Add the stock, bring to a boil. Then reduce to a simmer, cover lightly, and cook, stirring occasionally, for about 30 minutes or until the vegetables are tender.
2. In the container of a blender or food processor, purée the vegetables and liquid in batches until smooth. Return to the pot and heat through.
3. Adjust the salt and pepper to taste, and serve immediately, with the chives on the side for garnish.

Hint: Celery root, like broccoli, can be a terrific flavor enhancer. When I prepared this soup, I tried five different kinds of apples. Only the Granny Smith gave satisfactory results.

UKRAINIAN-STYLE FRUIT SOUP

Winter

Yield: about 6 servings

2 cups cold water
1 tablespoon fresh lemon juice
1½ tablespoons grated lemon zest
½ cup fresh white bread crumbs
1 pound fresh pippin or Newton apples
1 pound fresh Bartlett pears
½ pound fresh cherries, pitted
½ pound fresh plums, pitted
½ pound fresh peaches, skinned and diced
¼ cup raspberry jam or preserves
½ cup granulated sugar
¾ cup white port wine or sherry
1 cup cranberry juice

1. In a soup kettle or large saucepan, combine the water, lemon juice, lemon zest, and bread crumbs. Bring to boil, and add all at one time, the apples, pears, cherries, plums, and peaches. Bring to a boil. Then reduce to a simmer, cover lightly, and cook, stirring occasionally, for about 25 minutes, or until the fruit is soft. Remove from heat.
2. In the container of a blender or food processor, purée the mixture in batches, and then return to the pan. Add the jam, sugar, wine, and cranberry juice. Cover and refrigerate for at least 4 hours, and then serve chilled with a fruit pastry on the side.

16-ounce package frozen blueberries
1 cup water
¼ cup granulated sugar
pinch ground cinnamon
pinch ground nutmeg
pinch ground cloves
1 tablespoon cornstarch
1 tablespoon water
2 tablespoons lime or lemon juice
1 cup berry-flavored yogurt
½ cup soy milk
10-ounce package frozen berries, thawed

CREAMY BERRY SOUP

Autumn

Yield: about 4 to 6 servings

1. In a large saucepan or soup kettle, combine the 16 oz. of frozen berries, water, sugar, cinnamon, nutmeg, and cloves. Bring to a boil, then reduce to a simmer, and cook, stirring frequently, for about 5 minutes.
2. Blend the cornstarch with 1 tablespoon of water. Stir in the cornstarch mixture and continue to cook, stirring constantly, until thick and bubbly. Remove from heat, and stir in the lemon juice.
3. Cool to room temperature, adjust the sweetness to taste. Add the yogurt and milk. Cover and chill for about 3 to 4 hours.
4. When ready to serve, stir in the thawed berries, and ladle into well-chilled bowls.

1 pound pitted prunes
3 quarts water or unsweetened apple juice
3 tablespoons flour
1 cup sour cream or unflavored yogurt

CREAMY PRUNE SOUP

Autumn

Yield: about 6 servings

1. Place the prunes and water in a saucepan, and bring to a boil. Reduce to a simmer, and cook, stirring occasionally, until the prunes are very soft.
2. Meanwhile, in a bowl, beat together the flour and sour cream.
3. When the prunes are cooked, stir one cup of the hot liquid into the sour cream mixture, and the stir the sour cream mixture back into the soup. Bring to a slow boil, and cook, stirring frequently, until thickened. Remove from heat, and serve in heated bowls with a desired menu.

Hint: Here's a tasty way to enjoy nature's laxative.

CUBAN PLANTAIN SOUP

Year-Round
Yield: about 6 servings

4 large green plantains
6 cups vegetable stock or unsweetened apple juice
salt and pepper to taste
1 tablespoon fresh lime juice

1. Using a sharp knife, cut the plantains paper thin and arrange in the bottom of a 13 x 9-inch baking pan. Cover with water, and set aside at room temperature for about 1 hour.
2. When ready, drain, discarding the water, and pat the plantain slices dry using paper towels.
3. Place the slices in a bowl, and using the back of a large spoon, mash until smooth.
4. Heat the stock in a soup kettle or large saucepan. Bring to a boil. Add the plantain paste, a little at a time, stirring until smooth. Reduce to a simmer, cover lightly, and cook, stirring occasionally, for about 20 minutes. Remove from heat, adjust the salt and pepper to taste, and serve in heated bowls, with a sprinkle of lime juice on each bowl.

Hint: The plantain, popular in Latin American cooking, is a variety of banana with a squashlike taste.

DANISH FRUIT SOUP

Year-Round
Yield: about 6 to 8 servings

3½ cups dried mixed fruit, diced
¼ cup tapioca
½ cup granulated sugar
2 cups water or unsweetened apple juice
1 stick cinnamon
½ cup fresh lemon juice
½ cup grape jelly
pinch of ground cloves

1. In a soup kettle or large saucepan, combine the dried fruit with enough water to just cover by 1 inch. Cover tightly and set aside in a cool place for at least 8 hours.
2. When ready, place the kettle on the stove, and simmer gently, stirring occasionally, until the fruit is very soft.
3. Drain, returning the juices to the kettle, and beat in the tapioca, sugar, water, and cinnamon. Bring to a boil, and cook, stirring, for about 30 minutes, or until the tapioca is clear. Stir in the lemon juice, cloves, and jelly. Cook, stirring constantly, until the jelly is dissolved. Add the fruit, heat through, and serve in heated bowls with a sweet bread on the side.

1 cup cranberry juice
1 cup dry red wine
3-inch stick cinnamon
15-ounce package frozen berries
1 tablespoon fresh lemon juice
1 tablespoon granulated sugar
½ cup sour cream, or berry-flavored yogurt

EASY BERRY & WINE SOUP

Summer

Yield: about 2 to 4 servings

1. In a saucepan, combine the cranberry juice, wine and cinnamon. Bring to a boil, and reduce to 1 cup.
2. Meanwhile, in the container of a blender, purée the berries with lemon juice and sugar on low speed until smooth, and then using the back of a spoon, press through a sieve, discarding the seeds. Transfer to a saucepan.
3. Add lemon juice and sugar to the berry purée. Slowly add the cranberry and wine mixture. Bring just to a boil. Reduce to simmer, and cook, stirring constantly, for 5 minutes. Remove and discard the cinnamon stick.
4. Serve with sour cream or berry-flavored yogurt.

2 tablespoons raisins
1 tablespoon dry sherry or white port wine
2 small Bartlett pears, pared and diced
1½ cups water or unsweetened apple juice
1-inch cinnamon stick
pinch powdered anise
2 teaspoons granulated sugar
½ teaspoon fresh lemon juice

GERMAN PEAR SOUP

Summer

Yield: about 2 servings

1. In small bowl, combine raisins and sherry; then set aside.
2. In a soup kettle or Dutch oven, combine the pears, water, cinnamon stick, and anise. Bring to a boil, then reduce to a simmer, cover lightly, and cook for about 10 minutes, or until the pears are cooked tender.
3. Turn off the heat, remove and discard the cinnamon stick, and in the container of a blender or food processor, purée the soup in batches, until smooth. Pour into a large bowl, add the raisin mix, sugar, lemon juice. Cover and refrigerate for at least 4 hours. When ready, serve alone or as part of a menu.

Hint: The wine is used as a flavor enhancer. If you omit the wine, this is still a very good soup.

GERMAN-STYLE ELDERBERRY SOUP

Autumn

Yield: about 6 servings

2½ pounds elderberries
9¼ cups water or unsweetened apple juice
2 tablespoons lemon juice
1 teaspoon lemon zest
¾ cup granulated sugar
4 tablespoons cornstarch
4 tablespoons water

1. In a soup kettle or Dutch oven, combine the berries, water, lemon juice, and zest. Bring to a boil. Then reduce to a simmer, cover lightly, and cook, stirring occasionally, until the berries are mushy.
2. In the container of a blender or a food processor, purée the berry mix, in batches until smooth, and return to the pot.
3. In a cup, combine the sugar, cornstarch and water. Stir into the berry mixture, bring to a boil, heating briefly for about 2 minutes.
4. Turn off the heat, and adjust the sweetness to taste. Serve immediately, with a sweet cracker or cookie on the side.

GINGERED MELON SOUP

Summer

Yield: about 4 servings

2 large ripe cantaloupes, halved
2 tablespoons sliced fresh ginger root
16 individual fresh mint leaves
¾ cup fresh orange juice
1 ripe nectarine, thinly sliced

1. Using a melon baller, scoop out the pulp, being careful not to cut through the outer flesh. In the container of a blender or food processor, purée the melon balls, ginger, and half the mint leaves together, until very smooth, and then pour into a bowl.
2. Reserve the empty melon halves. Tightly cover them with plastic wrap and keep them in the refrigerator until serving the soup.
3. Stir in the orange juice, cover tightly, and chill for at least 4 hours. Then ladle into the empty melon halves, float the nectarine slices on the top, along with two mint leaves. Place each melon half in a larger bowl, and serve immediately.

Hint: Unsweetened fresh apple juice may be used in place of orange juice. A melon called a galia melon looks almost identical to cantaloupe, but tastes different.

2½ cups strawberry juice
1 large ripe banana, sliced
1 tablespoon bottled ginger juice
1 cup sparkling cider
¼ cup whipped strawberry yogurt
1 cup frozen mixed berries for garnish

GINGERED STRAWBERRY SOUP

Spring
Yield: about 4 to 6 servings

1. In the container of a blender, combine the strawberry juice, banana, and ginger juice. Process on HIGH until smooth . Pour into a bowl. Stir in the cider, cover and refrigerate for at least 2 hours.
2. When ready, ladle into well-chilled bowls, with a daub of yogurt on the top, and several berries sprinkled on each bowl.

2 pounds seedless grapes
1 cup water
2 tablespoons packed light brown sugar
1 teaspoon lime juice
1 tablespoon cornstarch or arrowroot

GRAPE SOUP

Autumn
Yield: about 3 to 4 servings

1. In a saucepan, combine the grapes, and ¾ cup water. Bring to a boil, then reduce to a simmer, cover tightly and cook, stirring, until the grapes are very soft. Remove from heat.
2. Meanwhile, blend the cornstarch into the remaining water until smooth.
3. In the container of a blender, purée the grape mixture in batches, and return to the pan. Add the sugar and lime juice. Return to the heat, bring to a slow boil, and stir in the cornstarch mixture. Cook, stirring constantly, until lightly thickened. Remove from heat, cool to room temperature, and chill in the refrigerator until needed.
4. When ready, garnish with additional sliced grapes, and finely crushed almonds.

Hint: The secret of this soup is to be sure the grapes you use are ripe. A little bruising or very soft grapes are preferred.

PAPAYA-ORANGE SOUP

Summer

Yield: about 4 to 5 servings

2 cups bottled tropical punch
7-gram envelope unflavored gelatin
1 large egg white
1 medium papaya, pared and chunked
1 cup fresh unsweetened orange juice
pinch ground cumin
2 tablespoons finely chopped almonds
½ cup grated coconut

1. Place the punch in a saucepan, and sprinkle the gelatin over the top. Set aside for about 5 minutes.
2. Meanwhile, in a bowl, using a wire whisk or electric mixer on high speed, beat the egg white until just a heavy foam.
3. Stir the egg into the punch mix, and tranfer to the stove. Using a wire whisk, and beating constantly, bring to a fast simmer, cooking until the gelatin is dissolved. The mixture with be frothy. Remove from heat and set aside for at least 10 minutes.
4. Meanwhile, in the container of a blender or food processor, combine one-third of the papaya and ⅓ cup of orange juice, processing until smooth. Repeat. Stir into the cooled punch mix, adjust the seasoning and sweetness to taste, cover and refrigerate for at least 8 hours.
5. One hour before ready, place the soup bowls in the freezer, and then when ready, ladle the chilled mixture into the bowls, garnish with almonds and coconut, and serve immediately.

PAPAYA LOVE

Autumn

Yield: about 4 servings

2 cups diced candied papaya
1 cup sour cream or unflavored yogurt
2 tablespoons real mayonnaise
½ cup water
6 fresh basil leaves
½ cup white port wine

1. In a saucepan or Crock Pot, combine the papaya, sour cream, mayonnaise, water, and basil. Bring to a boil, then reduce to a simmer, cover and cook slowly until the papaya is very soft.
2. Transfer the mixture to the container of blender or food processor, and purée until smooth. Return to the saucepan.
3. Add the wine, heat through, and serve as desired with a crusty bread on the side.

2 cups water or unsweetened apple juice
1 cup red port wine
½ cup granulated sugar
2 tablespoons lime juice
3-inch stick cinnamon
4 cups fresh strawberries, puréed
¼ cup strawberry-flavored yogurt
¼ cup heavy cream, beaten stiff
1 sprig fresh mint

PINK STRAWBERRY SOUP

Spring

Yield: about 6 to 8 servings

1. In a soup kettle or large saucepan, combine the water, wine, sugar, lime juice, and cinnamon. Bring to a boil, and cook for about 3 to 4 minutes. Stir in the strawberries, reduce to a simmer, cover and cook for about 5 minutes. Discard the cinnamon, remove from heat, and cool slightly.
2. Transfer to a bowl, stir in the yogurt, and fold in the cream. Cover tightly and refrigerate for at least 4 hours.
3. When ready, ladle into glass serving dishes, garnish with a sprig of fresh mint, and serve as desired.

Hint: The quality of this recipe is enhanced by the wine. Remember, no alcohol remains in this soup by the time it is served.

1 tablespoon all-purpose flour
½ cup cherry-flavored yogurt or unflavored sour cream
1 teaspoon granulated sugar
1½ cups pitted fresh Royal Ann cherries
3¾ cups water
¼ cup powdered sugar

POLISH SOUR CHERRY SOUP

Summer

Yield: about 4 servings

1. In a bowl, blend the flour, yogurt, and sugar until very smooth.
2. In a saucepan or soup kettle, combine the cherries, water, and powdered sugar. Simmer gently, stirring occasionally, for about 10 minutes. Remove from heat, and reserve about 2 tablespoons of the cooking liquid. Then slowly stir the flour mixture into the cherry mix, and return to the heat.
3. Bring to a boil, then reduce to a simmer, and cook, stirring frequently, for about 5 to 6 minutes, or until thickened. Remove from heat.
4. Cool to room temperature, cover tightly and refrigerate until chilled through.
5. When ready, drizzle on the reserved cooking liquid, swirl gently, and serve in chilled bowls.

Hint: This soup can be greatly enhanced by adding about 1 or 2 tablespoons of Cherry Heering liqueur, made in Denmark, during the last heating of the soup.

POMEGRANATE SOUP

Summer

Yield: about 4 servings

2 ripe pomegranates
1 tablespoon margarine
1 small white onion, chopped
2 teaspoons chopped fresh ginger root
20 fresh spinach leaves, washed and dried
½ teaspoon ground cumin
¾ cup water
salt and black pepper to taste
¼ cup heavy cream, sweetened to taste

1. Using a sharp knife, cut the pomegranates in half, and scoop out the small red seeds. Pick over and discard any white pith that may have come out with the seeds.
2. Melt the margarine in a large saucepan, and sauté the onion and ginger together until the onion is tender.
3. Reserve 1 tablespoon of the pomegranate seeds, and add the remainder to the onion mix. Then add the spinach leaves and cumin. Add the water, and bring to a boil. Reduce to a low simmer, cover and cook, without stirring, for about 5 minutes. Remove from heat, and cool slightly.
4. In the container of a blender or food processor, purée the mixture in batches until smooth. Adjust the salt and pepper to taste, and ladle into heated bowls. Swirl in a little of the cream, and a sprinkling of a few of the pomegranate seeds. Serve immediately.

Hint: This soup is traditionally known as Anarkali Shorba.

PRUNE SOUP

Summer

Yield: about 6 servings

1 pound pitted prunes, chopped
¼ teaspoon salt
3 quarts water
3 tablespoons all-purpose flour
½ pint sour cream
salt, pepper, and ground nutmeg to taste

1. In a soup kettle or Dutch oven, combine the prunes, salt, and water. Bring to a boil, and cook, stirring until the prunes are very soft.
2. In a bowl, blend the flour and sour cream. Stir in 1 cup of the hot liquid from the prunes until incorporated. Then stir into the hot mixture. Bring to a boil, stirring until thickened.
3. Turn off the heat, adjust any seasonings to taste, and serve immediately.

HUNGARIAN SPICED CHERRY SOUP

Spring
Yield: about 4 servings

1 pound Royal Ann cherries, pitted
2 strips of lemon rind
6 whole cloves
1 stick cinnamon
⅓ cup granulated sugar
3 cups water or unsweetened apple juice
3 tablespoons quick-cooking tapioca
1 cup red port wine
4 thin slices fresh lemon
1 cup sour cream or unflavored yogurt

1. Thoroughly wash the cherries and carefully remove the pits and stems.
2. Press the cloves into the lemon rind.
3. In a saucepan, combine the cherries, lemon rind, cinnamon, sugar, and water. Bring to a boil, then reduce to a simmer, and cook, uncovered, stirring occasionally, for about 15 minutes. Then stir in the tapioca, bring to a boil, and immediately remove from heat. Stir in the wine. Discard the lemon rind and cinnamon stick. Cool to room temperature, cover tightly and refrigerate for at least 4 hour, or until well chilled.
4. When ready, ladle into chilled soup bowls. Float the lemon slices on top with a daub of sour cream.

SPICY MELON & APPLE SOUP

Summer
Yield: about 4 servings

1 large honeydew melon, chunked
12-fluid-ounce bottle unsweetened apple juice
1 cup dry white wine
2 teaspoons lime or lemon juice
2 teaspoons finely minced crystallized ginger root
1 small honeydew melon, balled

1. Place the honeydew melon chunks in the container of a blender or food processor, and process on HIGH until smooth. Then add the apple juice, wine, lime juice, and ginger root. Process on LOW for a few seconds, and pour into a large bowl. Cover tightly, and refrigerate for at least 4 hours.
2. When ready, ladle into very cold chilled bowls, and add the honeydew melon balls from the smaller melon. Garnish with a sprig of mint.

Hint: Although this recipe calls for honeydew melon, it also works with other varieties of melon.

STRAWBERRY SOUP WITH CHERRIES

Spring

Yield: about 8 to 10 servings

4 cups frozen strawberry juice concentrate
4 cups water
2 tablespoons honey
½ cup fresh lime juice
½ cup white port wine (optional)
2 tablespoons cornstarch
2 tablespoons water
3 cups strawberries
1 cup frozen pitted cherries
½ cup light cream
½ cup sour cream or strawberry-flavored yogurt
chopped or sliced almonds for garnish

1. In a soup kettle or large saucepan, combine the strawberry juice, honey, lime juice, wine, and strawberries. Bring to a boil. Reduce to a simmer, and cook for about 5 minutes. Blend the cornstarch with 2 tablespoons water. Return the strawberry mixture to a boil, and stir in the cornstarch mixture, cooking and stirring until thickened.
2. Remove from heat, add the cream, and cool to room temperature, stirring occasionally. Strain through a sieve, discarding the pulp, and stir in the cherries. Cover tightly and refrigerate for about 2 hours.
3. When ready, ladle into well-chilled bowls, with a daub of sour cream on the top and garnished with chopped almonds.

TWO MELON SOUP

Autumn

Yield: about 6 servings

1 small cantaloupe, diced
2 tablespoons grated orange zest
2 tablespoons fresh orange juice
2 tablespoons sherry or white port wine
1 small honeydew melon, diced
2 tablespoons fresh lemon juice
3 tablespoons fresh mint leaves
sprigs fresh mint for garnish

1. In the container of a blender, combine the cantaloupe, orange zest, orange juice, and sherry. Process on HIGH until smooth. Pour into a bowl, cover tightly and refrigerate for about 4 hours.
2. Rinse out the container of the blender, and combine the honeydew, lemon juice and mint leaves. Process on HIGH until smooth. Pour into a bowl, cover and refrigerate for about 4 hours.
3. When ready, using two ladles, ladle one scoop of each into a chilled bowl at the same time, giving the soup a half-orange, half-green look. Garnish with mint sprigs, and serve immediately, with a sweet roll or cookie on the side.

CREAM SOUPS

Perhaps cream soup is the most difficult category into which to separate recipes. Many other recipes in this cookbook contain milk, cream, cheese, or other ingredients that give the finished preparation the look of a cream soup. Most cream soups are characterized by rich consistency, and many could easily be called hearty soups.

ALBUQUERQUE CORN SOUP

Year-Round

Yield: about 3 to 5 servings

1 cup vegetable stock
3½ cups frozen whole-kernel corn, thawed
¼ cup margarine
1 large clove garlic, peeled and chopped
2 cups milk
1 teaspoon crushed dried oregano
4-ounce can chopped green chilis
1 cup shredded Monterey Jack cheese
salt and ground white pepper to taste

1. In the container of a blender or food processor, combine the stock and 3 cups of the corn, and process on HIGH until smooth.
2. Melt margarine in a soup kettle or Dutch oven, and sauté the garlic until lightly colored. Stir in the remaining ½ cup of corn and continue to cook for about 2 minutes. Stir in the puréed corn, milk, oregano, and chilies. Bring to a boil, remove from heat, stir in the cheese, and adjust the salt and pepper to taste. Serve as desired.

ANATOLIAN SOUP

Winter

Yield: about 4 servings

2 tablespoons margarine
1 medium yellow onion, chopped
4 cups vegetable stock
¼ cup quick-cooking barley
1 cup unflavored yogurt
salt and pepper to taste
2 tablespoons chopped parsley
1 teaspoon crushed dried mint

1. Melt the margarine in a soup kettle or Dutch oven, and sauté the onions until translucent. Stir in the stock and bring to a boil. Reduce to a simmer, add the barley, cover lightly, and cook for about 15 to 20 minutes, or until the barley is tender.
2. In a bowl, combine 2 tablespoons of the hot liquid from the kettle, and yogurt, beating until blended, and then stir into the soup. Adjust the salt and pepper to taste, and remove from heat. Sprinkle with parsley and mint, and serve immediately as desired.

1 tablespoon olive oil
½ cup chopped yellow onions
1 cup sliced fresh mushrooms
8-ounce can artichoke hearts, drained and chopped
2 cups vegetable stock
½ cup fresh or frozen green peas
¼ cup unbleached flour blended with 2 cups evaporated skim milk
salt and pepper to taste

ARTICHOKE CHOWDER

Summer

Yield: about 4 to 5 servings

1. Heat the oil in a skillet and sauté the onion until golden. Add the mushrooms, artichokes, and stock. Bring to a boil, cover lightly, reduce to a simmer and cook for about 5 minutes. Add the peas, cover, and cook until tender. Stir in the milk mixture, return to a boil, and cook, stirring until thickened.
2. Turn off the heat, and adjust the salt and pepper to taste. Serve at once, alone or as part of a menu, with heated French bread slices or rolls on the side.

3 leftover baked potatoes
2 teaspoons margarine
1 medium yellow onion, chopped
3 cups vegetable stock
1 tablespoon chopped green onion
3 cups skim milk
1 cup half-and-half
whipped sour cream or unflavored yogurt
shredded colby cheese
3 green onions (whites and greens), finely chopped

BAKED POTATO SOUP

Winter

Yield: about 4 servings

1. Pare the potatoes, reserving the skins, and dice.
2. Melt the margarine in a skillet and sauté the onions until tender.
3. In the container of a blender, combine 1 cup of the stock and the potato skins. Process on high until smooth.
4. In a soup kettle or Dutch oven, combine the milk, potatoes, the sautéed onions, the mixture from the blender, and half-and-half. Bring to a boil, and immediately remove from heat.
5. Place a daub of sour cream in each bowl, sprinkle with a little cheese, and spoon the soup over the top. Garnish with green onion, and serve immediately.

BROCCOLI BREW

Winter

Yield: about 6 servings

½ cup water
2 instant vegetable bouillon cubes
10-ounce package frozen chopped broccoli
1 cup milk
1 cup light cream
1 teaspoon powdered onion
½ teaspoon ground nutmeg
salt and pepper to taste
snipped fresh chives for garnish (optional)

1. Heat the water and bouillon cubes together in a saucepan, stirring until the cubes are dissolved. Add the broccoli, bring to a boil. Then reduce to a simmer, cover tightly, and cook for about 3 to 4 minutes.
2. Remove from heat, and transfer half of the broccoli-bouillon mixture to the container of a blender or food processor, and purée until smooth. Then combine this broccoli mixture with ½ cup milk, ½ cup cream, onion powder, and nutmeg. Process until smooth.
3. Return to the pot. Add the remaining broccoli-bouillon mixture. Bring to a boil. Add the remaining ½ cup milk and ½ cup cream, stirring constantly, until incorporated.
4. Turn off the heat, and adjust the salt and pepper to taste. Serve immediately with a garnish of snipped fresh chives.

BROCCOLI CHEESE SOUP

Winter

Yield: about 6 servings

1 cup water
10-ounce package frozen chopped broccoli
2 vegetable bouillon cubes
2 cups milk
2 cups cubed Velveeta cheese
½ cup all-purpose flour
1 cup half-and-half
salt and pepper to taste

1. In a soup kettle or Dutch oven, combine the water, broccoli and stock cubes. Bring to a boil, reduce to a simmer, and cook for about 3 to 4 minutes.
2. Meanwhile, in the container of a blender or food processor, combine the milk, cheese, and flour. Process until smooth. Add the half-and-half.
3. Pouring in a narrow stream, and stirring constantly, pour the cheese mixture into the broccoli.
4. Bring the mixture to a boil, reduce to a simmer, and cook, stirring, to the desired thickness.
5. Turn off the heat, and adjust the salt and pepper to taste. Serve immediately.

1 cup margarine
1 cup all-purpose flour
2 pounds fresh broccoli, chopped and steamed until tender
8 ounces fresh mushrooms, trimmed, and sliced
4 cups vegetable stock or water
4 cups half-and-half or milk
1 teaspoon crushed tarragon
salt and pepper to taste

BROCCOLI & MUSHROOM CHOWDER

Winter
Yield: about 6 to 8 servings

1. Melt the margarine in a soup kettle or Dutch oven, sprinkle on the flour, stirring constantly, to make a roux. Then pouring in a narrow stream, and stirring constantly, add the stock. Bring to a boil. Reduce to a simmer, add the broccoli, mushrooms, half-and-half, and tarragon. Heat through, but do not allow to boil.
2. Turn off the heat, and adjust the salt and pepper to taste. Serve immediately.

Hint: The word chowder *usually refers to a thick, rich soup having chunks of food. This one has a thick creamy texture. Broccoli adds the flavor and tarragon enhances it.*

1½ cups boiling water
2 vegetable stock cubes
2 tablespoons margarine
1 medium white onion, chopped
two 8-ounce packages cream cheese, diced
2 cups milk
10-ounce package frozen chopped broccoli, thawed and drained
1 teaspoon fresh lemon juice
salt and pepper to taste

CREAM CHEESE & BROCCOLI SOUP

Spring
Yield: about 6 servings

1. In a bowl, combine the boiling water and stock cubes, stirring until dissolved.
2. Melt the margarine in a soup kettle or Dutch oven, and sauté the onion until lightly colored. Add the cream cheese and milk, and simmer for about 5 minutes, stirring frequently, until the cheese is incorporated. Stir in the broccoli, dissolved stock cubes, lemon juice, and heat through.
3. Turn off the heat, adjust the salt and pepper to taste. Serve immediately.

Hint: You can substitute fresh broccoli florets, if you wish.

BROCCOLI SWISS CHEESE SOUP

Winter

Yield: about 6 servings

1 tablespoon margarine
1 cup chopped shallots
3 cups broccoli florets, blanched and rinsed in cold water
1 cup broccoli stems, peeled and finely chopped
4 tablespoons all-purpose flour
4 cups vegetable stock or water
1 cup light cream
1 cup shredded Swiss or Emmenthaler cheese
⅛ teaspoon ground nutmeg
salt and pepper to taste

1. Melt the margarine in a soup kettle or Dutch oven, and sauté the shallots until tender. Sprinkle on the flour, stirring constantly, to make a roux. Then, while pouring in a narrow stream and stirring constantly, add the stock. Heat until just thickened. Add broccoli stems, bring to a boil, remove from heat. In the container of a blender or food processor, purée the soup, in batches, until smooth.
2. Return to the pot, heat through, stir in the cream and cheese, cooking until the cheese has melted.
3. Turn off the heat, add the nutmeg, and adjust the salt and pepper to taste. Just before serving, add the florets. Serve immediately.

BUTTERMILK GAZPACHO

Summer

Yield: about 4 to 6 servings

2 hard cooked eggs, halved
12-ounce can vegetable juice
1½ cups buttermilk
½ cup yellow onion, finely chopped
¼ cup celery, diced
½ cup green bell peppers, seeded and diced
1 tablespoon snipped fresh dill weed
salt and pepper to taste
1 lime, thinly sliced

1. In the container of a blender or food processor, combine the cooked egg yolks and vegetable juice, and process on HIGH until smooth. Pour into a bowl, and add the buttermilk, onion, celery, bell pepper, and dill weed.
2. In a small bowl, dice the cooked egg whites, and sprinkle evenly among the soup mugs or soup bowls. Ladle the soup over the top, and garnish with a slice of lime. Serve immediately.

Hint: Gazpacho has been popular in many restaurants. Cream gazpacho, however, is rare.

1 tablespoon all-purpose flour
1 tablespoon milk
4 cups buttermilk
½ cup seedless raisins
3-inch cinnamon stick
granulated sugar to taste
1 cup whipped cream

1. Blend the flour with the milk.
2. In a soup kettle or large saucepan, bring the buttermilk to a boil. Sprinkle on the flour-and-milk mixture, stirring until smooth. Add the raisins and cinnamon, and cook until the raisins are softened.
3. Turn off the heat. Serve immediately with a sprinkle of sugar and a daub of whipped cream.

Hint: You can use any dried fruit in place of the raisins.

2 cups fresh blueberries
1½ cups water
½ cup granulated sugar
½ teaspoon orange zest
2 tablespoons fresh orange juice
2 cups buttermilk

BUTTERMILK
SOUP WITH
BERRIES
Summer
Yield: about 6
servings

1. Reserve 6 large berries.
2. In a soup kettle or Dutch oven, combine the berries, water, sugar, orange zest and juice. Bring to a boil. Then reduce to a low simmer, cover lightly to just keep warm, and cook, stirring occasionally, for about 30 minutes.
3. Remove from heat, and in the container of a blender or food processor, purée until smooth. Pour into a bowl, add the buttermilk, cover and chill until ready to serve.
4. When ready, ladle into chilled bowls, float one berry on each bowl, and serve immediately with sweet crackers of choice on the side.

Hint: Most people throw away milk that turns sour in the refrigerator. Sour whole milk can be used as a substitute for buttermilk.

BUTTERNUT SQUASH SOUP

Autumn

Yield: about 6 servings

1 medium yellow onion, chopped
2 tablespoons margarine
2 to 3 pounds butternut squash, peeled and chopped
1 teaspoon English mixture spice
2 quarts vegetable stock
1 cup heavy cream
salt and pepper to taste
finely chopped celery for garnish

1. Melt the margarine in a soup kettle or Dutch oven, and sauté the onions until a golden color. Add the squash, English mixture spice, and stock. Bring to a boil. Then reduce to a low simmer, cover and cook, stirring occasionally, for about 40 minutes, or until the squash is very tender. Remove from heat and cool slightly.

2. In the container of a blender or food processor, purée the soup in batches, until smooth.

3. Return the mixture to the pot and stir in the cream. Heat through, but do not allow to boil.

4. Turn off the heat, and adjust the salt and pepper to taste. Serve immediately, alone or as part of a menu, with a garnish of chopped celery on the side.

Hint: For a chowder, just thicken this soup with a little flour or cornstarch.

1 stick margarine, at room temperature
⅔ cup all-purpose flour
1 tablespoon canola oil
½ green bell pepper, seeded and finely chopped
½ cup chopped celery
½ medium white onion, chopped fine
3 quarts milk
2 tablespoons chopped pimento
1 cup vegetable stock
½ teaspoon garlic powder
1½ pounds grated cheddar or Swiss cheese
½ pound grated Provolone cheese
½ cup beer or ale
¼ cup chopped parsley
salt and pepper to taste

1. In a cup or small bowl, and using the back of a spoon, blend the margarine and flour until smooth.
2. Heat the oil in a soup kettle or Dutch oven, and sauté bell pepper, onion, and celery, until the onion is tender. Add the flour mixture, stirring until incorporated. Then, pouring in a narrow stream, and stirring constantly, add the milk. Add the pimento, stock, and garlic powder.
3. Heat through (do not allow to boil), and stir in both cheeses until melted. Add the beer, reduce to a low heat, and cook, stirring occasionally, for about 15 minutes. Blend in the parsley, adjust the salt and pepper to taste. Serve immediately.

⅓ cup margarine
⅓ cup all-purpose flour
2½ cups milk
4 cups shredded Gouda cheese
1 cup unsweetened apple juice
salt and pepper to taste

1. Melt margarine in a soup kettle or Dutch oven, sprinkle the flour onto the margarine, stirring to make a roux. Then add the milk, pouring it in a narrow stream and stirring constantly. Cook until thickened.
2. Add the cheese, stirring constantly, until melted. Add the apple juice, adjust the salt and pepper to taste, and serve immediately.

Hint: Use other varieties of cheese to create other tastes. I discovered this soup in Bath, England, although it used mild cheese from the Netherlands.

CHEESY CHOWDER

Winter

Yield: about 2 servings

¼ cup margarine, at room temperature
⅓ cup all-purpose flour
4 cups vegetable stock
1½ cups diced potatoes
1 cup diced celery
1 cup diced carrots
½ cup diced yellow onions
3 cups milk
1 tablespoon soy sauce
8 ounces processed cheese spread, cubed

1. In a cup or small bowl, and using the back of a spoon, blend the margarine and flour together, and set aside.
2. In a soup kettle or Dutch oven, combine the stock, potatoes, celery, carrots and onions. Bring to a boil, then reduce to a simmer, and cover. Cook, stirring occasionally, for about 20 minutes, or until the potatoes are tender.
3. In a saucepan, melt the flour mixture to make a roux. Then, pouring in a narrow stream and stirring constantly, add the milk. Cook, stirring constantly, until thickened.
4. Stir the milk mixture into the cooking vegetables, before adding the soy sauce, and cheese. Continue to cook, stirring frequently, until the cheese has melted.
5. Turn off the heat, and adjust the salt and pepper to taste. Serve immediately.

Hint: This is a chowder lover's dream come true. Its flavor can easily be changed with the type of cheese used.

1 tablespoon cornstarch
1 tablespoon water
2 tablespoons margarine
1 cup minced yellow onion
½ cup minced green pepper
2⅓ cups milk
15-ounce can cream-style corn
1¼ cups shredded Monterey Jack cheese
⅛ teaspoon ground black pepper
⅛ teaspoon ground nutmeg

1. In a cup, combine the cornstarch and water until smooth. Set aside.
2. In a 2-quart microwave-safe casserole dish, combine margarine, onion and pepper. Cover and microwave on HIGH until the onion is tender, about 5 minutes.
3. Stir in the milk and creamed corn. Microwave on HIGH for about 8 to 9 minutes.
4. Stir in the cornstarch mix, cheese, pepper and nutmeg. Microwave on HIGH for about 1 to 2 minutes or until the cheese has melted. Remove from the microwave, cover lightly, and allow it to set for 5 minutes. Then serve immediately.

2 tablespoons canola oil
1 medium yellow onion, minced
½ cup dried potato flakes
3 cups water
2 cups frozen whole-kernel corn, thawed
3 cups milk
3 tablespoons margarine
salt and pepper to taste

CORN CHOWDER

Autumn

Yield: about 8 to 10 servings

1. Heat the oil in a soup kettle or Dutch oven, and sauté the onions until translucent. Add the potato flakes and water, cover lightly, and cook, stirring occasionally, for about 5 minutes.
2. Add the corn and milk and continue to simmer for about 5 minutes. Remove from heat. Add the margarine, adjust the salt and pepper to taste, and serve immediately.

CORN SOUP

Winter

Yield: about 6 servings

2 teaspoons peanut oil
½ green bell pepper, minced
1 small white onion, minced
1½ cups soy milk
2 teaspoons tamari sauce
1 tablespoon water or vegetable stock
2 teaspoons whole wheat flour
1½ cups frozen whole-kernel corn, thawed
salt and pepper to taste
dash of nutmeg for garnish
dash of parsley for garnish

1. Heat the oil in a large saucepan, and sauté the pepper and onion together until the onion is translucent.
2. In the container of a blender, combine the corn, milk and tamari sauce, and process until smooth. Add the flour, peppers and onions and continue to process until smooth.
3. Return to the pot, heat through, but do not allow to boil.
4. Turn off the heat, adjust the salt and pepper to taste, and garnish with nutmeg and parsley. Serve immediately.

Hint: The tamarai sauce and soy milk give this soup an Asian flavor.

CREAM-OF-ASPARAGUS SOUP

Spring

Yield: 4 to 6 servings

1½ cups chopped asparagus spears
2½ cups vegetable stock
1 large yellow onion, chopped
¼ teaspoon crushed dried tarragon
1 cup sour cream or unflavored yogurt
1 teaspoon ground nutmeg

1. In a pot, combine the asparagus, stock, onion, and tarragon. Bring to a boil, then reduce to a simmer, and cook for about 1 hour, or until the asparagus is very soft.
2. In the container of a blender or food processor, purée the soup, in batches, until smooth.
3. Return to the pot, bring to a boil, stir in the sour cream and nutmeg, and continue to cook for about 20 minutes.
4. Turn off the heat, and adjust the salt and pepper to taste. Serve immediately with a fresh, soft crust bread on the side.

3 hard cooked egg yolks
1 cup heavy cream or half-and-half
⅔ cup margarine
3 cups chopped yellow onion
3 medium cloves garlic, peeled and minced
⅔ cup all-purpose flour
8 cups milk
1 teaspoon crushed dried chervil
1 teaspoon crushed dried basil
1 teaspoon crushed dried tarragon
3 tablespoons chopped fresh parsley
salt, pepper and nutmeg to taste

COUNTRY-STYLE CREAM SOUP

Winter
Yield: about 8 servings

1. In a bowl, and using a wire whisk, beat the cream and egg yolks together until smooth. Chill until needed.
2. Melt the margarine in a soup kettle or Dutch oven, and sauté the onion until translucent. Add the garlic and continue to cook until the onion is lightly browned. Sprinkle on the flour, stirring constantly, to make a roux. Then, pouring in a narrow stream and stirring constantly, add the milk. Stir in the chervil, basil, tarragon and parsley. Bring to a boil, then reduce to a simmer, and cook, stirring frequently, for about 15 minutes.
3. Turn off the heat, and adjust the salt and pepper to taste, and using a wire whisk, beat in the cream mixture. Serve immediately.

Hint: The blending of herbs give this a real down-home flavor.

CREAM-OF-ALMOND SOUP

Autumn

Yield: about 6 servings

2 tablespoons margarine
1 celery stalk, minced
1 small clove garlic, peeled and crushed
3 cups unsweetened apple juice
⅔ cup ground almonds
⅛ teaspoon mace or nutmeg
1 cup heavy cream
salt and pepper to taste
2 tablespoons toasted slivered almonds

1. Melt the margarine in a large saucepan and sauté the celery and garlic together until tender. Add the apple juice, almonds, and mace, and bring to a boil. Then reduce to a simmer, cover lightly, and cook, stirring occasionally, for about 30 minutes.
2. Turn off the heat, and set aside undisturbed for at least 60 minutes.
3. In the container of a blender or food processor, purée the soup, in batches, until smooth.
4. Return to the pot, stir in the cream, and heat through. (Do not allow to boil.)
5. Turn off the heat, and adjust the salt and pepper to taste. Serve immediately, with the slivered almonds on the side for garnish.

Hint: You can add 2 tablespoons of amaretto just before serving to bring out the almond flavor.

CREAM-OF-BEER SOUP

Summer

Yield: about 4 servings

three 12-ounce bottles beer (1 dark and 2 light)
1 tablespoon granulated sugar
½ teaspoon confectioner's sugar
¼ teaspoon ground cinnamon
⅛ teaspoon ground nutmeg
3 eggs, separated
½ cup heavy cream
salt to taste

1. In a large saucepan, combine the beer, sugars, cinnamon, and nutmeg. Bring to a boil, then reduce to a simmer, cover lightly, and cook for about 10 minutes.
2. In a small bowl, and using a wire whisk, beat the egg yolks and cream together until smooth. Beat in 3 tablespoons of hot beer, and then stir the mixture back into the beer pot, stirring constantly, to avoid curdling.
3. Turn off the heat, adjust the salt and pepper to taste, and cool to room temperature. Cover tightly and refrigerate for at least 4 hours.
4. When ready, and using a wire whisk, beat the egg whites stiff but not dry. Gently fold into the chilled soup and serve immediately.

1 tablespoon margarine
1 cup minced yellow onion
¼ cup minced celery
¼ cup chopped celery leaves
3 cups beets, peeled and cut into julienne strips
2 cups vegetable stock
½ teaspoon Tabasco Sauce
1½ teaspoons granulated sugar
salt and pepper to taste
1½ cups buttermilk
2 teaspoons chopped fresh dill weed

CREAM-OF-BEET SOUP

Year-Round

Yield: about 6 servings

1. Melt the margarine in a large saucepan, and sauté the onions and celery together until tender. Add the celery leaves and cook for 2 more minutes. Add the beets, stock, Tabasco Sauce, and sugar. Bring to a boil. Then reduce to a simmer, cover lightly, and cook, stirring occasionally, for about 20 minutes, or until the beets are tender.
2. Turn off the heat, adjust the salt and pepper to taste, and cool slightly. Stir in the buttermilk and dill weed. When cooled to room temperature, cover tightly and refrigerate for at least 2 hours.
3. When ready, serve in chilled bowls, with a sprinkle of crushed dried dill over the top.

3 cups green tomatoes, peeled and finely chopped
1 medium yellow onion, chopped
¼ teaspoon ground cinnamon
⅛ teaspoon ground cloves
1 teaspoon granulated sugar
2 cups water or vegetable stock
3 tablespoons margarine
3 tablespoons all-purpose flour
4 cups milk
salt and pepper to taste

CREAM-OF-GREEN-TOMATO SOUP

Summer

Yield: about 4 servings

1. In a soup kettle or Dutch oven, combine the tomatoes, onion, cinnamon, cloves, sugar, and water. Bring to a boil, then reduce to a simmer, cover lightly, and cook for about 20 minutes.
2. Melt the margarine in a small saucepan, sprinkle on the flour, stirring to make a roux. Then, pouring in a narrow stream, and stirring constantly, add the milk, cooking until thickened.
3. Stir the milk mixture into the soup, and heat through.
4. Turn off the heat, and adjust the salt and pepper to taste. Serve immediately.

CREAM-OF-BROCCOLI SOUP

Year-Round

Yield: about 10 to 12 servings

½ cup margarine
2 pounds fresh broccoli
1 Herb Ox vegetable bouillon cube
2 tablespoons soy sauce
6 cups water
¾ pound Swiss cheese, grated
1 pound cheddar cheese, grated
16-fluid-ounce container sour cream
salt and pepper to taste
1 cup ground cashews

1. Thoroughly wash the broccoli, trimming the florets from the stalks. Then diced the stalks into smaller pieces.
2. Melt the margarine in a soup kettle or Dutch oven, and sauté the broccoli stems for about 10 minutes or until tender.
3. In the container of a blender or food processor, combine the broccoli, bouillon cube, soy sauce, and 1 cup water. Process on HIGH until smooth.
4. Return to the pot, add the remaining water, broccoli florets, cheese, and sour cream. Bring to a boil. Then reduce to a simmer, cover lightly, and cook for about 15 minutes, or until the cheese is melted.
5. Turn off the heat, and adjust the salt and pepper to taste. Ladle into soup bowls, sprinkle with ground cashews, and serve immediately with freshly baked muffins or corn bread on the side.

CREAM-OF-PEA SOUP

Winter

Yield: about 4 servings

2 tablespoons margarine
1 tablespoon chopped white onion
2 cups frozen peas
¼ teaspoon baking soda
½ teaspoon granulated sugar
2 cups water or vegetable stock
1 cup milk or cream
salt or pepper to taste

1. Melt the margarine in a soup kettle or Dutch oven, and sauté the onion, until translucent. Add the peas, baking soda, sugar, and water. Bring to a boil, then reduce to a simmer, cover lightly, and cook about 15 minutes, or until the peas are tender.
2. In the container of a blender or food processor, purée the mixture, in batches, until smooth. Return to the pot. Add the cream and heat through without boiling.
3. Turn off the heat, and adjust the salt and pepper to taste. Serve immediately.

ANISE
CREAM-OF-
BROCCOLI
SOUP

Winter

Yield: about 6
servings

2 tablespoons margarine
1 medium yellow onion, roughly diced
1½ pounds cooked broccoli, roughly chopped
1 tablespoon ground aniseeds
2 tablespoons dry white wine
3 quarts vegetable stock
3 cups milk or heavy cream
salt and pepper to taste
grated Swiss cheese

1. Melt the margarine in a soup kettle or Dutch oven, and sauté the onion until tender. Add the broccoli, aniseeds and wine. Continue to cook, stirring frequently, for about 10 minutes. Add the stock and milk. Bring to a boil, then reduce to a simmer, cover lightly, and cook for about 15 minutes.

2. In the container of a blender or food processor, purée the soup mix, in batches, until smooth.

3. Return to the pot, bring to a boil, and immediately remove from heat. Adjust the salt and pepper to taste, and ladle into soup bowls. Garnish with cheese, and serve immediately.

Hint: Although broccoli is a great flavoring ingredient, sometimes it can be overpowering. The aniseeds in this recipe take away the broccoli's harsh taste and leave a slight licorice taste in the background.

CREAM-OF-
CARROT
SOUP WITH
GINGER

Autumn

Yield: about 6 to 8
servings

4 tablespoons margarine
2 pounds carrots, peeled and minced
2 medium yellow onions, diced
2 cups vegetable stock
4 cups water
1 bay leaf
1½ tablespoons minced fresh ginger root
½ cup heavy cream
salt and pepper to taste

1. Melt margarine in a soup kettle or Dutch oven, and sauté together the carrots, onions, bay leaf and ginger. Cook, stirring constantly, until the onions are tender. Add the stock and water, and bring to a boil. Then reduce to a simmer, cover lightly, and cook for about 15 minutes, or until the carrots are fork tender. Remove and discard the bay leaf.

2. In the container of a blender or food processor, purée the hot mixture in batches until smooth.

3. Return to the pot, and heat through. Stir in the cream, adjust the salt and pepper to taste, and serve immediately in heated bowls, alone or as part of a menu.

CREAM-OF-CAULIFLOWER SOUP

Winter

Yield: about 6 to 8 servings

3 cups water
1 medium yellow onion, chopped fine
2 teaspoons crushed dried basil
2½ to 3 cups cauliflower florets
2 tablespoons margarine
2 tablespoons all-purpose flour
1 cup vegetable stock
2 cups milk
¼ pound cheddar cheese, cut into small pieces
salt and pepper to taste

1. In a soup kettle or Dutch oven, combine the water, onion, and basil. Bring to a boil. Then reduce to a simmer, cover lightly, and cook for about 5 minutes. Add the cauliflower, cover again, and cook, stirring occasionally, until the cauliflower is tender.
2. Melt the margarine in a second saucepan, sprinkle on the flour, and cook, stirring to make a roux. Then pouring in a narrow stream, and stirring constantly, add the 1 cup milk, cooking until thickened. Stir into the soup kettle.
3. Heat the remaining milk in the same saucepan (do not allow to boil), and stir in the cheese, cook until the cheese has melted. Stir into the soup kettle.
4. Heat the soup, until bubbles form around the edge of the pot. Then immediately remove from heat. Adjust the salt and pepper to taste, and serve immediately.

CREAM-OF-LIMA-BEAN SOUP

Year-Round

Yield: about 6 to 8 servings

1 cup dried lima beans, soaked overnight
6 cups cold water
2 small white onions, diced
2 small carrots, peeled and diced
½ teaspoon paprika
4 tablespoons margarine
2 tablespoons all-purpose flour
1 cup cream or milk
salt and pepper to taste

1. In a soup kettle or Dutch oven, combine the beans and water, and bring to a boil. Then reduce to a simmer, cover lightly, and cook for about 60 minutes, or until the beans are tender.
2. In the container of a blender, purée the beans and water, in batches, until smooth. Return to the soup kettle and bring to a boil.
3. In a saucepan melt 2 tablespoons of the margarine, and sauté the onions and carrots until the onions are translucent. Sprinkle on the flour and paprika, stirring until thickened and smooth. Then stir into the bean mixture. Heat through without boiling.
4. Turn off the heat, stir in the cream and remaining margarine, and adjust the salt and pepper to taste. Serve immediately.

1 tablespoon margarine
2 cups celery, chopped
1 medium yellow onion, chopped
1 medium potato, peeled and chopped
2 cups vegetable stock
1 teaspoon fresh dill weed
2 cups milk
2 tablespoons grated fresh carrot
2 tablespoons grated fresh celery
salt and pepper to taste

1. Melt the margarine in a soup kettle or Dutch oven, and sauté the chopped celery and onion together until the onion is tender. Add the potatoes, cover lightly, and cook over a low heat for about 10 minutes, or until the potatoes are fork tender. (Be careful not to brown the potatoes.) Add the stock and dill weed. Bring to a boil, then reduce to a simmer, and remove from heat.
2. In the container of a blender or food processor, purée the soup, in batches, until smooth. Return to the pot.
3. Stir in the milk, adjust the salt and pepper to taste, add the grated carrots and grated celery, Heat through; do not boil. Serve immediately.

Hint: This soup may convince you that celery isn't just for flavoring.

2 tablespoons margarine
2 medium white onions, diced
3 medium carrots, peeled and thinly sliced
½ cup celery, thinly sliced
2 tablespoons lemon zest
2 tablespoons fresh lemon juice
4 cups vegetable stock
⅔ cup light cream
salt and pepper to taste

CREAM-OF-LEMON SOUP

Year-Round

Yield: about 6 servings

1. Melt the margarine in a soup kettle or Dutch oven and sauté the onions, carrots, and celery together until the onions are translucent. Add the lemon zest, juice, and stock. Bring to a boil. Then reduce to a simmer, cover lightly, and continue to cook, stirring occasionally, for about 20 minutes.
2. In the container of a blender or food processor, purée the soup, in batches, and return to the pot.
3. Heat through, but do not boil. Stir in the cream, adjust the salt and pepper to taste, and serve immediately.

CREAM-OF-CHEESE & LEEK SOUP

Winter

Yield: about 6 servings

½ cup margarine
8 large fresh leeks (white parts only), trimmed and chopped
4 cups vegetable stock
½ cup all-purpose flour
4 cups half-and-half
1½ pounds chilled Brie, rind removed and diced
2 tablespoons snipped fresh chives
salt and fresh ground pepper to taste

1. Melt ½ of the margarine in a soup kettle or Dutch oven, and sauté the leeks until translucent. Add the stock, bring to a boil, then reduce to a simmer, cover lightly, and cook for about 5 minutes.
2. In the container of a blender or food processor, purée the soup, in batches, until smooth. Return to the pot.
3. Melt the remaining margarine in a small saucepan, sprinkle on the flour, stirring constantly, to make a roux. Then pouring in a narrow stream, and stirring constantly, add the half-and-half, stirring until smooth. Add the cheese, a little at a time, stirring after each addition, until melted.
4. Stir the cheese mix into the puréed mixture, and heat through without boiling. (Add more stock if needed to thin the soup.) Adjust the salt and pepper to taste, and ladle into soup bowls. Serve immediately, with chopped chives on the side.

CREAM-OF-CHEESE SOUP

Winter

Yield: about 3 servings

2 tablespoons margarine
3 green onions, thinly sliced
½ cup celery, thinly sliced
1¼ cups vegetable stock or water
½ cup half-and-half
⅔ cup processed cheese spread
1 teaspoon instant vegetable bouillon granules
⅛ teaspoon ground nutmeg
⅓ cup dry white wine
salt and white pepper to taste
toasted croutons for garnish

1. Melt margarine in soup kettle or Dutch oven, and sauté the onions and celery together until the onions are translucent. Add the water, half-and-half, cheese spread, instant bouillon, nutmeg, and wine. Bring to a boil, then reduce to a simmer, and cook, stirring constantly, for about 2 minutes.
2. Turn off the heat, and adjust the salt and pepper to taste. Serve immediately, with croutons on the side for garnish.

2 medium potatoes, peeled and diced
1 cup vegetable stock
1 teaspoon grated white onion
1 cup dry white wine
1 cup heavy cream
2 cucumbers, coarsely grated
4 celery stalks, coarsely grated
salt and pepper to taste

CREAM-OF-CUCUMBER SOUP

Summer

Yield: about 4 to 6 servings

1. In a soup kettle or Dutch oven, combine the potatoes, stock, onion, and wine. Bring to a boil, reduce to a slow boil, and cook for about 15 minutes, or until the potatoes are fork tender. Remove from heat and cool slightly.
2. In the container of a blender or food processor, purée the mixture in batches, until smooth. Return to the pot.
3. Bring to a boil, stir in the cream, cucumber and celery, and heat through (do not allow to boil).
4. Turn off the heat, adjust the salt and pepper to taste, cover tightly, and chill in the refrigerator for at least 4 hours before serving cold.

Hint: No matter how they are prepared, cucumbers should always be eaten cold.

2 tablespoons butter or margarine
2 medium white onions, chopped
1 small clove garlic, peeled and minced
2 heads (about 1 pound) fennel, thinly sliced
4 cups light vegetable stock
1 tablespoon orange zest
1 cup heavy cream

CREAM-OF-FENNEL SOUP

Summer

Yield: about 6 servings

1. Melt the butter in a saucepan or soup kettle, and sauté the onion and garlic together until the onion is translucent. Add the fennel, cover tightly, and cook, stirring occasionally, over a very low heat, for about 30 minutes. Add the stock, and orange zest. Bring to a boil, then reduce to a simmer, cover lightly, and cook for an additional 30 minutes, or until the fennel is fork tender.
2. Remove from heat, and purée in batches, using a blender or food processor, until smooth. Strain the mixture back into the pan, and stir in the cream. Adjust the salt and pepper to taste and reheat without boiling.
3. Remove from heat, and serve hot or cold with a light sprinkling of crushed sweet cookies.

Yogurt may be used in place of the cream.

Hint: Fennel has a taste similar to licorice or anise, but it is milder, sweeter, and more delicate.

CREAM-OF-GARLIC SOUP

Autumn

Yield: about 6 servings

1 medium head garlic, blanched, peeled, and minced
2 quarts water or vegetable stock
2 whole cloves
¼ teaspoon crushed dried thyme
4 sprigs fresh parsley
7 tablespoons olive oil
3 egg yolks, beaten
1 cup sour cream or unflavored yogurt
salt and pepper to taste

1. In a soup kettle or Dutch oven, combine the garlic, water, cloves, thyme, parsley, and 3 tablespoons of the olive oil. Bring to a boil, then reduce to a simmer, cover lightly, and cook for about 15 minutes.
2. Strain the soup through a fine sieve, pressing to extract the liquid from the ingredients. Return the liquid to the pot, and bring to a boil.
3. In a bowl, and using a wire whisk, beat the egg yolks and remaining olive oil until thickened. Stir in the sour cream. Then, beat in 3 tablespoons of the hot soup liquid, one at a time, into the mix, beating vigorously after each addition. Stir back into the hot soup.
4. Turn off the heat, and adjust the salt and pepper to taste. Serve immediately, with bread and cheese on the side.

Hint: Prepare sliced French bread, toasted, with 1 cup grated Swiss cheese melted on top.

CREAM-OF-ONION SOUP

Spring

Yield: about 18 to 28 servings

½ cup margarine
2 pounds yellow onions, diced
#10 can (6 pounds, 3 ounces) cheddar-cheese sauce
3 quarts water or vegetable stock
¼ cup white port wine
7-ounce can French's fried onions

1. Melt the margarine in a soup kettle or Dutch oven, sauté the yellow onions until lightly colored. Add the cheese sauce, water and wine, stirring until smooth. Bring to a slow boil, reduce to a simmer, and cook for about 10 minutes.
2. Turn off the heat, and adjust the salt and pepper to taste. Serve immediately, alone or as part of a menu, with chopped fried onions on the side to be used as garnish.

2 tablespoons margarine
1 tablespoon olive oil
4 large cloves garlic, peeled and minced
1 medium yellow onion, chopped
2 teaspoons paprika
4 cups vegetable stock
two 16-ounce cans crushed tomatoes, with juice
4-ounce can diced green chilis
¼ teaspoon chili powder
2 cups unflavored yogurt
salt and pepper to taste
4 ounces cheddar cheese, shredded
1 tablespoon chopped cilantro

CREAM-OF-GREEN-CHILI SOUP

Year-Round

Yield: about 6 servings

1. Melt the margarine in a soup kettle or Dutch oven, add the oil, and then sauté the garlic until lightly colored. Add the onion, and sauté until translucent. Add the paprika, stock, tomatoes, chilis, and chili powder. Bring to a boil, then reduce to a simmer, cover lightly, and cook, stirring occasionally, for about 20 minutes. Stir in the yogurt, and heat through. (Do not allow to boil.)
2. Turn off the heat, adjust the salt and pepper to taste, and ladle into soup bowls, with a sprinkle of cheese and cilantro. Serve immediately.

3 tablespoons margarine
1 pound fresh mushrooms, chopped
4 cups vegetable stock
½ teaspoon crushed dried basil
2 cups evaporated skim milk
½ cup all-purpose flour
¼ cup white wine
salt and white pepper to taste

CREAM-OF-MUSHROOM SOUP

Year-Round

Yield: about 6 servings

1. Melt the margarine in a soup kettle or Dutch oven, and sauté the mushrooms until lightly browned. Add the stock and basil. Bring to a boil, then reduce to a simmer, and cook for about 15 minutes. Turn off the heat.
2. Combine the skim milk and flour. Stir the milk-and-flour mixture into the stock-and-mushroom mixture. Return to the heat, and continue to simmer until the soup has thickened.
3. Turn off the heat, stir in the wine, and adjust the salt and pepper to taste. Serve immediately.

Hint: This soup can be used as a base when creating other soups.

CREAM-OF-GREEN-OLIVE SOUP

Summer

Yield: about 6 servings

2 cups pitted green olives
6 tablespoons olive oil
½ medium yellow onion, sliced
2 medium cloves garlic, peeled and crushed
4 cups vegetable stock
1 cup heavy cream
6 tablespoons all-purpose flour
4 drops Tabasco sauce
⅓ cup dry sherry
salt and pepper to taste
sliced pimento-stuffed green olives for garnish
garlic bread croutons for garnish

1. Put the olives a bowl, cover with cold water, and set aside for about 1 hour. Then drain and chop.
2. Heat 3 tablespoons of the olive oil in a soup kettle or Dutch oven, and sauté the onion, garlic and about two-thirds of the olives, cooking until the onions are translucent. Add 1 cup of the stock and bring to a boil. Remove from heat.
3. In the container of a blender or food processor, purée the mixture until smooth. Pour back into the pot, and add the remaining stock. Bring to a boil, then reduce to a simmer, cover lightly, and cook for about 20 minutes.
4. Blend the flour with 3 tablespoons of the olive oil. Using a wire whisk, beat the cream into the flour mixture. Then add the mixture to the stock-and-olives mixture, stirring constantly, until thickened. Add the remaining olives, Tabasco sauce, and sherry. Heat through.
5. Turn off the heat, and adjust the salt and pepper to taste. Serve immediately, with sliced stuffed olives and croutons on the side.

1 medium yellow onion, chopped
2 stalks celery, chopped
¼ cup margarine
3 tablespoons all-purpose flour
8 cups vegetable stock
2 cups creamy peanut butter
1 cup half-and-half, preheated
salt and pepper to taste
chopped peanuts for garnish

CREAM-OF-PEANUT SOUP

Winter

Yield: about 8 servings

1. Melt the margarine in a soup kettle or Dutch oven, and sauté the onion and celery together until the onions are golden brown color. Sprinkle on the flour, stirring until thickened and smooth. Then pouring in a narrow stream, and stirring constantly, add the stock, stirring until smooth. Bring to a boil, and cook, stirring constantly, until the liquid is thickened.
2. Strain through a sieve, returning the liquid to the pot, and discarding the vegetable matter.
3. Add the peanut butter and half-and-half, stirring until smooth. Heat through, but do not allow to boil.
4. Turn off the heat, and adjust the salt and pepper to taste. Serve at once, with chopped peanuts on the side as a garnish.

CREAM-OF-POTATO SOUP

Winter

Yield: about 4 servings

4 tablespoons margarine
2 small white onions, chopped
1 fresh leek (white part only), thinly sliced
3 celery stalks, diced
4 medium boiling potatoes, peeled and diced
1 teaspoon paprika
6 cups vegetable stock
½ teaspoon crushed dried thyme
1 teaspoon Worcestershire sauce
¾ cup heavy cream
salt and pepper to taste
1 tablespoon minced fresh parsley leaves (optional)

1. Melt the margarine in a soup kettle or Dutch oven, and sauté the onions until translucent. Add the leeks and celery, cooking for about 1 minute, and then add the potatoes and paprika. Heat through, and add the stock, thyme, and Worcestershire sauce. Bring to a boil, cover lightly and continue to cook, stirring occasionally, for about 30 minutes, or until the potatoes are fork tender.
2. Transfer about 1 cup of the vegetable matter into the container of a blender or food processor, and purée until smooth. Stir back into the pot.
3. Turn off the heat, add the cream, and adjust the salt and pepper to taste. Serve immediately, with parsley on the side.

CREAM-OF-POTATO & LOVAGE SOUP

Winter

Yield: about 6 servings

2½ cups finely chopped onions
5 cups vegetable stock
½ cup grated raw potatoes
1½ cups chopped lovage leaves
1 cup buttermilk
salt and pepper to taste

1. In a soup kettle or Dutch oven, combine the onion and stock. Bring to a boil, cover lightly, and cook until the onions are soft. Add the potato, about 1½ cups of the lovage leaves, and buttermilk. Increase to a very slow boil. Then reduce to a simmer, cover again, and continue to cook, stirring occasionally, for about 20 minutes, or until the potatoes are very tender.
2. Using a potato masher, mash the potatoes in the soup, and then whisk until smooth.
3. Turn off the heat, and adjust the salt and pepper to taste. Serve immediately.

Hint: Lovage, also called smallage or smellage, tastes like celery and comes in stalks with leaves. It can be found in health food stores and large supermarkets.

1 teaspoon safflower oil
1 pound fresh pumpkin, cut into chunks
1 medium yellow onion, chopped
1 small clove garlic, peeled and crushed
2 stalks celery, chopped
½ teaspoon crushed dried thyme
5 cups vegetable stock
1½ tablespoons cream cheese
1 tablespoon nonfat powdered milk
½ cup minced chives

1. Heat the oil in a soup kettle or Dutch oven, and sauté the pumpkin, onion, garlic, celery, and thyme together. Reduce to a very low heat, cover lightly, and cook for about 6 to 8 minutes. (Do not allow to brown.)

2. Add the stock, and bring to a boil. Then reduce to a simmer, and cook, uncovered for about 20 minutes, or until the pumpkin is tender.

3. Remove from heat, and in the container of a blender or food processor, purée the mixture, in batches, until smooth. Strain through a fine sieve pressing lightly with the back of a spoon.

4. Return to the pot, add the powdered milk, and bring to a boil, stirring constantly, and if too thick, add a little water, a quarter of a cup at a time.

5. Turn off the heat, and add the cheese, stirring until blended. Adjust the salt and pepper to taste, and serve immediately, with the chives on the side as a garnish.

Hint: For a richer soup, substitute a 16-ounce can pumpkin in place of the fresh pumpkin. Add the canned pumpkin to the mixture along with the stock.

CREAM-OF-SHIITAKE MUSHROOM SOUP

Year-Round

Yield: about 4 servings

6 fresh parsley sprigs
½ teaspoon dried thyme
½ bay leaf
1 quart milk
6 whole peppercorns
1 small white onion peeled and stuck with 2 cloves
4 tablespoons rice flour
4 tablespoons cold milk
8 ounces shiitake mushrooms
6 tablespoons heavy cream (optional)
2 tablespoons Madeira (optional)
reserved mushrooms slices (optional)

1. Tie the parsley, thyme, bay leaf, and peppercorn in a double thick square of cheesecloth.
2. In a soup kettle or Dutch oven, combine the quart of milk, onion, and herb bag. Bring to a slow boil, cover, and cook, stirring occasionally, for about 10 minutes.
3. In a bowl, blend the rice flour and 4 tablespoons of cold milk. Add 2 tablespoons of hot liquid from the pot, and then stir the mixture back into the soup. Continue to cook over a very low heat for about 20 minutes.
4. Meanwhile, wash and trim the tough ends of the mushrooms. Then slice several for garnish, and finely mince the remaining mushrooms. Stir the mushrooms into the soup, and continue to cook for about 5 minutes.
5. Turn off the heat, remove and discard the herb bag, stir in the cream and Madeira, and remove from heat. Serve immediately.

1 tablespoon butter or margarine
1 large yellow onion, chopped
3 tablespoons potato flakes
3 cups vegetable stock
2 teaspoons fresh lemon juice
2 medium heads spinach, chopped
2 teaspoons mace or nutmeg
½ cup milk
½ cup light cream

CREAM-OF-SPINACH SOUP

Year-Round

Yield: about 6 to 8 servings

1. Melt the butter in a saucepan or soup kettle, and sauté the onion until translucent. Sprinkle on the potato flakes and cook, stirring constantly, until thickened. (Do not allow to brown.) Add the stock, lemon juice, spinach and mace. Bring to a boil, then reduce to a simmer. Cook, stirring occasionally, uncovered for about 5 minutes, or until the spinach is completely wilted.
2. Remove from heat, and purée in batches, using a blender or food processor, until smooth.
3. Return the mixture to the pan, add the milk and cream, adjust the salt and pepper to taste, and heat through. Do not allow to boil. Remove from heat. Serve immediately, with herb cream garnish on the side.

Herb Cream Garnish

Whip ½ cup heavy cream until soft peaks form, and then fold in fresh herbs. Daub the cream on the top of soup bowls as a garnish.

5 tablespoons margarine
½ cup chopped yellow onion
4 tablespoons unbleached flour
4 cups milk
1 teaspoon crushed dried basil
1½ teaspoons granulated sugar
3 cups diced tomatoes
salt and pepper to taste

CREAM-OF-TOMATO SOUP

Year-Round

Yield: about 6 to 7 servings

1. Melt the margarine in a soup kettle or Dutch oven, and sauté the onion until translucent. Sprinkle on the flour, stirring until thickened and smooth. Then, pouring in a narrow stream, and stirring constantly, add the milk. Stir in the basil and sugar, and continue to cook, stirring occasionally, until thickened. Add the tomatoes, and continue to cook for about 3 minutes, or until heated through.
2. Remove from heat, and in the container of a blender or food processor, purée, in batches, until smooth. Adjust the salt and pepper to taste, and serve immediately.

Hint: Use vine-ripened, soft organic tomatoes for the best flavor.

QUICK CREAM-OF-VEGETABLE SOUP

Year-Round
Yield: about 4 servings

3 cups milk
2 cups vegetable stock or water
2 tablespoons instant minced onions
2 teaspoons vegetable bouillon granules
¼ cup diced fine celery
1⅓ cups instant mashed potatoes
10-ounce package frozen mixed vegetables
salt and pepper to taste

1. In a soup kettle or Dutch oven, combine the milk, stock, onion, bouillon granules, and celery. Bring to a boil, and then stir in the potatoes and vegetables. Return to a boil, reduce to a simmer, cover lightly, and cook, stirring occasionally, for about 15 minutes.

2. Turn off the heat, and adjust the salt and pepper to taste. Serve immediately.

CREAM-OF-ZUCCHINI SOUP

Autumn
Yield: about 6 servings

1 large yellow onion, chopped
¼ cup margarine
3 cups vegetable stock
6 medium zucchini, trimmed and diced
2 teaspoons crushed dried parsley
¼ teaspoon crushed dried thyme
1½ cups half-and-half
1 cup dry white wine
salt and pepper to taste

1. Melt the margarine in a soup kettle or Dutch oven, and sauté the onion until soft. Add the stock, zucchini, parsley, and thyme. Bring to a boil, then reduce to a simmer, and cook for about 10 minutes, or until the zucchini is tender.

2. In the container of a blender or food processor, purée the soup, in batches, until smooth. Return to the pot and heat through.

3. Turn off the heat, add the half-and-half and wine, adjust the salt and pepper to taste, and serve immediately.

Hint: Wine adds flavor to the mild-tasting zucchini.

1 pound fresh asparagus
5 cups vegetable stock
1 teaspoon curry powder
¼ teaspoon turmeric powder
¼ cup margarine
¼ cup all-purpose flour
¾ cup half-and-half
dash of lemon juice
salt and pepper to taste

1. Trim the asparagus, discarding the ends, and reserving the tips.
2. In a soup kettle or Dutch oven, combine stock and asparagus, curry, and turmeric. Bring to a boil, then reduce to a simmer, cover lightly, and cook, stirring occasionally, for about 30 minutes.
3. Place the asparagus tips in a small saucepan, add enough water to just cover, and boil for about 3 minutes. Drain and set aside.
4. In the container of a blender or food processor, purée the stock, in batches until smooth.
5. Melt the margarine in the same soup kettle, sprinkle on the flour, and cook stirring to make a roux. Add the puréed mixture, bring to a boil, and cook, stirring frequently, until thickened.
6. Turn off the heat, stir in the half-and-half, lemon juice, and salt and pepper to taste. Add the asparagus tips, and serve immediately.

Hint: This soup can also be chilled in the refrigerator and served cold. Many cooks insist that curry powder should never be used without turmeric powder.

DUCHESS SOUP

Year-Round

Yield: about 4 to 6 servings

2 tablespoons margarine
1 medium yellow onion, minced
1 tablespoon all-purpose flour
4 cups milk
1 large egg
6 ounces grated American cheese
salt and pepper to taste

1. Melt the margarine in the top of a double-boiler, add the onion, and cook over rapidly boiling water until the onion is translucent. Sprinkle on the flour, and cook, stirring until incorporated. Then, pouring in a narrow stream, add about 3½ cups of the milk, stirring constantly, until blended. Continue to cook, stirring frequently, for about 10 minutes, or until thickened.

2. Meanwhile, in a bowl, beat together the remaining milk and egg. Add about 3 tablespoons of the hot mixture, 1 tablespoon at a time, and then stir the egg mixture back into the soup, stirring until blended. Cook for about 2 to 3 minutes, then stir in the cheese, and continue stirring until melted. Remove from heat, adjust the salt and pepper to taste, and serve with a menu.

SCOTTISH CREAM-OF-LEEK SOUP

Winter

Yield: 6 to 8 servings

2 tablespoons margarine
2 cups leeks (whites only), coarsely chopped
½ cup chopped yellow onion
½ cup chopped celery
5 quarts vegetable stock
⅓ cup chopped fresh parsley
salt and pepper to taste
¾ cup heavy cream
finely chopped leek greens for garnish

1. Melt the margarine in a soup kettle or Dutch oven, and sauté the 2 cups of leeks, onion, and celery until the onion is translucent. Add the stock, bring to a boil, then reduce to a simmer, cover lightly, and cook, without stirring, for about 1 hour. Remove from heat.

2. In the container of a blender or food processor, process the soup in batches, until smooth. Return to the pot, add the parsley and leeks, stir in the cream, and heat through without boiling.

3. Remove from heat, and adjust the salt and pepper to taste. Serve immediately, with a sprinkling of finely chopped leek greens as a garnish.

Hint: In Gillespie's, a pub in Glasgow, Scotland, they make the very best cream-of-leek soup. Inspired by their soup, this version does not use beef or chicken stock.

2 tablespoons vegetable oil
1 medium yellow onion, thinly sliced
2 medium potatoes, peeled and diced
water
2 cups milk
1 cup white sauce mix
17-ounce can cream-style corn
salt and pepper to taste
1 tablespoon margarine
imitation bacon bits for garnish

1. Heat oil in a soup kettle or Dutch oven and sauté the onions until lightly colored. Add the potatoes, with enough water to just cover. Bring to a boil, then reduce to a simmer, and cook for about 20 minutes, or until the potatoes are very tender.
2. In a small saucepan, combine milk and white sauce mix, and cook over a low heat until thickened and smooth. Stir in cream-style corn, heat through, and then stir into the potato mixture.
3. Turn off the heat, adjust the salt and pepper to taste, and pour into a tureen, with a sprinkle of bacon bits, and dot with margarine. Serve immediately.

2 pounds fennel bulbs, peeled and finely minced
6 tablespoons canola oil
1 tablespoon crushed dried bouquet garni
4 cups vegetable stock
½ cup heavy cream (optional)
salt and pepper to taste

1. In a soup kettle or large saucepan, combine the fennel and oil, and sauté, stirring constantly, over a low heat for about 2 to 3 minutes. Cover and continue to cook for about 7 to 8 minutes. Then remove the cover, and continue to simmer, stirring frequently until, until the mixture starts to brown. Add the bouquet garni and stock, and bring to a boil. Then reduce to a simmer, cover and cook for abut 30 minutes. Remove from heat. Remove the bouquet garni.
2. In the container of a blender or food processor, purée the mixture in batches until smooth. Return to the pot, heat through, remove from heat, and stir in the cream. Adjust the salt and pepper to taste. Ladle into heated bowls, and serve immediately with an accompaniment of choice.

Hint: Bouquet garni is a bunch of herbs, usually parsley, thyme, and bay leaf, tied together or placed in a cheesecloth bag and used to flavor soups, stews, or broths. Tying and bagging the herbs allows them to be easily removed before the dish is served.

FOUR-CHEESE SOUP

Year-Round

Yield: about 6 servings

2 tablespoons margarine
1 medium leek, chopped
4 cups vegetable stock
1 medium potato, peeled and diced
2 cups half-and-half
¾ cup freshly grated Provolone cheese
¾ cup freshly grated fresh Parmesan cheese
¾ cup freshly grated Mozzarella cheese
¾ cup freshly grated fresh cheddar cheese
salt and pepper to taste
lightly toasted croutons

1. Melt margarine in a soup kettle or Dutch oven, and sauté the leeks until tender. Add the stock and potato, bring to a boil, then reduce to a simmer, cover lightly, and cook for about 20 minutes, or until the potato is tender.

2. In the container of a blender or food processor, purée the soup, in batches, until smooth. Return to the pot. Add the half-and-half, and continue to cook over a low heat. (Do not allow to boil.) Remove from heat, cover, and chill in the refrigerator for at least 8 hours.

3. When ready, reheat the soup to a simmer, add all the cheeses at one time, and cook, stirring until melted and incorporated into the soup. Adjust the salt and pepper to taste, and ladle into bowls, sprinkle with croutons, and serve immediately.

HARVEST CORN CHOWDER

Autumn

Yield: about 10 to 12 servings

1 tablespoon margarine
1 large white onion, chopped
two 14.5-ounce cans cream-style corn
4 cups whole-kernel corn
2 cups diced red potatoes
2 cups diced parsnips
10.75-ounce can cream-of-mushroom soup
6-ounce can sliced mushrooms, undrained
3 cups milk
½ medium green bell pepper, chopped
½ medium red bell pepper, chopped
salt and pepper to taste

1. Melt the margarine in a soup kettle or Dutch oven and sauté the onion until tender. Add the cream-style corn, whole corn, potatoes, parsnips, soup, mushrooms, milk, and peppers. Bring to a slow boil, reduce immediately to a simmer, cover lightly, and cook for about 30 minutes, or until the potatoes and parsnips are fork tender.

2. Turn off the heat, and adjust the salt and pepper to taste. Serve immediately. Garnish as desired.

5.25-ounce package dried au gratin potatoes, with cheese mix
15.25-ounce can whole-kernel corn, undrained
1 cup picante sauce
2 cups water
2 cups milk
1½ cups grated cheddar cheese
2.25-ounce can sliced ripe olives, drained
tortilla chips

1. In a large saucepan combine potatoes, corn, picante sauce, and water. Bring to a boil; reduce to a simmer, cover lightly, and cook for about 25 minutes, or until the potatoes are tender. Add dry cheese sauce mix, milk, cheddar cheese and olives. Cook until cheese is melted.
2. Turn off the heat, adjust the salt and pepper to taste, sprinkle with tortilla chips, and serve immediately.

1 tablespoon butter or margarine
1 small white onion, minced
½ cup sliced leeks
2 cups diced potatoes
2½ cups vegetable stock
½ cup chopped mustard greens
½ cup chopped watercress
½ teaspoon ground nutmeg or mace
¼ cup milk
⅓ cup light cream
salt and pepper to taste
whipped sour cream or yogurt for garnish
minced mustard greens and watercress for garnish

1. Melt the butter in a soup kettle or Dutch oven, add the onion, and sauté until transparent. Add the leeks and potatoes, and cook, stirring, for about 5 minutes. Add the stock, and bring to a boil. Then reduce to a simmer, cover tightly, and cook for about 15 minutes, or until the potatoes are tender. Add the mustard greens, watercress, nutmeg, and salt and pepper to taste. Heat gently for about 2 minutes, remove from heat, and cool slightly.
2. In the container of blender or food processor, purée the mixture in batches, until smooth. Return to the pot, add the milk and cream, and heat only until bubbles form around the edge of the pot. Ladle into warmed bowls, garnish, and serve immediately.

YOGURT NOODLE SOUP

Summer

Yield: about 6 servings

2 tablespoons arrowroot or cornstarch
2 cups unflavored yogurt
2 tablespoons safflower oil
1 medium yellow onion, chopped
2 quarts vegetable stock
5 large cloves garlic, peeled and minced
¼ cup soy sauce
3 medium carrots
1 teaspoon crushed dried mixed vegetables
1 teaspoon crushed dried thyme
5 sprigs fresh parsley, finely chopped
2 teaspoons crushed dried basil
6-ounce package wide egg noodles
7 green onions, chopped

1. In a small bowl, blend the arrowroot and yogurt, stirring until smooth.
2. Heat the oil in a soup kettle or Dutch oven, and sauté the onion until tender. Add the stock, garlic, soy sauce, carrots, dried mixed vegetables, thyme, parsley, and basil. Bring to a boil, and then reduce to a simmer. Cover lightly, and cook, stirring occasionally, for about 30 minutes.
3. Stir in the noodles and cook, stirring occasionally, for about 10 minutes or until the noodles are cooked al dente. Bring to a boil, add the yogurt, and return to a boil. Remove from heat and serve immediately, alone or as part of a menu, with a garnish of green onions on the side.

Quick Dumplings
Open a tube of refrigerator biscuits, arrange the biscuits over the top of a simmering soup, cover and cook for about 15 minutes.

2 pounds potatoes, peeled and diced

water

1 tablespoon margarine

1 pound kale, chopped

2 medium cloves garlic, peeled and chopped

1 cup heavy cream

5 teaspoons balsamic vinegar or to taste

salt and pepper to taste

1 bunch fresh chives

green onions, diced

1. Put the potatoes in a soup kettle or Dutch oven with enough water to cover. Bring to a boil, then reduce to a simmer, cover lightly, and cook for about 20 minutes, or until the potatoes are fork tender.
2. Using a masher, purée the potatoes (do not drain) in the pot. (They should be lumpy.)
3. Melt the margarine in a large skillet and sauté the kale and garlic together until the kale is well wilted. Stir into the potatoes.
4. Bring to a boil. Then reduce to a simmer, cover lightly, and cook, stirring occasionally, for about 10 minutes. Stir in the cream and vinegar. Heat through; do not boil.
5. Turn off the heat, and adjust the salt and pepper to taste. Serve immediately, alone or as part of a menu, with the chives and onions on the side.

Hint: I like to have at least one large potato cooked and diced, which I add to the soup just before serving.

4 large egg yolks

⅜ cup heavy cream

1/4 cup dry sherry or white port wine

16 cups boiling vegetable stock

1. In a bowl, beat the egg yolks, and while still beating and pouring in a narrow stream, beat in the cream, and then the wine. Pour into a large, pre-heated soup tureen.
2. Then, stirring constantly, add the stock, until incorporated. Add dumplings if desired, and serve as part of a dinner menu.

SASSY SPINACH SOUP

Summer
Yield: about 6 servings

½ cup chopped red onion
1 large clove garlic, peeled and crushed
2 tablespoons margarine
4 cups water
5 instant vegetable bouillon cubes
½ cup broken thin noodles, uncooked
10-ounce package frozen chopped spinach, thawed and drained
3 cups milk
½ teaspoon dried pepper flakes, or to taste
½ cup shredded cheddar cheese
½ cup shredded Swiss cheese
salt and pepper to taste

1. Melt the margarine in a soup kettle or Dutch oven and sauté the onion and garlic together until the onion is a golden color. Add the water and bouillon cubes. Bring to a boil, stirring to dissolve the bouillon cubes. Add the noodles. Return to a boil, and continue to cook, stirring occasionally, for about 10 minutes or until the noodles are al dente. Stir in the spinach and continue to cook for about 3 minutes before adding the pepper flakes, milk, and two cheeses. Heat through, stirring constantly, until the cheese has melted, but do not boil.
2. Turn off the heat, adjust the salt and pepper to taste, and serve immediately.

EASY CREAM-OF-POTATO SOUP

Year-Round
Yield: about 4 servings

3 cups vegetable stock
2 tablespoons powdered onions
1½ cups dried potato flakes
1 tablespoon margarine
1 cup sour cream
½ teaspoon crushed dried basil
salt and pepper to taste
3 tablespoon chopped chives for garnish

1. In a soup kettle or Dutch oven, and using a wire whisk, beat together the stock, onion powder, and potato flakes. Bring to a boil, and add the margarine. Reduce to a simmer, and cook, stirring frequently, until the mixture is thickened. Add the sour cream and basil, and adjust the salt and pepper to taste. Cover lightly, and cook for about 10 minutes.
2. Turn off the heat, and serve immediately.

Hint: This soup will show you how to use potato flakes to thicken soups.

3 cups water
3 vegetable bouillon cubes
¼ cup chopped onion
½ cup chopped celery
1 cup chopped broccoli
6 cups milk
7 tablespoons cornstarch
1 pound Velveeta cheese, cubed
salt and pepper to taste

1. In a soup kettle or Dutch oven, combine the water and bouillon cubes, bring to a boil, and cook, stirring until the cubes are dissolved. Add the onions, celery, and broccoli. Return to a boil. Reduce to a simmer, cover lightly, and cook, stirring occasionally, until the vegetables are fork tender.
2. Meanwhile, in a bowl, and using a wire whisk, beat the milk and cornstarch together until smooth. Then pouring in a narrow stream, pour into the hot soup mixture, stirring slowly until thickened.
3. Add the cheese cubes, stirring only until the cheese is melted. Remove from heat, adjust the salt and pepper to taste, and serve immediately.

Hint: This recipe was originally actually two recipes. The first was vegetable soup and the second cheese soup. The cook made a mistake, and the result was this very good, flavorful soup.

1½ quarts water
1 small white onion, chopped
1 cup chopped celery
2½ cups diced potatoes
1½ cups diced carrots
5 vegetable bouillon cubes
1½ cups chopped broccoli
1½ cups cauliflower
two 10¾-ounce cans cream-of-mushroom soup
1 pound Velveeta cheese
salt and pepper to taste

1. In a soup kettle or Dutch oven, combine the water, onion, celery, potatoes, carrots, bouillon cubes, broccoli, and cauliflower. Bring to a boil and then reduce to a simmer. Cover lightly and cook, stirring occasionally, for about 20 minutes, or until the vegetables are tender. Stir in the soup and the cheese, and cook stirring frequently for about 6 to 8 minutes or the until cheese melts. (Do not allow to boil.)
2. Remove from the heat, and adjust the salt and pepper to taste. Serve immediately.

Hint: The key ingredient, Velveeta, is one of the easiest cheeses for making soup. It is so soft, and melts to a smoothness that's unbelievable.

VICHYSSOISE

Year-Round

Yield: about 6 servings

2 tablespoons unsalted butter
11 ounces leeks, trimmed and sliced
8 ounces potatoes, peeled and thinly sliced
2 cups water
1¼ cups milk
1¼ cup heavy cream
salt and white pepper to taste
ground almonds for garnish

1. Melt the butter in a soup kettle or Dutch oven. Sauté the leeks and potatoes together, covered, stirring occasionally, for about 10 minutes.
2. Add the water, and bring to a boil. Reduce to a simmer, cover, and continue to cook for about 15 to 20 minutes, or until the potatoes are very tender. Remove from heat and cool slightly.
3. When ready, in the container of a blender or food processor, purée the mixture in batches, until smooth. Return to the pot, stir in the milk and cream, and adjust the salt and pepper to taste. Chill in the refrigerator for at least 3 hours.
4. When ready, ladle into well-chilled bowls. Drop a daub of unflavored yogurt on top, swirl it around a little, and garnish with ground almonds. Serve immediately.

Hint: It's reported that the first vichyssoise was created in Manhattan in the Ritz Carlton Hotel by chef Louis Diat. Vichyssoise is simply a leek-and-potato soup, prepared in French cooking. White pepper is preferred; black pepper would alter the creamy appearance.

HEARTY SOUPS

Hearty soups seem to stick to your ribs. You'll want to prepare many of these soups on a cold day to complement a light meal. They're often bulky or chunky, and provide comfort and nutrition in equal measure.

ACORN SQUASH CHOWDER

Winter

Yield: about 6 to 8 servings

3 large carrots, trimmed, peeled, and sliced
1 large red onion, sliced
4 acorn squash, cooked and pulp removed from skin
⅓ cup vegetable stock or water
2 tablespoons margarine
1 tablespoon all-purpose flour
salt and pepper to taste
2½ cups vegetable stock
¼ cup unflavored yogurt or sour cream
½ cup sherry or white port wine
½ teaspoon ground nutmeg
⅛ teaspoon paprika powder
dash ground allspice
dash of red pepper
1 cup half-and-half
1½ tablespoons brandy (optional)

1. In a soup kettle or Dutch oven, combine the carrots, onion, and water. Bring to a boil, then reduce to a simmer, cover, and cook for about 15 minutes. Remove from heat, and drain.

2. In a food process or blender, combine the carrot mixture and squash. Process on HIGH until smooth.

3. Melt the margarine in a soup kettle or Dutch oven, sprinkle on the flour, stirring to make a roux. Pouring in a narrow stream, stir in the stock until smooth. Add the yogurt, sherry, nutmeg, paprika, allspice, red pepper and vegetable purée.

4. Bring to a boil, then reduce to a simmer, cover, and continue to cook for about 40 minutes. Stir in the half-and-half, brandy, and heat through. Remove from heat, keep warm, and serve immediately, alone or with a menu.

Hint: The alcohol from the port wine and brandy is burned off during cooking, which leaves only the wonderful flavor.

¼ cup melted margarine
¼ cup all-purpose flour
pinch grated mace
1½ quarts enriched soy milk or milk
20 ounces fresh asparagus, sautéed tender, drained, and diced
3 cups shredded cheddar or other cheese
paprika to taste
shredded fresh Romano cheese for garnish

ASPARAGUS
CHEESE
SOUP

Spring

Yield: about 4 to 6 servings

1. In a bowl, and using a pastry blender or two knives, blend the margarine, flour and mace together. Pouring in a narrow stream, stir in the milk, before transferring to a soup kettle or Dutch oven.
2. Over medium heat, bring to a boil, and cook, stirring until thickened. Add the asparagus and cheese, stirring until melted. Remove from heat. Immediately garnish with Romano cheese and paprika. Serve immediately.

3 tablespoons margarine
2 pounds fresh asparagus, cut diagonally into 1-inch pieces
1 medium clove garlic, peeled and chopped
3 leeks, sliced
4 green onions, finely chopped
1 small red potato, peeled and chopped
4 cups water
3 Herb Ox vegetable stock cubes
1 tablespoon soy sauce
1 cup light cream
2 tablespoons chopped fresh tarragon
2 tablespoons chopped fresh basil
salt and pepper to taste

ASPARAGUS
SOUP

Summer

Yield: about 6 servings

1. Melt the margarine in a soup kettle or Dutch oven, and sauté the asparagus, garlic, leeks, and onion until tender. Add the potatoes, water, and stock cubes. Bring to a boil, then reduce to a simmer, and cook, stirring frequently, until the stock cubes have completely dissolved. Add the soy sauce, cream, tarragon, and basil.
2. Turn off the heat, and adjust the salt and pepper to taste. Serve immediately.

Hint: Vegetable stock can be used in place of the water. I prefer Herb Ox vegetable stock cubes because of their consistent good taste and uniform solubility. They appear to contain fewer additives (also no MSG) than other stock cubes and granules.

AUTUMN RAREBIT SOUP

Autumn

Yield: about 4 to 6 servings

5 cups cooked pumpkin or winter squash
2½ cups hot vegetable stock
1½ cups beer or ale
2 tablespoons margarine
1 large yellow onion, chopped
3 medium cloves garlic, peeled and crushed
1 cup shredded cheddar cheese
¼ cup pumpkin seeds, hulled and lightly toasted
salt and pepper to taste

1. In a large saucepan, combine the pumpkin and stock. Set aside briefly, and then, in the container of a blender or food processor, purée the mixture in batches until smooth.
2. In a soup kettle or Dutch oven, combine pumpkin purée and beer. Bring to boil, reduce to simmer, cover lightly, and cook for about 5 minutes.
3. Meanwhile, melt the margarine in a skillet and sauté the onions and garlic until lightly colored. Stir into the pumpkin mix in the soup kettle. Add the cheese. Cover again and simmer for about 15 minutes.
4. Turn off the heat, and adjust the salt and pepper to taste. Serve immediately, alone or as part of a menu, with toasted pumpkin seeds on the side.

AUTUMN SOUP

Autumn

Yield: about 4 to 6 servings

1 tablespoon margarine
1 cup chopped red onion
1 cup chopped carrots
1 cup chopped celery stalks and leaves
1 cup chopped potato
3 cups water
1 teaspoon Kitchen Bouquet (optional)
1 bay leaf
¼ teaspoon crushed dried basil
28-ounce can diced tomatoes
2 cups diced zucchini
salt and pepper to taste

1. Melt the margarine in a soup kettle or Dutch oven, and sauté the onion until tender. Add the carrots, celery, potato, water, Kitchen Bouquet, bay leaf, basil, tomatoes, and zucchini. Bring to a boil. Reduce to a simmer, cover lightly, and cook for about 30 minutes, or until tender.
2. Turn off the heat, discard the bay leaf, and adjust the salt and pepper to taste. Serve immediately.

½ cup long-grain rice

2 cups milk

2 tablespoons cornstarch

6 egg yolks

4 cups vegetable stock

¼ cup margarine

1 tablespoon crushed dried parsley

1 tablespoon grated lemon or lime zest (optional)

1 cup fresh lemon juice

salt and pepper to taste

1. Put the rice in a sieve, and wash under running water until the water runs clear.
2. In a bowl, and using a wire whisk, beat together the milk, cornstarch, and egg yolks.
3. In a soup kettle or Dutch oven, bring the stock to a boil. Add the rice, cover, and cook, stirring frequently, until the rice is tender, about 20 to 25 minutes.
4. Remove from the heat, and using a wire whisk, beat in the egg mixture. Return to the heat, bring to a boil, and cook, stirring until thickened. Add the margarine, parsley, lemon zest, and juice. Return to a boil, then remove from heat, and adjust the salt and pepper to taste. Serve immediately.

two 10-ounce packages frozen whole-kernel corn

3½ cups vegetable stock

large tomato, peeled and seeded

¼ cup yellow onion, coarsely chopped

½ teaspoon crushed dried oregano

2 tablespoons margarine

½ cup heavy cream

green pepper matchsticks for garnish (optional)

1. In a soup kettle or Dutch oven, combine the corn and stock. Bring to a boil. Reduce to a simmer, cover, and cook for about 5 minutes.
2. Turn off the heat, and using a slotted spoon, remove ½ cup of the corn. Purée the remaining liquid and corn mixture in a blender or food processor, until smooth. Return the liquid to the pot.
3. In the container of a blender or food processor, purée the tomato, onion, and oregano, and process until smooth.
4. Melt the margarine in a skillet and sauté the tomato mixture until thickened. Then stir into the hot soup in the pot.
5. Bring the mixture to a boil, reduce to a simmer, and cook, stirring occasionally, for about 5 minutes. Stir in the cream, and cook until just heated through. (Do not boil.)
6. Remove from heat, and serve immediately, alone or as part of a menu, with the reserved corn and pepper matchsticks on the side.

BAKED BEAN SOUP

Winter

Yield: about 4 to 6 servings

3 tablespoons margarine
½ cup chopped yellow onion
1 medium clove garlic, peeled and minced
3 tablespoons all-purpose flour
¼ teaspoon dry mustard
2 cups tomato juice or V-8 vegetable juice
1 cup vegetable stock or water
2 teaspoons Worcestershire sauce
21-ounce can baked beans
salt and pepper to taste
shredded cheddar cheese for garnish

1. Melt the margarine in a soup kettle or Dutch oven, and sauté the onion and garlic together until the onion is translucent. Sprinkle on the flour and mustard powder, stirring to make a roux. Pouring in a narrow stream, stir in the tomato juice and stock until smooth. Add the Worcestershire sauce and beans, cover lightly, and cook, stirring frequently, until thickened. Reduce to a simmer and continue to cook, undisturbed, for about 30 minutes.
2. Turn off the heat, and adjust the salt and pepper to taste. Serve immediately, alone or as part of a menu, with cheese garnish.

It was once said that the way beans are prepared nearly defined the Mason-Dixon Line. In the North they were prepared in one way, and in the South another way. This soup marries both cuisines.

3 medium white or red potatoes, peeled
4 tablespoons margarine
2 medium yellow onions, diced
¼ cup all-purpose flour
4 cups vegetable stock
1 cup dried potato flakes
2 cups half-and-half
1 teaspoon dried basil
¼ teaspoon garlic powder
¼ teaspoon Tabasco Sauce
¼ cup imitation bacon bits
½ cup shredded Provolone cheese
3 tablespoons chopped chives or scallions

1. Peel the potatoes. Steam or cook the potatoes in enough water to cover until fork tender. Drain and dice. Set aside.
2. Melt the margarine in a soup kettle or Dutch oven, and sauté the onion, until translucent. Sprinkle on the flour, and stir to make a roux. Add 1 cup of the stock, a little at a time, and cook, stirring until thickened. Add the remaining stock, and bring to a boil. Reduce to a simmer, and cook for about 10 minutes.
3. Add the potato flakes, half-and-half, basil, garlic powder, Tabasco Sauce, and bacon bits. Simmer for an additional 10 minutes, add the cooked potatoes, and heat through.
4. Turn off the heat, and adjust the salt and pepper to taste. Serve immediately with the cheese and chives sprinkled over the top.

4 cups vegetable stock
1 cup quick-cooking pearl barley
4 teaspoons crushed fresh basil
1 teaspoon minced celery
1½ teaspoons Worcestershire sauce
salt and pepper to taste

BARLEY GRUEL

Winter

Yield: about 4 to 6 servings

1. In a saucepan, combine the stock, barley, basil, celery, and Worcestershire sauce. Bring to a boil. Then reduce to a simmer, cover, and cook over a low heat until the barley is very tender. Cooking time will be 30 minutes to 1 hour, depending on the type of barley.
2. Remove from heat, and adjust the salt and pepper to taste. Serve with chilled stalks of celery on the side.

Hint: Prepare the soup in the morning, and let it stew slowly all afternoon. This can be prepared in a Crock Pot. When ready to serve, add thinly sliced onions to each bowl. Have a variety of crackers at hand.

BARLEY SOUP

Winter

Yield: about 4 to 5 servings

3 tablespoons canola oil
1 large yellow onion, chopped
2 medium cloves garlic, peeled and chopped
2 large carrots, peeled and diced
2 celery stalks, diced
¾ cup pearl barley
6 cups vegetable stock or water
¼ teaspoon ground English mixture spice
3 tablespoons margarine
⅓ pound fresh white mushrooms, chopped
3 teaspoons fresh lemon juice
1 tablespoon minced fresh parsley
salt and pepper to taste

1. Heat the oil in a soup kettle or Dutch oven, and sauté the onions and garlic until tender. Add the carrots and celery, and cook, stirring for about 1 minute. Stir in the barley, stock, and English mixture spice. Bring to a boil, then reduce to a simmer, cover lightly, and cook, for about 40 to 50 minutes, or until the barley is tender.
2. Meanwhile, melt the margarine in a skillet, and sauté the mushrooms until tender. Add the lemon juice, and transfer to the hot soup.
3. Stir the parsley into the soup, and continue to simmer for about 5 minutes. Remove from heat, adjust the salt and pepper to taste. Serve immediately in heated bowls.

2 **Herb Ox vegetable stock cubes**
1½ **cups boiling water**
1 **cup (from 16-ounce can) diced tomatoes with juice**
4.5-**ounce package small-shell macaroni**
14–**ounce can red kidney beans, rinsed and drained**
1 **cup frozen chopped spinach, thawed**
½ **teaspoon crushed dried oregano**
½ **teaspoon crushed dried basil**
¾ **ounce (about 1¼ tablespoons) grated Parmesan cheese**
salt and pepper to taste

BEAN & PASTA SOUP

Summer

Yield: about 4 servings

1. In a soup kettle or Dutch oven, combine the stock cubes and water. Heat, stirring until dissolved. Add the tomatoes. Cook until bubbles form around the edge of the pot.
2. Add the macaroni and cook for about 7 minutes before adding the beans, spinach, oregano and basil. Cover lightly, and cook, stirring occasionally, until the macaroni is al dente, about 7 to 10 minutes. (If the soup seems thick, add ¼ cup of water.) Remove from heat, adjust the salt and pepper to taste, and serve immediately alone or as part of a menu, with Parmesan cheese on the side.

Hint: Pasta does not add much flavor to a soup, but it adds texture.

1 **pound navy beans, soaked in water overnight**
1 **pound pitted prunes**
2 **cups carrots thinly sliced**
5 **cups potatoes, diced**
1 **tablespoon vegetable oil**
1 **medium yellow onion, chopped**
¼ **teaspoon ground cloves**
½ **cup unsweetened apple juice**
salt and pepper to taste

BEAN & PRUNE SOUP

Summer

Yield: about 4 servings

1. In a soup kettle or Dutch oven, combine the beans and enough water to cover by 1½ inches. Bring to a boil, then reduce to a simmer, cover tightly, and cook for about 30 minutes, or until just tender. Add the prunes, carrots, and potatoes.
2. Heat the oil in a skillet and sauté the onions until tender. Then stir into the bean mixture.
3. Add the cloves and apple juice, return to a boil, reduce to a simmer, and continue to cook for about 10 minutes. Remove from heat, adjust the salt and pepper to taste, and serve immediately.

BEAN SOUP WITH PISTOU

Year-Round

Makes about 4 to 6 servings

1 cup dried navy beans
1 cup dried cannellini beans
1 large yellow onion, chopped
5 cups boiling vegetable stock
2 large carrots, peeled and minced
1 cup shredded cabbage
2 small red potatoes, peeled and diced
10-ounce package frozen cut green beans, thawed

PISTOU

4 tablespoons minced garlic
3 tablespoons chopped basil leaves
6 tablespoons virgin olive oil
4 tablespoons grated fresh Romano cheese

1. The night before, place the navy beans and cannellini beans in separate large bowls or saucepans. Cover with cold water, and set aside until needed.

2. When ready, position the rack to the center of the oven and preheat to 400°F. Drain the soaked beans, and rinse several times. Place together in a large bean pot, or saucepan. Add the onion and enough water to cover the beans. Cover tightly, and cook in the oven for about 1½ to 2 hours, or until the beans are very tender.

3. Remove from the oven and drain. And then, using a blender or food processor, purée the mixture in batches until smooth. Return to the bean pot, slowly add the vegetable stock, carrots, cabbage, chopped potatoes, and beans. Adjust the seasoning to taste, cover again, and return the pot to the oven. Reduce the heat to 350°F. and cook for an additional 1 hour.

4. Meanwhile, using a mortar and pestle, or a small bowl and large spoon, press the garlic cloves and basil together until very smooth. Gradually blend in the oil, and stir in the cheese.

5. Remove the soup from the oven, and stir in one half of the pistou. Ladle into warmed bowls, and serve with the remaining pistou as a garnish on the side.

¾ cup vegetable oil
1½ pounds yellow onions, chopped
1¼ pounds red potatoes, peeled and diced
1 pound carrots, trimmed, peeled and diced
1 pound celery, sliced
#10 can (6 pounds, 3 ounces) cheddar cheese sauce
2 cups beer
4 cups vegetable stock
two 10-ounce packages frozen mixed vegetables, thawed
½ teaspoon paprika
2 tablespoons chopped parsley
salt and pepper to taste

BEER SOUP WITH CHEESE

Summer

Yield: about 25 to 30 servings

1. Heat the oil in a soup kettle or Dutch oven, and sauté the onion until transparent. Reduce to a low heat setting, add the potatoes, carrots, and celery, cover tightly, and continue to cook for about 20 minutes, or until the vegetables are tender.
2. Add the cheese sauce, beer, stock, thawed vegetables, paprika, and parsley. Bring to a boil. Reduce to a simmer, cover again and continue to cook, stirring occasionally, for about 15 to 20 minutes.
3. Remove from heat, adjust the salt and pepper to taste, and serve immediately.

1 teaspoon extra virgin olive oil
1 large yellow onion, chopped
2 large carrots, peeled and chopped
4 medium garlic cloves, peeled and chopped
four 15-ounce cans black-eyed peas, drained
8 cups vegetable stock
¼ pound fresh watercress
salt and pepper to taste

BLACK-EYED PEAS & WATERCRESS SOUP

Summer

Yield: about 6 to 8 servings

1. Heat the oil in a soup kettle or Dutch oven, and sauté the onion until translucent. Add the carrots and garlic, heat through, and then add the beans, and stock. Bring to a boil, then reduce to a simmer, and cook, stirring occasionally, for about 7 to 8 minutes, or until the vegetables are tender.
2. Meanwhile, thoroughly wash the watercress, and discard any discolored leaves and stems. Separate about 2 cups (loosely packed) of the tender watercress sprigs, and coarsely chop the remaining watercress.
3. When the soup is ready, remove from heat, and reserve about 1 cup of the solid ingredients. Then, in the container of a blender, purée in batches, until smooth.
4. Return everything to the pan, and bring to a boil. Remove from heat, stir in the watercress sprigs and pieces, and adjust the salt and pepper to taste. Ladle into heated bowls. Serve immediately, with dark bread on the side.

BLACK BEAN SOUP

Autumn

Yield: about 6 servings

1 pound dried black beans, soaked in water overnight
2 whole bay leaves
3 quarts vegetable stock or water
1 cup olive or canola oil
3 small shallots, peeled and diced
1 small white onion, diced
1 large red pepper, trimmed, seeded, and diced
1 large green pepper, trimmed, seeded, and diced
3 cloves garlic, peeled and minced
1 tablespoon ground cumin
2 teaspoons crushed dried oregano
2 tablespoons fresh parsley
2 tablespoons light brown sugar
salt and pepper to taste

1. Drain the soaking beans. Transfer them to a soup kettle or Dutch oven. Add the bay leaves and stock, and bring to a boil. Then reduce to a simmer, cover lightly, and cook, stirring occasionally, for about 2½ to 3 hours, or until the beans are very tender. Add more water if necessary during cooking.
2. Meanwhile, heat the oil in a skillet and sauté the shallots and onion until translucent. Add the red pepper, green pepper, and garlic, and continue to cook, stirring frequently, for about 3 minutes. Add the cumin, oregano, and parsley. Heat through and add the sugar. Remove from heat and cool slightly.
3. In the container of a blender or food processor, purée the sautéed ingredients until smooth, and then stir into the cooking beans. Cover again, and continue to cook for an additional 30 minutes.
4. Turn off the heat, remove and discard the bay leaves, and adjust the salt and pepper to taste. Serve immediately.

Hint: By tradition, this soup is made very thick.

2 tablespoons vegetable oil
2 medium yellow onions, chopped
4 medium cloves garlic, peeled and minced
8 jalapeños, seeded and chopped
1 tablespoon fresh red chili, crushed; or dried red chili powder
2 cups black beans, soaked in water overnight
1 cup canned diced tomatoes
2 teaspoons ground cumin
1 teaspoon ground ezpazote
1 teaspoon ground coriander
¼ teaspoon ground cloves
1 tablespoon red wine vinegar
6 to 8 cups water
3 tablespoons tequila (optional)

TEX-MEX BLACK BEAN SOUP WITH JALAPEÑOS

Autumn
Yield: about 6 to 8 servings

1. Heat the oil in a saucepan, and sauté the onions and garlic together until the onions are tender.
2. In a soup kettle or Dutch oven, combine the onions and garlic with the jalapeños, red chili powder, beans, tomatoes, cumin, ezpazote, coriander, cloves, vinegar, and water. Bring to a boil. Then reduce to a simmer, cover lightly, and cook for about 2 hours, or until the beans are tender.
3. Turn off the heat, divide the soup in half, and then in the container of a blender or food processor, purée one half of the soup until smooth. Pour the puréed portion back into the hot mixture, and continue to simmer for about 15 minutes, or until thickened to desired consistency.
4. Turn off the heat, and stir in the tequila. Serve immediately, alone or as part of a menu, with a garnish of sour cream on the side.

Hint: This soup is south-of-the-border hot and spicy. Dried chili powder will be hotter than fresh red chilis. Ezpazote is also sold under the name Mexican tea. Since jalapeños and other chili peppers can burn the skin, wear gloves while handling them.

BLACK BEAN SOUP WITH ORANGE

Autumn

Yield: about 6 servings

2 cups black beans, soaked in water overnight
7 cups water
2 Herb Ox vegetable bouillon cubes
freshly ground pepper
2 leeks, sliced
2 medium carrots, peeled and chopped
1 medium yellow onion, chopped
¼ cup fresh chopped cilantro
1 cup fresh orange juice
2 tablespoons orange zest

1. Drain the beans, and put them in a soup kettle or Dutch oven. Add about 5 cups of water, bouillon cubes, and pepper. Bring to a boil. Then reduce to a simmer, cover lightly, and cook, stirring occasionally, for about 2 to 2½ hours, or until the beans are very tender.

2. Meanwhile, in a saucepan, combine the leeks, carrots, and onion. Add the remaining 2 cups of water, bring to a boil, then reduce to a simmer, and cook until the carrots are tender.

3. Remove 2 cups of cooked beans with their liquid from the pot, and purée in the container of a blender or food processor. Then stir back into the pot of beans.

4. Add the cooked vegetables with their cooking water to the beans, and bring to a boil. Remove from heat, stir in the cilantro, orange juice, and orange zest. Serve alone or as part of a menu.

Hint: For best results, use Herb Ox cubes rather than the granules.

1 pound black beans, soaked in water overnight
8 cups water
2 teaspoons celery salt
2 cups vegetable stock
2 pounds turnips, peeled and finely diced
1½ tablespoons olive oil
1½ cups green peppers, seeded and chopped
1½ cups minced red onions
1½ tablespoons crushed garlic
1 teaspoon ground cumin
16-ounce can diced tomatoes with juice
¼ cup red wine vinegar

BLACK BEAN SOUP WITH TURNIPS

Autumn

Yield: about 6 servings

1. In a soup kettle or Dutch oven, combine the beans, 8 cups of water, and celery salt. Bring to a boil, then reduce to a simmer, cover lightly, and cook, stirring occasionally, for about 2½ hours, or until the beans are very tender.

2. Strain the beans through a fine sieve, reserving the liquid. Add 2 cups vegetable stock to the reserved liquid, putting the beans and stock back into the soup kettle. Add the turnips and bring to a boil. Then reduce to a simmer, and continue to cook, stirring occasionally, for about 10 minutes.

3. Heat the oil in a skillet and sauté the peppers, onions, garlic, and cumin, stirring constantly, until the onions are a golden color. Add the tomatoes and vinegar. Reduce the heat to the lowest setting cover and cook for about 15 minutes. Stir the tomato mixture into the beans, and heat through.

4. Turn off the heat, and adjust the salt and pepper to taste. Serve immediately. Garnish as you wish.

Hint: The secret of this combination is to dice the turnips very small. That way, they add to the soup's texture.

BLACK BEAN SOUP WITH VEGETABLES

Autumn
Yield: about 6 to 8 servings

2 cups dried black beans, soaked in water overnight
1 medium white onion, finely diced
3 tablespoons margarine
1 small carrot, peeled and finely minced
1 celery stalk and leaves, finely minced
6 cups vegetable stock
1 teaspoon chopped fresh basil
¼ cup lemon juice
¼ cup white port wine
salt and pepper to taste
sour cream for garnish
finely chopped almonds for garnish (optional)

1. Melt the margarine in a soup kettle or Dutch oven, and sauté the onion until lightly colored. Add the carrot and celery, and continue to cook, stirring frequently, for about 5 minutes. Add the beans (undrained), stock, and basil. Bring to a boil, and then reduce to a simmer. Cover lightly, and cook, stirring occasionally, for about 2 hours, or until the beans are tender.

2. Remove from heat, and in the container of a blender or food processor, purée the mix in batches until smooth.

3. Return to the pot, add the lemon juice and wine, and heat through. Remove from the heat, and adjust the salt and pepper to taste. Serve immediately with sour cream and chopped dill on the side.

Hint: Putting the vegetables through a blender helps them complement the soup's texture.

1 cup dried kidney beans, soaked in water overnight
8½ cups vegetable stock
3 large carrots, peeled and finely chopped
1 large yellow onion, finely chopped
½ cup fresh parsley, chopped
1 medium clove garlic, peeled and minced
1 teaspoon dry mustard
4 ounces cheddar cheese, shredded
1 ounce blue cheese, crumbled
1½ cups red cabbage, shredded
salt and pepper to taste

BLUE CHEESE MINESTRONE

Spring

Yield: about 6 to 8 servings

1. In a soup kettle or Dutch oven, combine the beans (undrained) and vegetable stock. Bring to a boil, and then reduce to a simmer. Cover lightly, and cook, stirring occasionally, for about 2 hours, or until the beans are tender.
2. Add the carrots, onions, parsley, garlic, mustard, cheddar cheese, and blue cheese. Return to a boil. Reduce to a simmer, cover lightly, and continue to cook for about 40 minutes, or until the vegetables are tender.
3. Add the cabbage, cook for about 5 minutes, and then remove from heat. Adjust the salt and pepper to taste, and serve immediately.

Hint: The two cheeses complement the musty taste of the beans.

1 pound dried navy beans, soaked in water overnight
4 quarts vegetable stock or water
3 cups chopped celery stalks and leaves
1½ cups minced carrots
2 large yellow onions, chopped
1 tablespoon lemon zest
¼ cup lemon juice
salt and pepper to taste

BOUNTIFUL BEAN SOUP

Spring

Yield: about 10 to 12 servings

1. In a soup kettle or Dutch oven, combine the beans (undrained), stock, celery, carrots, onions, and lemon zest. Bring to boil. Reduce to a simmer, cover lightly, and cook, stirring occasionally, until the liquid evaporates just below the surface and the beans are tender. Remove from heat.
2. In the container of a blender or food processor, purée the beans in batches until smooth, and then return to the pot.
3. Stir in the lemon juice, adjust the salt and pepper to taste, and serve immediately.

Hint: Oranges or limes in place of lemons produces a flavor variation.

If well cooked, beans are a natural thickening agent.

BRAZILIAN VEGETARIAN RICE SOUP

Autumn

Yield: about 4 servings

2 tablespoons vegetable oil
1 medium yellow onion, quartered
¼ teaspoon powdered cloves
2 large ripe tomatoes, quartered
1 medium carrot, peeled and diced
¼ cup chopped celery leaves
½ teaspoon black pepper
10 cups vegetable stock or water
½ cup uncooked white pearl rice
salt and pepper to taste
3 medium carrots, sliced thin on the diagonal
¼ cup flat leaf parsley, finely chopped

1. Heat the oil in a soup kettle or Dutch oven, and sauté the onion until lightly colored. Add the cloves, tomatoes, diced carrots, celery, pepper, and vegetable stock. Bring to a boil, then reduce to a simmer, cover lightly, and cook, stirring occasionally, for about 20 minutes.

2. Thoroughly wash and drain the rice through a fine sieve, rinsing until the water runs clear.

3. Add the rice to the soup, cover lightly, and continue to simmer for about 10 minutes. Add the thinly sliced carrots and parsley. Bring to a boil, then reduce to a simmer, and cook for about 10 minutes, or until the rice is tender. Remove from heat, and adjust the salt and pepper to taste. Serve immediately.

5-ounce package dried lima beans, soaked overnight
2.5-ounce package dried white beans, soaked overnight
1 tablespoon virgin olive oil
1 small white onion, chopped
1 medium clove garlic, peeled and minced
4 cups vegetable stock
2 teaspoons tomato sauce
8-ounce can diced tomatoes
1 tablespoon packed light brown sugar
1 teaspoon crushed sage
½ cup enriched soy milk
1 tablespoon evaporated milk

1. Melt the butter in a saucepan or soup kettle, and sauté the onion and garlic together until the onion is translucent. Add the stock, tomato sauce, lima beans, and diced tomatoes. Bring to a boil, then reduce to a simmer, cover lightly, and cook, stirring occasionally, until the beans are tender.
2. Remove from heat and purée in batches, using a blender or food processor, until smooth. Return to pan, add the white beans, sugar, and sage. Simmer over low heat for about 40 minutes, or until the white beans are tender. Add more water if necessary during cooking.
3. Remove from heat. Stir in the soy milk and evaporated milk, and adjust the salt and pepper to taste. Serve immediately.

1¾ cups vegetable stock
10-ounce package frozen broccoli florets, thawed, drained, and minced
¼ cup Minute Rice (uncooked)
⅛ teaspoon ground nutmeg
salt and pepper to taste

1. In a soup kettle or Dutch oven, combine the vegetable stock and broccoli. Bring to a boil, and stir in the rice and nutmeg. Cover tightly, remove from heat, and set aside, undisturbed for about 5 minutes.
2. Adjust the salt and pepper to taste, and serve immediately.

BROCCOLI APPLE SOUP

Summer

Yield: about 4 servings

1 tablespoon olive or vegetable oil
2 cups fresh broccoli stems, peeled and diced
¾ teaspoon crushed dried lemon thyme
1 cup sliced yellow onion
1 cup McIntosh apple, pared, cored, and diced
½ cup diced celery
4 cups vegetable stock or unsweetened apple juice
½ cup plumped seedless raisins
salt and pepper to taste
¼ cup unflavored yogurt or sour cream for garnish
2 tablespoons minced parsley for garnish

1. Heat the oil in a soup kettle or Dutch oven, and combine the broccoli, thyme, onion, apple, and celery. Cover lightly, and cook, stirring occasionally, until the onions are translucent.
2. Add the stock to the vegetables, and bring to a boil. Then reduce to a simmer, cover lightly, and cook for about 30 minutes.
3. Remove from heat and cool slightly. Then in the container of a blender or food processor, purée the mixture in batches, until smooth.
4. Return to the pot, heat through, add the raisins, and adjust the salt and pepper to taste. Serve immediately, alone or as part of a menu, with yogurt and parsley on the side.

Hint: This soup can be made with vegetable stock rather than apple juice. If you use apple juice, the soup can be served hot or cold.

1 small carrot, peeled and thinly sliced
1 celery stalk and leaves, sliced
1 small white onion, chopped
1 medium clove garlic, peeled and minced
½ teaspoon crushed dried marjoram
¼ teaspoon crushed dried basil
½ cup vegetable stock
2 cups skim milk
2 cups coarsely chopped broccoli
½ cup vegetable-flavored pasta, cooked al dente and drained
ground nutmeg to taste for garnish
1 cup unflavored yogurt or whipped sour cream for garnish

BROCCOLI VEGETARIAN SOUP

Summer

Yield: about 4 servings

1. In a soup kettle or Dutch oven, combine the carrots, celery, onions, garlic, marjoram, basil, and stock. Bring to a boil, then reduce to a simmer, cover lightly, and cook for about 10 minutes.
2. Add the milk and broccoli, and bring to a boil. Then reduce to a simmer, cover lightly, and simmer for about 5 minutes, or until the broccoli is tender.
4. Remove from heat, and in the container of a blender or food processor, purée the soup, in batches, until smooth.
5. Return to the pot, add the pasta, and heat through.
6. Turn off the heat, and adjust the salt and pepper to taste. Serve immediately, with the nutmeg and yogurt as a garnish.

Hint: The use of freshly snipped herbs will heighten this soup's taste and aroma.

CABBAGE & BEET SOUP

Year-Round

Yield: about 8 servings

two 16-ounce cans diced tomatoes
3 teaspoons instant vegetable bouillon granules
2½ cups fresh beets, sliced
3 medium carrots, peeled and diced
1 large yellow onion, sliced
2 celery stalks, coarsely chopped with tops
water
3 medium cloves garlic, peeled and minced
1 medium head cabbage, sliced or cut in wedges
granulated sugar to taste
salt and pepper to taste
2 tablespoons fresh lemon juice

1. In a soup kettle or Dutch oven, combine the tomatoes, bouillon granules, beets, carrots, onion, celery, and enough water to cover by at least 1 inch. Bring to a boil, then reduce to a simmer, cover lightly, and cook, for about 20 minutes, or until the vegetables are tender. Add the garlic, cabbage, and sugar. Continue to cook for about 10 minutes.
2. Turn off the heat, adjust the salt and pepper to taste, and stir in the lemon juice. Serve immediately.

CABBAGE-CARROT SOUP

Year-Round

Yield: about 8 servings

1 tablespoon margarine
1 large clove garlic, peeled and chopped
2 celery stalks and leaves, chopped
16-ounce can red kidney beans, drained
½ small head cabbage, chopped
3 medium carrots, peeled and chopped
28-ounce can diced tomatoes
1½ cups vegetable stock or unsweetened apple juice
salt and pepper to taste
chopped parsley for garnish

1. Melt the margarine in a soup kettle or Dutch oven and combine the garlic, celery, beans, cabbage, carrots, tomatoes, and stock. Bring to a boil, then reduce to a simmer, cover lightly, and cook, stirring occasionally, for about 20 minutes.
2. Remove from heat. Adjust the salt and pepper to taste, and serve in hot bowls with a garnish of parsley.

Hint: This soup takes only 30 minutes to prepare.

7½ cups water
½ teaspoon crushed dried oregano
5 whole peppercorns
2 bay leaves
1 pound tofu, diced
16-ounce can diced tomatoes
16-ounce can cut green beans
2 medium carrots, thinly sliced
1 medium white onion, chopped
½ cup red wine
½ teaspoon red pepper flakes (optional)
1 small head cabbage, chopped

CABBAGE & TOFU SOUP

Year-Round

Yield: about 6 to 8 servings

1. In a soup kettle or Dutch oven, combine water, oregano, peppercorns and bay leaves. Bring to a boil, then reduce to a simmer, cover lightly, and cook, stirring occasionally, for about 10 minutes.
2. Remove from heat, strain and discard the vegetable matter, and return the liquid to the pot. Add the tofu, tomatoes, beans, carrots, onions, and wine. Return to a boil, reduce to a simmer, and continue to cook, stirring, for about 10 minutes. Add the pepper flakes and cabbage, and continue to cook for about 20 minutes longer, or until all the vegetables are tender.
3. Turn off the heat, and adjust the salt and pepper to taste. Serve immediately.

Hint: Using vegetable stock in place of the water will give the soup a richer flavor.

2 tablespoons margarine
1 medium yellow onion, sliced
4 medium carrots, peeled and diced
2½-quarts vegetable stock
1 small head cabbage, coarsely chopped
1 cup zucchini, finely diced
salt and pepper to taste

CABBAGE SOUP WITH ZUCCHINI

Autumn

Yield: about 9 servings

1. Melt the margarine in a soup kettle or Dutch oven, and sauté the onion until lightly colored.
2. Add the carrots and stock, and bring to a boil. Then reduce to a simmer, cover lightly, and cook, stirring occasionally, for about 10 minutes. Add the cabbage and zucchini, and cook for about 10 minutes.
3. Turn off the heat, and adjust salt and pepper to taste. Serve immediately.

CABBAGE BEAN SOUP WITH RIVELS

Year-Round
Yield: about 6 servings

1 cup all-purpose flour
2 tablespoons milk
1 egg, beaten
4 cups water or vegetable stock
5 cups shredded green cabbage
1⅓ cups shredded carrots
2 tablespoons imitation bacon bits
1 tablespoon Herb Ox vegetable bouillon granules
1 tablespoon cider vinegar
1 teaspoon caraway seeds
1 large onion, chopped
1 medium apple, coarsely chopped
15.5-ounce can great northern beans, rinsed
salt and pepper to taste

1. To make the rivels, in a bowl, using a fork or pastry blender, combine the flour, milk, and egg until coarse crumbs (about the size of raisins) forms. Set aside.

2. In a soup kettle or Dutch oven, combine the water, cabbage, carrots, bacon bits, bouillon granules, vinegar, caraway seeds, onion, apple, and beans. Bring to a boil, then reduce to a simmer, cover lightly, and cook for about 5 minutes.

3. Sprinkle on the rivels, stirring to separate, and cover the pot again. Continue to simmer for about 20 minutes or until the vegetables are tender.

4. Turn off the heat, and adjust the salt and pepper to taste. Serve immediately.

Hint: Rivels are small chunks of homemade pasta or very tiny dumplings. Flavor the rivels by sprinkling them with finely chopped or ground basil or another herb.

4 tablespoons margarine
1 medium onion, chopped
6 cups chopped cauliflower
1 large potato, peeled and diced
1 quart vegetable stock or water
2 tablespoons fresh snipped chives
½ teaspoon herbes de Provençe
few drops hot pepper sauce
salt and pepper to taste
1 cup heavy cream
2 egg yolks, at room temperature
2 tablespoons brandy or rum
½ pound Roquefort
chives for garnish

CAULIFLOWER & ROQUEFORT SOUP

Year-Round

Yield: about 4 to 6 servings

1. Melt margarine in soup kettle or Dutch oven, and sauté the onions until tender. Tightly cover the pot, turn off the heat, and allow to set, undisturbed for about 10 minutes.

2. When ready, adjust the heat under the pot to medium, add the cauliflower, potato, and sautéd onions, and cook, stirring constantly, for about 2 to 3 minutes. Add the stock, chives, herbes de Provençe, pepper sauce and salt and pepper to taste. Bring to a boil. Then reduce to a simmer, cover and cook, stirring occasionally, for about 10 minutes, or until the vegetables are tender.

3. Remove from heat, and in the container of a blender or food processor, purée in batches, and then return to the pot.

4. In the container of a blender or food processor, combine the cream, yolks and brandy and blend until smooth. With the blender running, and pouring in a narrow stream, add 1 cup of the hot soup, and blend until smooth.

5. Stir back into the pot, add half the Roquefort, and cook, stirring constantly, until the cheese melts. (Do not allow to boil.) Remove from heat, and serve immediately, alone or as part of a menu, garnished with hot toasted croutons, the remaining Roquefort, and chives.

CAULIFLOWER SOUP WITH CHEESE

Autumn

Yield: about 4 servings

4 tablespoons margarine
3 medium carrots, trimmed, and diced
3 medium celery stalks and leaves, diced
1 medium yellow onion, minced
3 tablespoons all-purpose flour
1½ cups vegetable stock or water
2 cups cauliflower florets
2 cups grated mild cheddar cheese
1½ cups half-and-half
¼ teaspoon cayenne pepper
salt and pepper to taste
½ cup finely diced colby cheese for garnish

1. Melt the margarine in a soup kettle or Dutch oven, and sauté the carrots, celery, and onion until tender. Sprinkle on the flour, and cook, stirring constantly, until incorporated.
2. Then, pouring in a narrow stream and stirring constantly, add the stock, until smooth. Add cauliflower. Bring to a boil, then reduce to a simmer, cover lightly, and cook for about 5 minutes, or until the cauliflower is tender.
3. Stir in the cheddar cheese, and cook, stirring until melted. (Do not allow to boil.) Stir in the half-and-half, cayenne, and salt and pepper to taste. Remove from heat and serve immediately with a garnish of colby cheese.

Hint: Garnish this soup with a sprinkling of ground nutmeg.

8 cups vegetable stock
1 stalk celery with leaves, coarsely chopped
1 medium carrot, coarsely chopped
1 medium yellow onion, quartered
2 sprigs fresh parsley
1 bay leaf
2 cups uncooked cheese-filled tortellini
2 medium zucchini, cut in half lengthwise and sliced
salt and pepper to taste

CHEESE TORTELLINI SOUP

Summer

Yield: about 6 to 8 servings

1. In a soup kettle or Dutch oven, combine the 6 cups of the stock, celery, carrot, onion, parsley, and bay leaf. Bring to a boil, then reduce to a simmer, cover, and cook for about 10 minutes. Strain through a fine sieve, discarding the vegetable matter, and returning the liquid to the pot.
2. Add the remaining stock, bring to a boil, and then add the tortellini and zucchini. Return to a boil. Reduce to a simmer, cover lightly, and cook, stirring occasionally, for about 20 minutes, or until the tortellini is al dente.
3. Turn off the heat, adjust the salt and pepper to taste. Serve immediately.

½ cup boiling water
3 tablespoons Herb Ox vegetable bouillon granules
1 tablespoon margarine
1 cup chopped white onions
1⅓ pounds potatoes, peeled and diced
2 cups water
10-ounce package frozen broccoli florets, thawed and drained
½ cup shredded cheddar or colby cheese
salt and pepper to taste

CHEESE, POTATO & BROCCOLI SOUP

Summer

Yield: about 4 servings

1. In a cup, combine the ½ cup boiling water and bouillon granules. Stir until dissolved. Set aside.
2. Melt the margarine in a soup kettle or Dutch oven, and sauté the onion until tender. Add the potatoes, the 2 cups of water and the bouillon-and-water mix. Bring to a boil. Then reduce to a simmer, cover and cook until the potatoes are tender.
3. Using a slotted spoon, remove about 1 cup of potatoes and set aside.
4. In the container of a blender or food processor, purée the remaining soup, in batches, until smooth. Return to the pot, and add the reserved potatoes. Stir in the broccoli, reheat over a medium heat (do not allow to boil) and add the cheese, stirring until melted. Remove from heat, adjust the salt and pepper to taste, and serve immediately with a fresh loaf of bread on the side.

CHEESY CABBAGE SOUP

Summer

Yield: about 6 to 8 servings

1 cup dried kidney beans, soaked in water overnight
8½ cups vegetable stock
3 large carrots, peeled and minced
1 large yellow onion, minced
½ cup chopped fresh parsley
1 medium clove garlic, peeled and minced
1 teaspoon dry mustard
1 ounce blue cheese, crumbled
2 cups cole slaw
salt and pepper to taste

1. In a soup kettle or Dutch oven, combine the undrained beans and stock, bring to a boil, then reduce to a simmer, cover lightly, and cook, stirring occasionally, for about 2 hours, or until the beans are tender.
2. Add the carrots, onions, parsley, garlic, mustard, and blue cheese. Return to a boil, reduce to a simmer, cover lightly, and continue to cook for about 40 minutes, or until the vegetables are tender.
3. Add the cole slaw, cook for about 5 minutes, and then remove from heat. Adjust the salt and pepper to taste, and serve immediately.

Hint: Believe it or not, cole slaw is an ingredient for this surprising soup.

CHICKPEA & SPINACH SOUP

Summer

Yield: about 4 servings

1 tablespoon margarine
1 large yellow onion, chopped
4 small cloves garlic, peeled and minced
1 cup milk
16-ounce can chickpeas, drained and rinsed
4 to 5 cups fresh spinach, shredded
⅛ teaspoon cardamom powder
⅛ teaspoon ground nutmeg
1 teaspoon curry powder
¼ teaspoon turmeric
salt and pepper to taste

1. Melt the margarine in a soup kettle or large saucepan, and sauté the onion and garlic until the onion is translucent. Stir in the milk, bring to a boil. Then reduce to a simmer, add the chickpeas, spinach, cardamom, nutmeg, curry powder, and turmeric, and cook, stirring occasionally, for about 15 minutes.
2. Transfer about 1½ cups of the soup into the container of a blender, and purée until smooth. Return to the pot, and heat through.
3. Turn off the heat, and adjust the salt and pepper to taste. Serve immediately.

⅓ pound dried chickpeas, soaked in water 2 days
4 tablespoons olive oil
1 large white onion, chopped
2 celery stalks and leaves, chopped
2 large carrots, peeled and diced
1 leek, thinly sliced
2 medium cloves garlic, peeled and minced
2 cups shredded cabbage
16-ounce can diced tomatoes
2 teaspoons tomato paste
7 cups vegetable stock
1 fresh zucchini, peeled and chopped
⅓ cup elbow macaroni, cooked al dente and drained
salt and pepper to taste

CHICKPEA & VEGETABLE SOUP

Summer

Yield: about 6 servings

1. Heat the oil in a soup kettle or Dutch oven, and sauté the onion until lightly browned. Add the celery, and cook, stirring frequently, for about 1 minute. Add the carrots, leek, garlic and cabbage. Cover lightly, and cook for about 2 to 3 minutes, or until the cabbage has softened.
2. Add the tomatoes, tomato paste, stock, and chickpeas (drained of soaking water and rinsed). Bring to a boil, and cook for about 3 minutes. Reduce to a simmer, cover tightly, and cook, stirring occasionally, for about 1½ hours, or until the chickpeas are very tender.
3. Stir in the zucchini and macaroni. Heat through, remove from heat, and adjust the salt and pepper to taste. Serve immediately.

CHILI CARNE SOPA

Year-Round
Yield: about 6 servings

2 tablespoons vegetable oil
¼ cup all-purpose flour
1 medium clove garlic, peeled and finely chopped
1 medium yellow onion, chopped
¼ cup canned chopped green chilis
1 teaspoon crushed dried oregano leaves
2 teaspoons chili powder
16-ounce can pinto beans, drained
2 cups V-8 vegetable juice
2 cups quick-cooking pearl barley
salt and pepper to taste
¼ cup fresh chopped cilantro

1. Heat the oil in a soup kettle or Dutch oven, and sauté the garlic and onion until the onion is translucent. Sprinkle on the flour, and continue to cook, stirring until smooth. Add the chilis, oregano, chili powder, and beans. Heat through, reduce the heat to a simmer, cover lightly, and cook for about 10 minutes.
2. Add the vegetable juice and barley, bring to a boil, then reduce to a simmer, cover and cook, stirring occasionally, for about 30 minutes, or until the beans and barley are very tender.
3. Turn off the heat, adjust the salt and pepper to taste before stirring in the cilantro. Serve immediately, alone or as part of a menu, with heated fresh tortillas on the side.

Hint: Serve this in warmed bowls, on the patio with a tall, cold drink.

CHUNKY PIZZA SOUP

Year-Round
Yield: about 4 servings

1 tablespoon olive or vegetable oil
1 medium yellow onion, minced
½ cup sliced fresh mushrooms
¼ cup green peppers, cut into matchsticks
14-ounce can diced tomatoes
1 cup vegetable stock
1/2 teaspoon crushed dried basil
1 cup shredded mozzarella cheese

1. Preheat the oven broiler.
2. Heat the oil in a soup kettle or Dutch oven, and sauté the onion, mushrooms, and green peppers together until the onion is translucent. (Do not allow to brown.) Add the tomatoes, stock, and basil. Bring to a boil.
3. Remove from heat. Ladle into oven-proof bowls, sprinkle with cheese, and put the individual bowls under the broiler until the cheese melts. Remove from the broiler and serve immediately with crusty bread or bread sticks.

2 tablespoons margarine
1 medium yellow onion, diced
2 medium carrots, peeled and diced
8 cups vegetable stock
1 cup crunchy peanut butter
1 small fresh ripe tomato, quartered
4 small potatoes, peeled and diced
1 small green pepper, roasted, peeled, seeded, and diced
3 tablespoons minced fresh parsley
1 large (about 3 pounds) zucchini, diced
two 8-ounce cans sliced button mushrooms
3 tablespoons freshly squeezed lemon juice
salt and cayenne pepper to taste

CHUNKY PEANUT SOUP

Year-Round

Yield: about 8 servings

1. Melt the margarine in a soup kettle or Dutch oven, and sauté the onion until just tender. Add the carrots, and continue to cook, stirring occasionally, for about 5 minutes.

2. Meanwhile in a bowl, using a wire whisk, beat 1 cup of the stock with the peanut butter until smooth.

3. Add the remaining stock, tomato, potatoes, green pepper, and 2 tablespoons of the parsley to the pot. Bring to a boil, add the peanut butter mixture, and return to a boil. Then reduce to a rolling simmer, cover lightly, and cook for about 15 minutes, or until the potatoes are fork tender. Add the zucchini and mushrooms, and cook, stirring, until the zucchini is tender.

4. Turn off the heat, add the lemon juice, and adjust the salt and pepper to taste. Ladle into soup bowls and sprinkle with the remaining parsley just before serving.

CHUNKY POTATO LEEK SOUP

Summer

Yield: about 4 servings

2 teaspoons margarine
1 cup sliced leeks
2 cups vegetable stock
2 cups cubed potatoes
1 cup canned whole-kernel corn
2 tablespoons fresh dill weed, chilled
2 teaspoons grated Parmesan cheese
red pepper sauce to taste

1. In a 2-quart microwave casserole, combine the leeks and margarine, and microwave on HIGH, stirring once, for about 3 minutes. Add the stock, potatoes, cover lightly with a vented cover, and microwave, stirring twice, on HIGH for about 4 minutes.
2. Add the corn, dill, cheese, and pepper sauce. Once more cover with the vented cover, and cook on HIGH for about 4 minutes, or until the potatoes are tender.
3. Turn off the heat, adjust the salt and pepper to taste, and set aside for 2 to 3 minutes before serving.

CHUNKY VEGETABLE SOUP

Year-Round

Yield: about 4 to 5 servings

1½ cups water
4 green onions
3 asparagus spears
1 medium (about 1½ pounds) zucchini, quartered lengthwise
1 broccoli stalk, peeled and quartered lengthwise
1 cup milk
¼ cup margarine
1 medium yellow onion, minced
1 celery stalk, minced
2 tablespoons all-purpose flour
salt and pepper to taste

1. Put the water in the base of a steamer, bring to a boil. In the upper section of the steamer, combine the onions, asparagus, zucchini, and broccoli. Cover and steam for about 5 to 7 minutes, or until the vegetables are tender.
2. Reserve the water (steaming liquid) from the base of the steamer. Transfer the vegetables to a platter. When they are cool to the touch, dice, and then set aside.
3. Add enough milk to the reserved steaming liquid to measure 2 cups.
4. Melt the margarine in a large saucepan, and sauté the onion, and celery until tender. Sprinkle on the flour, stirring until incorporated. And then, pouring in a narrow stream, and stirring constantly, add the remaining milk. Bring to a boil, stir in the vegetables, heat through, adjust the salt and pepper to taste. Serve immediately.

Hint: Asparagus spears were once called the arrows of the gods.

¼ pound soba noodles or thin spaghetti, cooked al dente
2 teaspoons coconut milk
2 cups unsweetened apple juice or vegetable stock
1 stalk lemon grass, cut into 1-inch lengths
4-inch piece fresh ginger root, peeled and thinly sliced
1 tablespoon curry powder
½ teaspoon turmeric
2 teaspoons grated lime zest
2 tablespoons fresh lime juice
2 teaspoons Chinese-style chili sauce
1 tablespoon sesame oil
8 white button mushrooms, trimmed
salt and pepper to taste
cilantro sprigs for garnish

THAI COCONUT CURRY SOUP

Year-Round

Yield: about 4 servings

1. In a soup kettle or Dutch oven, combine the coconut milk, apple juice, lemon grass, ginger, curry, turmeric, lime zest and juice, and chili sauce. Bring to a boil. Then reduce to a simmer, cover lightly, and cook, stirring occasionally, for about 20 minutes.
2. Add the oil, mushrooms and noodles to the hot soup.
3. Turn off the heat, and adjust the salt and pepper to taste. Serve immediately, alone or as part of a menu, with cilantro sprigs on the side as a garnish.

Hint: Soba noodles and Chinese chili sauce can be found in Asian food stores or very large supermarkets.

5 cups vegetable stock
2 cups day-old cole slaw
¼ cup minced fresh carrots
½ teaspoon A-1 steak sauce
salt and pepper to taste

COLE SLAW SOUP

Autumn

Yield: about 4 to 6 servings

1. In a Crock Pot, combine the stock, cole slaw, carrots, and steak sauce. Bring to a boil, reduce to low, and cook for about 1 hour, or until the carrots are tender.
2. Turn off the heat, and adjust the salt and pepper to taste. Serve immediately.

Hint: Mince rather than shred the cole-slaw cabbage in a food processor. Add chopped onion or garlic if desired.

COLONIAL POTATO & WATERCRESS SOUP

Year-Round

Yield: about 4 to 6 servings

4 potatoes, peeled and diced
4 cups cold water
1 bunch fresh watercress, chopped
1 tablespoon butter or margarine
½ cup milk
salt and pepper to taste

1. In a soup kettle or Dutch oven, combine the potatoes and water, bring to a boil, and cook for about 20 minutes, or until the potatoes are fork tender.
2. Drain and reserve the water. Press the potatoes through a fine sieve. Return them to the pot along with the reserved potato water, add the watercress, and bring to a slow boil. Reduce to a simmer, and cook for about 5 minutes. Add the margarine and milk. Heat through.
3. Turn off the heat, and adjust the salt and pepper to taste. Serve immediately.

Hint: For variations, substitute unsweetened apple juice or vegetable stock for the water. To create a rich, thick soup, use heavy cream instead of milk.

CONFETTI SOUP

Year-Round

Yield: 12 to 14 servings

Confetti refers to the multitude of colors visible in the soup bowl.

1 tablespoon canola oil
2 medium yellow onions, minced
4 large carrots, peeled and diced
2 large fennel bulbs, diced
10 cups vegetable stock or water
1 teaspoon crushed dried tarragon
1 teaspoon crushed dried thyme
1 large red bell pepper, stemmed, seeded, and diced
2 medium zucchini, peeled and diced
12 large fresh mushrooms, quartered
salt and pepper to taste
grated Parmesan cheese for garnish

1. Heat the oil in soup kettle or Dutch oven, and sauté the onions, cooking until soft. Add the carrots, fennel, stock, tarragon, and thyme. Bring to a boil, then reduce to a simmer, cover lightly, and cook, stirring occasionally, for about 20 minutes, or until the vegetables are tender.
2. Add the red bell pepper, zucchini, and mushrooms. Cover lightly, and cook for about 10 minutes.
3. Turn off the heat, and adjust the salt and pepper to taste. Serve immediately, with Parmesan cheese on the side.

¼ cup vegetable oil
2 cups yellow onions, sliced
2 teaspoons minced garlic
4 cups frozen corn, thawed
4 cups vegetable stock
¼ teaspoon ground nutmeg
½ cup instant milk powder
¾ cup cooked navy beans
salt and pepper to taste

1. Heat the oil in soup kettle or Dutch oven, and sauté the onions and garlic until the onions are lightly colored. Add 3 cups of the corn, stock and nutmeg. Bring to a boil, then reduce to a simmer, cover lightly, and cook, stirring occasionally, until the corn is tender.
2. Meanwhile, in the container of a blender or food processor, purée the remaining corn with ½ cup of hot liquid from the pot, and process until smooth. Add the milk powder, and stir back into the soup. Add the beans. Bring to a boil, then reduce to a simmer, and cook until heated through.
3. Turn off the heat, and adjust the salt and pepper to taste. Serve immediately.

two 15-ounce cans pinto beans, drained and rinsed
½ cup beer
1½ cups vegetable stock
½ medium yellow onion, sliced
3 medium cloves garlic, peeled and minced
½ cup fresh cilantro leaves
1 fresh jalapeño pepper, sliced thin
salt and pepper to taste

1. In a soup kettle or Dutch oven, combine the beans, beer, stock, onion, garlic, cilantro, and pepper. Bring to a boil. Then reduce to a simmer, cover lightly, and cook for about 30 minutes, or until the beans are tender.
2. Turn off the heat, and adjust the salt and pepper to taste. Serve immediately.

CUBAN BLACK BEAN SOUP WITH MARINATED RICE

Year-Round

Yield: about 6 to 7 servings

⅔ cup cooked brown rice
½ cup tomatoes, finely chopped
¼ cup green onion, chopped
2 teaspoons lemon juice
1 teaspoon olive oil
1 pound dried black beans, soaked in water overnight
9 cups water
5 cloves garlic, peeled and crushed
1½ cups green bell pepper, seeded and finely chopped
2 tablespoons lemon juice
1½ teaspoons ground cumin
oregano to taste
2 to 4 drops hot sauce

1. In a bowl combine the rice, tomatoes, green onions, lemon juice, and oil. Cover tightly and chill in the refrigerator until needed.
2. Drain the beans, and in a soup kettle or Dutch oven, combine the beans, water, and 2 cloves of crushed garlic. Bring to a boil, then reduce to a simmer, cover lightly, and cook for about 1½ to 2 hours, or until the beans are tender.
3. Add the pepper, lemon juice, cumin, oregano, 3 cloves of crushed garlic, and hot sauce. Return to a boil. Reduce to a simmer, cover, and continue to cook for at 30 minutes, or until the vegetables are tender.
4. When ready, spoon the rice into the bowls, and ladle the soup over the top. Serve immediately.

2 tablespoons margarine
1 cup chopped yellow onion
½ cup chopped green bell pepper
1 medium clove garlic, peeled and minced
½ teaspoon ginger powder
½ teaspoon curry powder
¼ teaspoon turmeric powder
1¾ cups vegetable stock
½ cup water
two 10-ounce packages frozen chopped broccoli, thawed and drained
½ to ¾ cup half-and-half
salt and white pepper to taste.

CURRIED BROCCOLI SOUP

Year-Round

Yield: about 6 servings

1. Melt the margarine in a soup kettle or Dutch oven, and sauté the onion, pepper, and garlic together until the onion is translucent. Sprinkle on the ginger, curry powder, and turmeric, and continue to cook, stirring constantly, for about 1 minute. Add the stock, water, and broccoli. Bring to a boil, then reduce to a simmer, cover lightly, and cook, stirring occasionally, for about 30 minutes, or until the broccoli is tender.
2. In the container of a blender or food processor, purée the soup, in batches, until smooth.
3. Return to the pot, and add enough half-and-half to a desired consistency.
4. Turn off the heat, and adjust the salt and pepper to taste. Serve immediately.

5.5 ounces quick-cooking barley
2 ounces canned green beans, or fresh, chopped
3⅔ cups vegetable stock or water
2 cups white potatoes, diced
1 small cabbage, shredded
3 tablespoons cream
1 tablespoon all-purpose flour
salt and pepper to taste

ENGADINER GERSTENSUPPE (BARLEY SOUP)

Winter

Yield: about 4 servings

1. In a soup kettle or Dutch oven, combine the barley, beans, and water. Bring to a boil. Then reduce to a simmer, cover lightly, and cook, stirring occasionally, for about 2 hours.
2. Add the cabbage and potatoes, and cook for about 20 minutes, or until the potatoes are fork tender. In a separate bowl, blend the cream with the flour. Add the cream-and-flour mixture into the soup kettle, stirring until the soup is thickened.
3. Turn off the heat, and adjust the salt and pepper to taste. Serve immediately with freshly baked crusty bread on the side.

CURRIED CORN & TOMATO SOUP

Autumn

Yield: about 6 servings

1 tablespoon margarine
1 cup white onion, finely chopped
2 teaspoons minced garlic
1 tablespoon curry powder
¼ teaspoon turmeric powder
3 tablespoons all-purpose flour
1 large tomato, seeded and diced
4 cups vegetable stock
1 bay leaf, crushed
2 cups corn kernels
1 cup unflavored yogurt
chopped chives

1. Heat the margarine in a saucepan and sauté the onion until tender. Add the garlic, curry powder, turmeric, and flour, stirring until incorporated. Add the tomato, stock, and bay leaf. Bring to a boil, then reduce to a simmer, cover and cook, stirring occasionally, for about 30 minutes.
2. In the container of a blender or food processor, purée the soup, in batches, until smooth.
3. Return to the pot, add the corn, bring to a boil, then remove from the heat.
4. Stir in the yogurt, and serve immediately, with the chopped chives on the side.

CURRIED LENTIL SOUP

Year-Round

Yield: about 6 to 8 servings

1 tablespoon canola oil
1 cup red onion, chopped
2 medium cloves garlic, peeled and crushed
2 tablespoons curry powder
¼ teaspoon turmeric powder
3 cups vegetable stock
2½ cups water
16-ounce can diced tomatoes
2 cups uncooked lentils
1 cup carrots, finely chopped
½ cup dry red wine
1 cup chopped parsley
salt and pepper to taste

1. Heat the oil in a soup kettle or Dutch oven, and sauté the onion and garlic until soft. Add the curry powder and turmeric, stirring briefly, and then add the stock, water, tomatoes, lentils, carrots, and wine. Bring to a boil. Then reduce to a simmer, cover lightly and simmer, about 40 minutes, or until the lentils are tender. Stir in the parsley.
2. Turn off the heat, and adjust the salt and pepper to taste. Serve immediately.

2 tablespoons canola oil

3 medium cloves garlic, peeled and chopped

1 tablespoon red curry paste

½ cup thick coconut cream

½ cup coconut milk

2½ cups vegetable stock

2 teaspoons curry powder

¼ teaspoon turmeric powder

3 tablespoons Thai fish sauce (nam pla) (optional)

1 teaspoon granulated sugar

1 cup shredded cabbage

1½ teaspoons lemon juice

1 pound Chinese-style thin noodles, cooked, drained, and rinsed

2 green onions, coarsely chopped, for garnish

2 lemons, cut into wedges, for garnish

THAI CURRY NOODLE SOUP

Summer

Yield: about 4 servings

1. Heat the oil in a saucepan, and sauté the garlic until lightly colored. Add the curry paste, heat through, and add the coconut cream; stir continuously until oily. Add the coconut milk, stock, curry powder, turmeric, fish sauce, and sugar. Continue to cook, stirring for about 4 to 5 minutes. Add the cabbage, stirring briefly to incorporate. Remove from heat, and stir in the lemon juice.

2. Divide the cooked noodles between the soup bowls, and ladle the hot soup over the top. Garnish with green onions, and serve immediately with lemon wedges on the side.

3 generous tablespoons vegetable shortening

4 tablespoons all-purpose flour

1½ quarts vegetable stock or water

2 medium white onions, chopped

¼ teaspoon caraway seeds

¼ teaspoon crushed dried French thyme

½ teaspoon crushed dried savory

½ teaspoon crushed dried marjoram

salt and pepper to taste

GERMAN-STYLE FLOUR SOUP

Year-Round

Yield: about 4 servings

1. Melt the shortening in a soup kettle or Dutch oven, sprinkle on the flour, stirring to make a roux. Stir in the chopped onion and sauté briefly.

2. Pouring in a narrow stream, add the stock, stirring until the mixture thickens. Add the caraway seeds, thyme, savory, and marjoram. Bring to a boil, and immediately remove from heat. Adjust the salt and pepper to taste and serve immediately.

ENGLISH BORSCHT

Year-Round

Yield: about 4 to 6 servings

1½ cups fresh beets, peeled and grated
1½ cups red cabbage, finely shredded
3 tablespoons tomato paste
2 tablespoons red wine vinegar
3 tablespoons butter or margarine
4 cups vegetable or chicken stock
1 large red onion, minced
1 large carrot, peeled and grated
1 tablespoon molasses
salt and pepper to taste
whipped sour cream or unflavored yogurt for garnish

1. In a large saucepan or soup kettle, combine the beets, cabbage, tomato paste, vinegar, 1½ tablespoons of the butter, and stock. Bring to a boil. Then reduce to a simmer, cover and cook, stirring occasionally, for about 55 to 60 minutes, or until the beets are very tender.

2. Melt the remaining butter in a skillet, and sauté the onion and carrots together until the onions are browned. Transfer to the soup kettle, and continue to cook for about 10 to 12 minutes. Adjust the salt and pepper to taste, stir in the molasses, and serve with a garnish of sour cream.

GARBANZO BEAN SOUP

Year-Round

Yield: about 4 servings

3 tablespoons margarine
¼ cup minced white onion
3 cups vegetable stock
15-ounce can chickpeas (garbanzo beans), drained
¼ teaspoon garlic salt
¼ teaspoon crushed dried mint leaves
¼ cup uncooked macaroni
salt and pepper to taste
grated Parmesan cheese
minced parsley for garnish

1. Melt the margarine in a soup kettle or Dutch oven, and sauté onion until a golden color. Add the stock, garbanzo beans, garlic salt, mint leaves and pepper. Bring to a boil. Then reduce to a simmer. Add the macaroni, cover lightly, and simmer for about 20 minutes, or until the noodles are al dente.

2. Turn off the heat, and adjust the salt and pepper to taste. Serve immediately, alone or as part of a menu, with the cheese and parsley on the side as a garnish.

¼ cup plus 2 tablespoons extra virgin olive oil
2 medium yellow onions, coarsely chopped
3 medium cloves garlic, peeled and minced
2 celery stalks, chopped
three 16-ounce cans diced tomatoes
3 pieces day-old Italian bread, crusts removed
4 cups hot vegetable stock
½ cup chopped fresh basil leaves
2 tablespoons fresh chopped parsley
2 tablespoons fresh chopped marjoram
salt and pepper to taste

1. Heat the oil in a soup kettle or Dutch oven, and sauté the onions, garlic, and celery together until the onions are tender. Reduce the heat to low, add the tomatoes, cover lightly, and cook for about 10 minutes.
2. Place the bread in a bowl, and pour 1 cup of hot stock over the top. Using the back of a spoon, mash the bread until blended with the stock.
3. Stir the softened bread and remaining stock into the tomatoes, and cook, stirring frequently, for about 30 minutes.
4. Add the basil, parsley, and marjoram during the last 5 minutes of cooking time. Remove from heat, and in the container of a blender or food processor, purée the soup, in batches, until smooth. Return to the pot and heat through.
5. Turn off the heat, and adjust the salt and pepper to taste. Serve immediately; garnish as desired.

FIVE-BEAN SOUP

Autumn

Yield: about 6 servings

1 cup dried pinto beans, soaked in water overnight
1 cup dried navy beans, soaked in water overnight
1 cup dried red beans, soaked in water overnight
1 cup dried great northern beans, soaked in water overnight
1 cup dried black-eyed peas, soaked in water 2 days
10 cups water
1 cup vegetable stock or unsweetened apple juice
1 cup diced yellow onion
1 tablespoon chili powder
2 teaspoons garlic powder
¾ teaspoon crushed dried lemon thyme
¼ teaspoon pepper
16-ounce can diced tomatoes
2 crushed bay leaves
¼ teaspoon Worcestershire sauce
1 medium carrot, peeled and grated
salt and pepper to taste

1. In a soup kettle or Dutch oven, combine the beans and water. Bring to a boil. Then reduce to a simmer, cover lightly, and cook for about 2 hours, or until the beans are just tender. Add the stock, onion, chili, garlic powder, thyme, pepper, tomatoes, bay leaf, Worcestershire sauce, and carrots. Cover and simmer for about 40 minutes.
2. Turn off the heat, adjust the salt and pepper to taste, and remove the bay leaf. Serve immediately, alone or as part of a menu, with cornbread on the side.

Hint: Repeatedly rinse the beans. Then soak them and change the soaking water a few times to reduce the amount of gas they produce.

2 tablespoons canola oil
¾ cup cabbage, chopped
½ cup onion, chopped
½ cup celery, chopped
½ cup carrots, chopped
¾ cup turnips, diced
¾ cup acorn squash, diced
4 cups tomatoes, diced
4 cups vegetable stock
¼ cup quick-cooking barley
¼ cup pearl rice
2 cups white sauce
½ cup vinegar
1 clove garlic, peeled and minced
1 teaspoon caraway seeds
2 teaspoons Worcestershire sauce
¼ teaspoon thyme
1 cup sour cream or unflavored yogurt

GERMAN-STYLE SOUR CREAM SOUP

Summer

Yield: about 6 servings

1. Heat the oil in a soup kettle or Dutch oven, and sauté the cabbage, onion, celery, carrots, turnips, and squash, until the onion is translucent. Cover tightly and cook on a low heat for about 15 minutes, or until the turnips are fork tender. Add the tomatoes, stock, barley, and rice. Cover tightly, and continue to cook for about 90 minutes.

2. In a bowl, blend the white sauce, vinegar, garlic, caraway seed, Worcestershire sauce, and thyme. Stir into the soup mixture, and bring to a boil. Then reduce to a simmer, recover and cook, stirring occasionally, for about 10 minutes.

3. Turn off the heat, and adjust the salt and pepper to taste. Serve immediately with the sour cream on the side.

GINGER SQUASH SOUP

Summer

Yield: about 6 servings

2 tablespoons margarine
1 large yellow onion, chopped
1 small clove garlic, peeled and chopped
2 teaspoons grated fresh ginger root
2 tablespoons all-purpose flour
1½ cups vegetable stock
2 cups cooked summer squash
½ cup fresh orange juice
2 teaspoons grated orange zest
salt and pepper to taste
¼ teaspoon ground nutmeg
fresh chopped parsley

1. In a 2-quart microwave-proof casserole, combine the margarine, onions, garlic, and ginger root together and microwave on HIGH, stirring once, for about 4 to 5 minutes, or until the onion is tender.
2. Blend the flour with the stock, and add to the casserole dish. Also add the squash, and microwave on HIGH, stirring once, for about 7 to 9 minutes, or until the liquid is boiling and thickened.
3. In the container of a blender or food processor, purée the soup, in batches, until smooth. Add the orange juice and zest, and process until incorporated.
4. Return to the casserole, adjust the salt and pepper to taste, and stir in the nutmeg. Microwave on HIGH for about 2 minutes, before ladling into heated bowls. Sprinkle with parsley and serve immediately.

Hint: Ginger and garlic bring alive the flavor of the squash which might otherwise remain bland.

1 medium yellow onion, sliced
1 stalk celery, thinly sliced
1 green bell pepper, seeded and sliced
¼ teaspoon crushed garlic
2 teaspoons minced fresh ginger root
½ cup water
4 cups vegetable stock
8-ounce can tomato sauce
2 white potatoes, peeled and diced
1 teaspoon crushed dried basil
1 teaspoon paprika
⅓ teaspoon ground black pepper
1 small zucchini, halved lengthwise and sliced
2 cups frozen whole corn kernels
salt and pepper to taste.

GINGER
VEGETABLE
SOUP

Summer
Yield: about 4
servings

1. In a soup kettle or Dutch oven, combine the onion, celery, green pepper, garlic, and ginger root. Add the water, bring to a boil, and cook for about 5 minutes, or until the celery is tender.
2. Add the stock, tomato sauce, potatoes, basil, paprika, pepper, zucchini, and corn. Return to a boil, cover lightly, and cook, stirring occasionally, until the potatoes are tender. Remove from heat, adjust the salt and black pepper to taste, and serve immediately.

2½ cups milk
2 tablespoons all-purpose flour
a little margarine
1 tablespoon minced white onion
1¼ cups hot vegetable stock or water
pinch herbes de Provençe
2 tablespoons finely grated Stilton cheese

GLASGOW
CHEESE
SOUP

Winter
Yield: about 6
servings

1. In a cup, blend ½ cup of the milk and the flour until smooth. Set aside.
2. Melt the margarine in a soup kettle or Dutch oven, and sauté the onions until tender. Add the vegetable stock, bring to a boil, and stir in the remaining milk. Cook until bubbles form around the edge of the pot, bring to a slow boil, stir in the milk-and-flour mix, and cook, stirring occasionally, until thickened. Add the cheese, stirring until melted and smooth.
3. Turn off the heat, stir in the herbs, adjust the salt and pepper to taste, and pour into a tureen. Serve immediately.

GOAT CHEESE SOUP

Autumn

Yield: about 6 servings

2 medium yellow onions, peeled and minced
6 cups vegetable stock
⅓ cup dry white wine
1 medium red bell pepper, seeded and diced
1 large McIntosh apple, pared and diced
2 teaspoons crushed dried basil
5 ounces creamy goat cheese, without rind
salt and pepper to taste

1. In a soup kettle or Dutch oven, combine the onions, and ½ cup of the stock. Bring to a boil, and cook, stirring occasionally, for about 10 minutes, or until most of the stock has evaporated. Add the wine, deglazing the pan, and cook, stirring constantly, for about 3 minutes. Add the remaining stock, peppers, apples, basil, salt and pepper to taste. Cover lightly, and simmer for about 30 minutes, or until the apple and vegetables are tender.

2. Remove from heat, cool slightly, and then in the container of a blender, purée the mixture, in batches, until smooth. Passing the mixture through a fine sieve, return to the pan.

3. Heat though, remove from heat, and stir in the goat cheese, beating until melted. Readjust the salt and pepper to taste, and serve in heated bowls as desired, with a garnish of choice.

Hint: Only use pure goat cheese ("pur chèvre") for this recipe. A combination goat and cow's milk cheese won't do. Old goat cheese has a very sour taste. Always look for one that's fresh with a slightly tart taste.

1 cup red lentils
1 cup brown lentils
6 cups vegetable stock
½ small white onion, diced
1 large carrot, peeled and diced
1 stalk celery, diced
⅛ teaspoon celery seed
3 tablespoons dried potato buds
1 large white potato, peeled and diced
2 tablespoons olive oil
½ teaspoon crushed dried oregano
pinch dill weed
2 teaspoons red wine vinegar, (optional)
salt and pepper to taste

1. In a soup kettle or Dutch oven, combine the lentils, stock, onion, carrot, celery, celery seeds, potato buds, potato, olive oil, oregano, and dill weed. Bring to a boil, then reduce to a simmer, and cook, stirring occasionally, for about 1 hour.
2. Turn off the heat, stir in the vinegar, and adjust the salt and pepper to taste. Serve immediately.

1 tablespoon margarine
1 medium yellow onion, chopped
2 tablespoons whole wheat flour
4 cups vegetable stock
2 medium carrots, peeled and sliced
¼ teaspoon crushed dried marjoram
3 cups Brussels sprouts, trimmed and halved
2 cups cooked baby lima beans
2 tablespoons minced parsley
salt and pepper to taste

1. Melt the margarine in a soup kettle or Dutch oven, and sauté the onion until lightly colored. Sprinkle on the flour, and cook, stirring to make a roux. Add the stock, carrots, and marjoram, stirring until smooth. Bring to a boil, then reduce to a simmer, cover lightly, and cook for about 10 minutes. Add the Brussels sprouts, return to a boil, and reduce to a simmer. Cover and cook for about 10 minutes longer. Add the beans and parsley, and heat through.
2. Turn off the heat, adjust the salt and pepper to taste, and serve immediately. Garnish as desired.

GREEN PEPPER & TOMATO SOUP

Summer

Yield: about 4 servings

1 tablespoon garlic paste
1 tablespoon crushed dried basil
2 tablespoons crushed dried parsley
¼ teaspoon crushed dried thyme
2 teaspoons sweet paprika
1 tablespoon tomato paste
2 tablespoons olive oil
salt and pepper to taste
1 large yellow onion, quartered and sliced
pinch saffron threads
two 16-ounce cans diced tomatoes; reserve juice
2 medium green bell peppers, seeded and diced
6 cups vegetable stock or water
⅓ cup Minute Rice
salt and pepper to taste
fresh chopped basil or parsley for garnish
fresh grated Parmesan cheese for garnish

1. In a bowl, blend the garlic paste, basil, parsley, thyme, paprika, and tomato paste.
2. Heat the oil, in a soup kettle or Dutch oven, and sauté the garlic blend and onions together until the onions are tender. Sprinkle on the saffron, and cook, over a low heat, stirring constantly, for about 3 minutes. Stir in the peppers, tomatoes, and stock. Bring to a boil, then reduce to a simmer, cover lightly, and cook, stirring occasionally, for about 25 minutes.
3. Stir the rice and reserved juice from the diced tomatoes into the soup. Heat through.
4. Turn off the heat, adjust the salt and pepper to taste. Set aside for about 5 minutes, and then serve immediately. Garnish as desired.

1 tablespoon chopped chives
2 tablespoons finely crushed sunflower seeds
8-ounce carton sour cream or unflavored yogurt
cayenne pepper to taste
2 tablespoons canola oil
1 large white onion, minced
two 10-ounce packages frozen mixed vegetables, thawed
3½ cups vegetable stock
1 small head lettuce, shredded into strips
10-ounce package frozen chopped spinach, thawed
½ teaspoon cumin powder
salt and pepper to taste

SHREDDED
GREENS
SOUP

Year-Round

Yield: about 4
servings

1. In a bowl, blend the chives, sunflower seeds, sour cream and cayenne to taste. Refrigerate until ready to use.
2. Heat the oil in a soup kettle or Dutch oven, and sauté the onions until tender. Add the mixed vegetables, heat through, and stir in the stock. Bring to a boil, then reduce to a simmer, and cook, stirring frequently, for about 2 minutes.
3. Add the lettuce, spinach, and cumin. Bring to a boil, and immediately remove from heat. Adjust the salt and pepper to taste. Serve immediately, with sour cream on the side as a garnish.

10 cups water or vegetable stock
1 cup yellow split peas
1 cup green split peas
½ teaspoon crushed dried basil
1 medium yellow onion, peeled and minced
2 medium carrots, peeled and diced
1 cup minced celery
salt and pepper to taste

1. In a soup kettle or Dutch oven, combine the water and peas, bring to a boil, and cook, stirring for about 3 minutes. Remove from heat, cover, and set aside for about 1 hour.
2. When ready, add the basil, onion, carrots, and celery to the peas. Return to the heat, and bring to a boil. Reduce to a simmer, cover lightly, and cook, stirring occasionally, for about 90 minutes, or until the peas are very soft.
3. Turn off the heat, and adjust the salt and pepper to taste. Serve immediately.

HARVEST BOWL SOUP

Year-Round

Yield: about 6 to 8 servings

1 tablespoon olive oil
2 cups yellow onion, chopped
1½ cups carrots, thinly sliced
1 cup celery, thinly sliced
4 medium cloves garlic, peeled and minced
2 teaspoons crushed dried Italian seasoning
3 cups vegetable stock
3 cups V-8 vegetable juice
¼ pound fresh green beans, cut into pieces
½ teaspoon crushed dried basil
½ teaspoon crushed dried tarragon
two 16-ounce cans red kidney beans, rinsed and drained
2 cups yellow pumpkin, coarsely chopped
salt and pepper to taste

1. Heat the oil in a soup kettle or Dutch oven, and sauté the onions, carrots, celery, garlic, and Italian seasoning together until the carrots are tender. Add the stock, vegetable juice, beans, basil, and tarragon. Bring to a boil, then reduce to a simmer, cover lightly, and cook, stirring occasionally, for about 30 minutes.
2. Add the kidney beans and squash. Return to a boil, and cook for about 5 additional minutes.
3. Turn off the heat, and adjust the salt and pepper to taste. Serve immediately.

HEARTY VEGETABLE BARLEY SOUP

Winter

Yield: about 6 servings

1 tablespoon olive oil
½ cup yellow onion, chopped
1 medium clove garlic, peeled and minced
7 cups water or vegetable stock
16-ounce can diced tomatoes
½ cup quick-cooking barley
½ cup sliced celery
½ cup sliced carrots
2 teaspoons vegetable bouillon granules
½ teaspoon crushed dried basil
10-ounce package frozen mixed vegetables
salt and pepper to taste

1. Heat the oil in a soup kettle or Dutch oven, and sauté the onions until tender. Add garlic and heat through. Add the stock, tomatoes, barley, celery, carrots, bouillon granules, and basil. Bring to a boil. Then reduce to a simmer, cover lightly, and cook, stirring occasionally, for about 30 to 40 minutes or until the barley is very soft.
2. Add the mixed vegetables, cook for about 10 minutes, adding more water if too thick.
3. Turn off the heat, and adjust the salt and pepper to taste. Serve immediately.

1 tablespoon margarine
1 pound parsnips, peeled and thinly sliced
1 pound McIntosh apples, pared and sliced
1 medium yellow onion, chopped
2 teaspoons curry powder
1 teaspoon ground cumin
1 teaspoon ground coriander
½ teaspoon cardamom powder
1 large clove garlic, peeled and crushed
1¼ cups vegetable stock
⅔ cup heavy cream
salt and pepper to taste
chopped chives or parsley

IRISH-STYLE PARSNIP & APPLE SOUP

Autumn

Yield: about 6 servings

1. Melt the margarine in a soup kettle or Dutch oven and sauté the parsnips, apples, and onions together until the onions are translucent. Add the curry powder, cumin, coriander, cardamom, and garlic. Cook, stirring constantly, for about 3 minutes. Pouring in a narrow stream and stirring constantly, add the stock. Bring to a boil, then reduce to a simmer, cover lightly, and cook for about 30 minutes, or until the parsnips are very tender.

2. Turn off the heat, and in the container of a blender or food processor, purée the soup, in batches, until smooth. Return to the pot, add the cream, and heat through. (Do not allow to boil.) If too thick, add water, ¼ cup at a time.

3. Turn off the heat, and adjust the salt and pepper to taste. Serve immediately. Garnish as desired.

ITALIAN BEAN SOUP

Year-Round

Yield: about 6 to 8 servings

1 cup navy beans
8 cups water
8-ounce can tomato sauce
1 cup white onions, minced
1 cup carrots, minced
½ cup green bell peppers, seeded and minced
2 medium cloves garlic, peeled and minced
2 vegetable bouillon cubes
1½ teaspoons crushed dried basil
1½ teaspoons crushed dried oregano
½ cup elbow macaroni
salt and pepper to taste

1. The night before, thoroughly rinse the beans under running water, place in a soup kettle or Dutch oven, and add the water. Set aside until the next day.
2. When ready, do not drain, but place on the heat, and bring to a boil. Add the tomato sauce, onions, carrots, peppers, garlic, bouillon cubes, basil, and oregano. Return to a boil, reduce to a simmer, cover lightly, and cook, stirring occasionally, for about 80 to 90 minutes. About 15 minutes before the mixture is cooked through, add the macaroni.
3. When ready, ladle into heated bowls, and serve with thick slices of hot Italian bread.

Hint: The macaroni may also be cooked separately until al dente and added just before serving.

NEW ENGLAND-STYLE PUMPKIN SOUP

Autumn

Yield: about 4 to 6 servings

1 tablespoon margarine
1 small onion, finely chopped
1 pound fresh pumpkin, steamed, drained, and puréed
2 cups vegetable stock
½ teaspoon thyme
1 teaspoon crushed dried basil
1 cup cream
¼ cup dry sherry
salt and pepper to taste
chopped parsley or chives for garnish

1. Melt the margarine in a soup kettle or Dutch oven, and sauté the onion until a golden brown color. Stir in the pumpkin, stock, thyme, and basil. Bring to a boil, then reduce to a simmer, cover lightly, and cook, stirring occasionally, for about 15 minutes.
2. Cool slightly, and stir in the cream and sherry. Return to the heat, and heat through.
3. Turn off the heat, adjust the salt and pepper to taste, garnish with parsley, and serve immediately.

1 cup dried black beans, soaked overnight and drained

8 cups water

1 medium yellow onion, chopped

1 large green bell pepper, seeded and chopped

2 medium cloves garlic, peeled and crushed

1 teaspoon crushed dried oregano

1 teaspoon ground cumin

6-ounce can tomato paste

3 tablespoons red wine vinegar

1 tablespoon tamari soy sauce

2 cups cooked brown rice

¼ cups chopped green chilis

¼ teaspoon pepper sauce

2 tablespoons fresh, chopped coriander

LATIN BLACK BEAN SOUP

Year-Round

Yield: about 6 servings

1. In a soup kettle or Dutch oven, combine the beans and water, onion, garlic, pepper, oregano, and cumin. Bring to a boil, cover lightly, and cook for about 90 minutes. Add the tomato paste, vinegar, and tamari soy sauce. Cover again and cook for an additional 30 minutes. Add the chilis, rice, pepper sauce, and coriander. Heat through, but do not boil.

2. Turn off the heat, and adjust the salt and pepper to taste. Serve immediately. Garnish if desired.

3 tablespoons butter or margarine

1 medium white onion, minced

3 large leeks, sliced

2 medium Idaho or russet potatoes, peeled and diced

4-ounce package dried green split peas, soaked overnight

3½ cups vegetable stock

LEEKIE PEA SOUP

Year-Round

Yield: about 6 to 8 servings

1. Melt the butter in a saucepan or soup kettle, and sauté the onion and leeks together until softened. Add the potatoes, peas, and stock. Bring to a boil, then reduce to a simmer, cover lightly, and cook, stirring occasionally, for about 40 minutes, or until the peas are very tender.

2. At this point, the soup may be eaten as is, or it can be puréed in batches, using a blender or food processor until smooth.

3. If the soup is puréed, return it to the pan, reheat, adjust the salt and pepper to taste, and serve immediately with a variety of bread on the side.

Hint: This soup was popular in my uncle's St. Helena Hotel in California. If you add 1½ cups sour cream, this makes a great cream soup, too.

LENTIL VEGETABLE SOUP

Year-Round

Yield: about 6 to 8 servings

3 tablespoons olive oil
1 medium yellow onion, chopped
3 medium cloves garlic, peeled and minced
1 medium green bell pepper, seeded and chopped
8 cups water
1½ cups quick-cooking lentils
1 cup dry white wine
3 stalks celery, sliced
2 fresh zucchini, peeled and sliced
1 teaspoon crushed dried basil
three 8-ounce cans tomato sauce
1 cup brown rice
2 cups sliced carrots
2 medium red potatoes, diced
1 teaspoon crushed dried thyme
salt and pepper to taste

1. Heat the oil in soup kettle or Dutch oven and sauté the onions, garlic, and bell pepper together until tender. Add the water, lentils, and wine. Cook for about 30 minutes, or until the lentils are just tender.

2. Add the celery, zucchini, basil, tomato sauce, rice, carrots, potatoes, and thyme. Continue to cook, stirring, until the potatoes are fork tender.

3. Turn off the heat, and adjust the salt and pepper to taste. Serve immediately. Garnish if desired.

1 tablespoon olive oil
1 medium yellow onion, chopped
2 medium tomatoes, peeled and chopped
2 tablespoons chopped celery leaves
1 tablespoon snipped fresh cilantro
½ teaspoon ground ginger
½ teaspoon ground turmeric
1 teaspoon ground cinnamon
7½ cups vegetable stock or unsweetened apple juice
½ cup green lentils
½ cup canned chickpeas, drained and rinsed
3-ounce package soup noodles
2 large egg yolks
1 tablespoon fresh lemon or lime juice
seasoning to taste
snipped fresh cilantro leaves for garnish

LIBYAN-
STYLE SPICED
SOUP

Year-Round

Yield: about 6 to 8
servings

1. Heat the oil in a saucepan, and sauté the onion until transparent. Add the tomatoes, celery, cilantro, ginger, turmeric, cinnamon, and cook, stirring for about 1 minute. Add the stock, lentils, and chickpeas. Bring to a boil, then reduce to a simmer, and cook for about 1½ to 2 hours, or until the chickpeas are very tender.

2. Adjust the seasoning to taste, and add the soup noodles, cooking until al dente, adding more water or stock should it become necessary.

3. In a bowl, using a wire whisk, beat the egg foamy, and then beat in the lemon juice. Add to the soup, stirring constantly, until thickened. Transfer to a serving bowl or soup tureen. Garnish with cilantro leaves, and serve immediately with a crusty bread on the side.

MEDITERRANEAN-STYLE LEEK & TOMATO SOUP

Year-Round

Yield: about 4 to 6 servings

2 tablespoons virgin olive oil
2 large leeks (green part only), chopped
½ teaspoon crushed coriander
¼ teaspoon dried red pepper flakes
3 small red potatoes, peeled and thickly sliced
16-ounce can diced tomatoes
2½ cups vegetable stock
⅔ cup white port wine
¼ teaspoon ground anise
¼ teaspoon saffron threads
seasoning to taste
snipped fresh parsley for garnish

1. Heat the oil in a saucepan, and sauté the chopped green portion of the leeks for about 1 minute. Add the coriander and pepper flakes, and continue to cook until the greens are very soft.
2. Add the potatoes, tomatoes, stock, and wine. Bring to a boil. Then reduce to a simmer, sprinkle on the anise and saffron. Cover lightly and simmer for about 20 minutes, or until the potatoes are fork tender. Adjust the seasoning to taste. Ladle into heated soup bowls, and sprinkle with parsley.

SUPER-FAST SOUP

Year-Round

Yield: about 3 to 4 servings

10.75-ounce can condensed cream soup
10-ounce package frozen chopped vegetables, thawed
10.75-ounce soup can water, soy milk, or unsweetened apple juice
seasoning to taste
2 slices lightly buttered toast

1. In a saucepan, combine the canned soup, vegetables, and water. Bring to a boil.
2. Remove from the heat, and adjust the seasoning to taste. Serve immediately in warmed bowls with the buttered toast on the side.

Hint: This recipe can create a variety of soups, depending on the canned cream soup and vegetable(s) you choose. Chop a green vegetable to use as a garnish. Serve with bread or crackers.

¼ cup margarine
3 medium fresh leeks, chopped
5 cups vegetable stock
1 medium potato, thinly sliced
2 egg yolks
1 cup shredded Jarlsberg cheese
salt and pepper to taste

MELLOW CHEESE SOUP

Year-Round

Yield: about 6 servings

1. Melt the margarine in a soup kettle or Dutch oven and sauté the leeks until tender. Add the stock and potato, and bring to a boil. Then reduce to a simmer, cover lightly, and cook, stirring occasionally, until potato is fork tender.
2. In a blender or food-processor container, purée the soup in batches until smooth. Return to the pot.
3. In a bowl, and using a wire whisk, beat together the egg yolks and ¼ cup of the hot soup. Slowly stir back into the soup.
4. Add ¾ cup of the cheese to the soup and heat through (do not boil), stirring until melted.
5. Turn off the heat, and adjust the salt and pepper to taste. Serve immediately with the remaining ¼ cup cheese as a garnish.

Hint: For another flavor, use another type of mild cheese.

1 cup peanut butter
2 tablespoons vegetable oil
1 medium yellow onion, minced
1½ cups cooked diced potatoes
4 cups vegetable stock
½ cup cream (optional)
salt and pepper to taste
2 tablespoons chopped chives
coarsely chopped peanuts for garnish

PEANUT SOUP

Autumn

Yield: about 4 servings

1. Heat the oil in a soup kettle or Dutch oven and sauté the onion until it is transparent. Add the peanut butter, potatoes and 1 cup of stock, stirring to make a paste.
2. In the container of a blender or food processor, purée the mixture until smooth. Return to the pot, and stir in the remaining stock. Bring to a boil, then reduce to a simmer, and cook, stirring frequently, for about 5 minutes.
3. Turn off the heat, stir in the cream, and adjust the salt and pepper to taste. Serve immediately. Garnish with chives and peanuts as desired.

MINNESOTA WILD RICE SOUP

Autumn

Yield: about 4 to 5 servings

2 tablespoons margarine
1 cup sliced celery stalks
½ cup coarsely chopped carrot
½ cup chopped onion
½ cup seeded and chopped green bell pepper
3 tablespoons all-purpose flour
1½ cups cooked wild rice
1 cup water
1¼ cups vegetable stock
1 cup half-and-half
⅓ cup toasted slivered almonds
¼ cup fresh chopped parsley
salt and pepper to taste

1. Melt the margarine in a soup kettle or Dutch oven, and sauté the celery, carrot, onion, and pepper together until the onion is lightly colored. Sprinkle on the flour, and cook, stirring until incorporated. Add the rice, water, and stock. Bring to a boil, then reduce to a simmer, cover lightly, and cook, stirring occasionally, for about 15 minutes. Stir in the half-and-half, almonds, and parsley, and heat through.
2. Turn off the heat, and adjust the salt and pepper to taste. Serve immediately.

MOROCCAN PUMPKIN SOUP

Autumn

Yield: about 3 to 4 servings

1 tablespoon safflower oil
1 tablespoon margarine
1 medium white onion, chopped
1½ cups sliced carrots
1½ cups chopped parsnips or turnips
2½ cups diced fresh pumpkin or 1½ cups fresh purée
3½ cups vegetable stock
salt and pepper to taste

1. Heat the oil and margarine in a soup kettle or Dutch oven, and sauté the onion until lightly colored. Add the carrots and parsnips, cover lightly, and cook, stirring occasionally, until the vegetables are crisp tender.
2. Add the pumpkin to the pan and cook for about 3 minutes.
3. Add the stock, bring to a boil. Then reduce to a simmer, cover, and cook for about 30 minutes, or until the vegetables are very tender. Remove from heat and cool slightly.
4. In the container of a blender or food processor, purée the mixture, in batches, until smooth. Return to the pan, adjust the salt and pepper to taste, and reheat, but do not boil. Ladle into heated bowls, and garnish with chopped fresh parsley.

Hint: This is one of the smoothest vegetable soups I've ever found. It gets that texture from both the pumpkin and the parsnips. At the same time, the carrots add a slight chunkiness.

10 ounces dried mixed beans, soaked overnight
1 tablespoon butter or margarine
1 large yellow onion, chopped
1 small leek, trimmed and sliced
4 medium cloves garlic, peeled and minced
1 cup vegetable stock
3 cups water
14-ounce can crushed tomatoes
3-ounce can sliced mushrooms, with liquid
5-ounce package frozen green peas
1 teaspoon crushed dried oregano

1. Put the beans and soaking water in a saucepan, and bring to a boil. Then reduce to a simmer, cover lightly, and cook, stirring occasionally, for about 50 minutes, or until the beans are very tender. Then drain.

2. Melt the butter in a saucepan or soup kettle, and sauté the onion, leek, and garlic together, until the onion is lightly colored. Add the stock, water and beans. Bring to a boil, then reduce to a simmer, and cook, stirring occasionally, for about 15 minutes. Add the tomatoes, mushrooms, green peas, and oregano. Cover again, and continue to simmer for about 15 minutes longer, or until the beans are very tender.

3. Remove from heat, and purée about half of the mixture, using a blender or food processor, until smooth. Return the purée to the remaining soup mixture, and continue to simmer for about 10 minutes.

4. Remove from heat, cool to room temperature, and then refrigerate for at least one day before reheating and serving.

Hint: This soup is a blend of nine flavors. Like so many soups, it improves with age. It's a good soup the day it is made, but it's a great soup the next day.

MOROCCAN TOMATO SOUP

Autumn

Yield: about 6 servings

2 tablespoons olive oil
1 onion, chopped
5 cloves garlic, peeled and minced
28-ounce can crushed tomatoes
1 cup creamy or chunky peanut butter
1 teaspoon cumin
1 tablespoon hot pepper sauce
2 tablespoons cayenne
1 tablespoon chili powder
2 tablespoons white vinegar
1 tablespoon granulated sugar
¼ cup tomato paste
2 cups water
salt and pepper to taste

1. Heat the oil in a soup kettle or Dutch oven, and sauté the onion and garlic together until lightly browned.
2. In the container of a blender, or food processor, purée the tomatoes and their liquid until smooth. Then pour into the pot. Add the peanut butter, and cook, stirring constantly, until incorporated. Add cumin, hot sauce, cayenne, chili powder, white vinegar, sugar, tomato paste, and water. Cover lightly, and continue to cook over a low heat, stirring frequently, for about 15 minutes.
3. Turn off the heat, and adjust the salt and pepper to taste. Serve immediately.

Hint: Unlike other tomato-based soups, this one has an underlying flavor of peanuts. This soup burns easily, so do not allow it to come to a full boil.

2 tablespoons butter or margarine
1 small white onion, chopped
1 medium clove garlic, peeled and chopped
2 tablespoons all-purpose flour
2½ cups vegetable stock
9 to 10 ounces fresh, white button mushrooms, sliced
1 tablespoon snipped fresh cilantro
⅔ cup light cream

SCOTTISH MUSHROOM- GRUEL SOUP

Winter
Yield: about 4 to 6 servings

1. Melt 1 tablespoon of butter in a saucepan or soup kettle, and sauté the onion and garlic together until the onion is translucent. Sprinkle on the flour, and stir to make a roux. Then pouring in a narrow stream, and stirring constantly, add the stock. Add half the mushrooms, and cilantro. Bring to a boil, then reduce to a simmer, and cook, stirring frequently, for about 10 minutes.

2. Remove from heat, and purée in batches, using a blender or food processor, until smooth. Return to the pan.

3. Melt the remaining butter in a skillet or saucepan, and sauté the remaining mushrooms, stirring constantly, until lightly colored, and then add to the soup.

4. Heat until bubbles form around the edge of the pan., remove from heat, and add the cream. Adjust the salt and pepper to taste, and serve immediately, with a garnish of snipped fresh parsley.

Although this recipe is made with small white button mushrooms, almost any type of mushroom can be used. As the mushroom aficionado can attest, different varieties of mushrooms can alter a recipe from slight variations in taste to a complete change in character.

NUTTY CARROT SOUP

Spring

Yield: about 4 servings

2 pounds fresh carrots, peeled and chopped
4 cups vegetable stock
1 medium potato, peeled and chopped
1 tablespoon margarine
1 large yellow carrot, peeled and chopped
4 cloves garlic, peeled and chopped
¾ cup hazelnuts or pecans, chopped
1 cup yogurt
1 teaspoon fresh ginger root, peeled and chopped
¼ cup sherry

1. In a soup kettle or Dutch oven, combine the carrots, stock, and potato. Bring to a boil, then reduce to a simmer, cover lightly, and cook, stirring occasionally, for about 15 minutes. Set aside and cool to room temperature.

2. Melt the margarine in a skillet and sauté the onions and garlic together until the onion is translucent. Stir into the cooled carrot mixture.

3. In the container of a blender or food processor, purée the carrot and onion mixture until smooth. Return to the pot, add the nuts, yogurt, and ginger, heat through, but do not boil.

4. Turn off the heat, stir in the sherry, and serve immediately.

Hint: Nuts can be used in almost any dish if you purée them.

¾ cup extra virgin olive oil

4 medium cloves garlic, peeled and minced

9 pounds ripe tomatoes, skinned, seeded, and quartered

1 tablespoon cocoa powder

salt and pepper to taste

granulated sugar to taste

2 cups water

2 loaves stale Italian bread, crusts removed

1. Heat the oil in a large saucepan or soup kettle, and sauté the garlic until tender. Add the tomatoes, adjust the heat to a simmer, and cook, stirring occasionally, for about 20 minutes, or until the tomatoes are rendered to a purée. Add the cocoa powder, and adjust the salt and pepper to taste before stirring in the sugar.

2. Stir in the water, and bring to a boil.

3. Break the bread into pieces and stir into the soup. Add more boiling water, should the mixture become too dry. Remove from heat, cool slightly, and stir in the garnish. Serve as desired.

Garnish

⅓ cup extra virgin olive oil

3 small springs fresh basil, chopped

Remove the soup from the heat, and drizzle the oil and basil into each bowl.

2 teaspoons olive oil

½ cup chopped onion

2 cloves garlic, peeled and minced

½ cup canned chopped Italian tomatoes, drained

8-ounce can chickpeas, drained; reserve ½ cup liquid

½ cup cooked elbow macaroni

1½ teaspoons chopped fresh basil

salt and pepper to taste

fresh basil sprigs for garnish

1. Heat the oil in a soup kettle or Dutch oven and sauté the onion and garlic together until the onion is translucent. Add tomatoes, bring to a boil, then reduce to a simmer, and cook, uncovered for about 5 minutes. Add chickpeas with reserved liquid, macaroni, and basil, and heat through.

2. Turn off the heat, and adjust the salt and pepper to taste. Serve immediately, with a sprig of fresh basil on each bowl.

Hint: The secret of making this soup is to be sure that the chickpeas are cooked through and the pasta is al dente.

PLOMEEK SOUP

Year-Round

Yield: about 6 to 7 servings

2 tablespoons margarine
2 medium onions, sliced
1 pound carrots, peeled and sliced
½ pound turnips, peeled and sliced
10 ounces potatoes, peeled and sliced
5 tablespoons tomato paste
4 cups water
2 cloves garlic, peeled and sliced
¾ teaspoon dried basil
¼ teaspoon nutmeg
salt and pepper to taste
sour cream for garnish
fresh parsley, finely chopped, for garnish

1. Melt the margarine in a soup kettle or Dutch oven, and sauté the onions until a golden color. Add the carrots, turnips, potatoes, tomato paste, 3 cups water, garlic, basil, and nutmeg. Bring to a boil, then reduce to a simmer, cover lightly, and cook, stirring occasionally, for about 20 minutes, or until the turnips are tender.
2. In the container of a blender or food processor, purée the mixture, in batches, until smooth. Then return to the pot. Add the remaining water, and heat through.
3. Turn off the heat, and adjust the salt and pepper to taste. Serve immediately, with a daub of sour cream and sprinkle of parsley on each bowl.

Hint: It's been reported that Mr. Spock from "Star Trek" favors a soup much like this one.

6 tablespoons olive oil
2 medium new potatoes, peeled and diced
3 medium carrots, peeled and shredded
2 tablespoons tomato paste
2 medium celery stalks, cut in halves
3 quarts vegetable stock
1 tablespoon chopped fresh basil
1 cup Arborio rice or long-grain rice
salt and pepper to taste
grated fresh Parmesan cheese for garnish

POTATO & RICE SOUP

Winter
Yield: about 8 to 10 servings

1. Heat the oil in a soup kettle or Dutch oven, and sauté the potatoes until lightly colored. Add carrots and tomato paste and cook over a low heat until carrots soften. Add the celery, stock, and basil. Bring to a boil, then reduce to a simmer, cover lightly, and cook, stirring occasionally, for about 40 minutes.
2. Add the rice and continue to cook for about 20 minutes, or until the rice is tender, and then discard the celery.
3. Turn off the heat, and adjust the salt and pepper to taste. Serve immediately, with the cheese on the side.

Hint: Arborio rice adds a creamier texture than ordinary rice.

2 large onions, chopped
1 medium head of cauliflower, chopped
5 cups diced potatoes
8 cups water
2 teaspoons dried dill weed
2 bay leaves, crushed
2 tablespoons soy sauce
freshly ground pepper to taste
chopped fresh cilantro for garnish

POTATO CAULIFLOWER SOUP

Winter
Yield: about 6 to 8 servings

1. In a soup kettle or Dutch oven, combine the onions, cauliflower, potatoes, water, and dill. Bring to a boil, then reduce to a simmer, cover lightly, and cook, stirring occasionally, for about 30 minutes, or until the potatoes are tender.
2. In the container of a blender or food processor, purée the soup in batches, until smooth. Return to the pot.
3. Add the bay leaves, and soy sauce. Bring to a boil, then reduce to a simmer, cover again, and cook for about 15 minutes.
4. Turn off the heat, and adjust the salt and pepper to taste. Serve immediately, with the chopped cilantro garnish.

POTATO SKIN SOUP

Autumn

Yield: about 4 servings

4 tablespoons margarine
1 large white onion, chopped
2 cups chopped potato skins
4 cups vegetable stock
light cream
salt and pepper to taste
parsley or chives for garnish

1. Melt the margarine in a soup kettle or Dutch oven, and sauté the onion, and potato skins (scrubbed clean) until lightly colored. Add the stock, and bring to a boil. Then reduce to a simmer, cover lightly, and cook, stirring occasionally, until the potato skins are fork tender.

2. In the container of a blender or food processor, purée the soup, until smooth, adding enough light cream to obtain the desired taste. Return to the pot.

3. Heat through, adjust the salt and pepper to taste, and serve immediately, with a sprinkling of chives over the top.

Hint: Most people discard potato skins along with their nutritional ingredients. Hand pare the potato skins and make thick pieces.

2 tablespoons margarine
½ cup chopped white onion
1½ cups chopped leeks
1 teaspoon minced garlic
1 quart vegetable stock
13.75-ounce can artichoke hearts, drained and quartered
2½ cups baking potatoes, peeled and cubed
2 small sprigs fresh thyme
1½ cups milk
¾ teaspoon Tabasco Sauce
salt and black pepper to taste
chopped fresh watercress for garnish

POTATO ARTICHOKE SOUP

Autumn
Yield: 6 to 8 servings

1. Melt the margarine in a soup kettle or Dutch oven, and sauté the onion and leeks together until the onion is translucent. Add the garlic and continue to cook until the onion is lightly colored. Add the stock, artichokes, potatoes, and thyme. Bring to a boil, then reduce to a simmer. Cover lightly, and cook, stirring occasionally, for about 15 minutes, or until the potatoes are fork tender. Add the milk, Tabasco Sauce, and continue to cook for about 5 minutes longer.

2. Turn off the heat and discard the thyme. In the container of a blender or food processor, purée the soup, in batches, until very smooth. Adjust the salt and pepper to taste. Serve immediately, with a sprinkle of watercress on the side.

Hint: For a smoother, milder taste, use fresh artichoke hearts rather than canned artichoke hearts.

RATATOUILLE SOUP

Autumn

Yield: about 6 servings

1 tablespoon virgin olive oil
1 large yellow onion, minced
1 medium clove garlic, peeled and minced
2 cups diced eggplant
2½ cups diced zucchini
1 cup chopped green onions
1½ cups diced green bell peppers
1½ cups diced red bell peppers
16-ounce can crushed tomatoes
3 tablespoons tomato sauce
1 tablespoon honey
pinch cayenne or chili pepper
3 cups vegetable stock
1 cup sun-dried tomatoes

1. Heat the oil in a saucepan or soup kettle, and sauté the onion and garlic together until the onion is translucent. Add the 1½ cups of the eggplant, 2 cups of the zucchini, green onion, 1 cup of the green onions, 1 cup of the red peppers, tomatoes, tomato sauce, honey, cayenne, and stock. Bring to a boil, then reduce to a simmer, cover lightly, and cook, stirring occasionally, for about 10 to 12 minutes.
2. Remove from heat, and purée in batches, using a blender or food processor, until smooth. Return the mixture to the pan.
3. In a separate saucepan, combine the remaining vegetables, cover with lightly salted water, bring to a boil, and drain immediately. Add the vegetables to the soup pan. Heat through and serve.

Hint: If the vegetables were kept intact and not liquefied, you'd have a casserole. You can substitute molasses for the honey.

6 tablespoons olive oil
2 tablespoons margarine
2 medium onions, chopped
2 medium cloves garlic, peeled and minced
4 ounces Parmesan cheese, grated
2½ quarts basic vegetable stock
¾ cup Arborio rice or other long-grain rice
1 pound fresh spinach, chopped and blanched
salt and fresh ground black pepper to taste

RICE & SPINACH SOUP

Year-Round

Yield: about 8 servings

1. Heat the oil and margarine in a soup kettle or Dutch oven, and sauté the onion and garlic until the onion is translucent. Add the stock. Bring to a boil, add the rice, reduce to a simmer, cover lightly, and cook for about 20 minutes or until the rice is tender.
2. Turn off the heat, stir in the spinach, and adjust the salt and pepper to taste. Sprinkle with cheese. Serve immediately.

2 tablespoons canola oil
2 medium red onions, sliced
2 medium green bell peppers, chopped
1 small head of cabbage, cored and thinly sliced
1 tablespoon chopped dill weed
1½ quarts water
2 egg yolks
½ cup heavy cream
1 tablespoon cider vinegar
salt and pepper to taste

ROMANIAN-STYLE CABBAGE SOUP

Autumn

Yield: about 6 servings

1. Heat the oil in a soup kettle or Dutch oven, and sauté the onion until translucent. Add the peppers and continue to cook, stirring frequently, until tender.
2. In the same pot, layer in the cabbage, onion, peppers, and dill. Add the water, return to the heat, and bring to a boil. Reduce to a simmer, cover lightly, and cook for about 30 minutes, or until the vegetables are tender.
3. Meanwhile in a bowl, beat the egg yolks, cream, and vinegar together until blended. Continue beating, add ¼ cup of the hot liquid from the pot, and then stir the egg-and-cream mixture tempered with hot liquid back into the soup pot.
4. Turn off the heat, adjust the salt and pepper to taste, and ladle into bowls. Serve immediately, alone or as part of a menu, with freshly baked bread on the side.

ROOT VEGETABLE SOUP

Autumn

Yield: about 6 servings

2 tablespoons finely minced chives for garnish
2 tablespoons finely minced parsley for garnish
4 tablespoons margarine
2½ tablespoons all-purpose flour
6 cups vegetable stock
2 large leeks (white part only), thinly sliced
3 medium carrots, peeled and cubed
3 medium turnips, peeled and cubed
2 medium parsnips, peeled and cubed
2 medium red potatoes, peeled and cubed
2 hearts of bibb lettuce leaves, separated
2 cups fresh spinach
salt and pepper to taste
½ cup heavy cream

1. In a cup, combine the chives and parsley. Chill in the coldest part of the refrigerator until ready to use.
2. Melt the margarine in a soup kettle or Dutch oven, and sprinkle on the flour, stirring to make a roux. Add the vegetable stock, stirring until blended. Add the leeks, carrots, turnips, parsnips, and potatoes. Bring to a boil, reduce heat, and simmer. Cover lightly, and cook, stirring occasionally, until the vegetables are tender. Add the lettuce and spinach leaves (without stems). Cover and cook until the lettuce leaves are tender. Do not overcook. Stir in the cream, do not boil, but heat through.
3. Turn off the heat, adjust the salt and pepper to taste. Serve immediately, with the chilled chive-parsley mix and black bread on the side.

Hint: There is little acid in the soup, so it will retain much of its color.

4 tablespoons margarine
1 medium yellow onion, chopped
1 medium cauliflower
1 large boiling potato, peeled and diced
1-quart vegetable stock
2 tablespoons snipped chives
2 tablespoons herbes de Provençe
liquid pepper salt and pepper to taste
1 cup heavy cream
2 egg yolks, at room temperature
2 tablespoons Armagnac
½ pound Roquefort, crumbled
chives for garnish

RIVIERA ROQUEFORT & CAULIFLOWER SOUP

Autumn
Yield: about 4 servings

1. Melt the margarine in a soup kettle or Dutch oven, and sauté the onion for briefly. Cover, and then cook over a very low heat for 10 minutes.
2. Meanwhile, trim and core the cauliflower, chopping to make about 6 cups. Add the cauliflower to the onions before stirring in the stock, chives, and herbes de Provençe. Adjust liquid pepper salt and pepper to taste. Bring to a boil, then reduce to a simmer, cover lightly, and cook, stirring occasionally, for about 10 minutes.
3. In the container of a blender or food processor, purée the soup, in batches, until smooth, and then return to the pan.
4. In a bowl, using a wire whisk, beat the cream, yolks, and Armagnac together until smooth. Then whip in 1 cup hot soup, before stirring the mixture back into the hot soup. Add half of the Roquefort, and continue to cook, stirring constantly, until the cheese melts. (Do not allow to boil.)
5. Turn off the heat, and adjust the salt and pepper to taste. Serve immediately, and sprinkle the remaining Roquefort on top.

Hint: Herbes de Provençe are available at most specialty shops. Although the recipe calls for Roquefort, any blue cheese can be used.

RUSSIAN VEGETABLE SOUP

Autumn

Yield: about 6 to 8 servings

1 tablespoon butter or margarine
1 medium red onion, chopped
3 medium potatoes, peeled and thinly sliced
2 parsnips, peeled and sliced
1 cup sliced carrots
2 cups finely sliced red cabbage
2 tablespoons minced fresh parsley
pinch crushed dried basil
pinch crushed dried oregano
pinch crushed dried rosemary
½ teaspoon fresh grated nutmeg
4 cups vegetable stock
salt and pepper to taste

1. Melt 1 tablespoon butter in a saucepan, add the onion, potatoes, parsnips, carrots, and cabbage. Cover and simmer over a low heat, stirring several times, for about 10 minutes. Add the parsley, basil, oregano, rosemary, nutmeg, and stock. Bring to a boil, then reduce to a simmer, cover and cook, stirring occasionally, for about 30 minutes.

2. Remove from heat, cool slightly, and purée in a blender or food processor.

3. Return to the heat, heat through, and serve.

Leek Garnish

1 small leek, trimmed and cut into matchsticks
1 tablespoon butter or margarine

Melt the butter in a skillet or saucepan, and sauté the leeks, stirring frequently, until crisp. Garnish the soup.

2 tablespoons butter or margarine
6 large leeks, trimmed and cut into strips
¼ teaspoon curry powder
4 medium potatoes, peeled and sliced ¼ inch thick
1 stalk celery, cut into matchsticks
4 cups vegetable stock
1 cup dry white wine
1 teaspoon saffron powder, or to taste
1 teaspoon crushed dried parsley
8-ounce carton heavy cream
1 tablespoon lemon juice
salt and pepper to taste

SAFFRON SOUP

Winter
Yield: about 4 to 6 servings

1. Melt the butter in a soup kettle or Dutch oven, and sauté the leeks and curry together until the leeks are tender. Add the potatoes and celery. Heat through, and then add 2 cups of the stock. Bring to a boil, then reduce to a simmer, cover lightly, and cook, stirring occasionally, for about 15 minutes or until the vegetables are tender.

2. Meanwhile, in a separate saucepan, combine the wine, saffron, and parsley. Bring to a boil, and cook, stirring frequently, for about 10 minutes. Remove from heat and set aside.

3. When the vegetables are ready, remove from heat, and cool slightly. The pour into the container of a blender or food processor, and purée in batches until smooth. Return to the soup kettle.

4. Strain the saffron mix through a fine sieve into the vegetable mix. Add the remaining 2 cups of stock to the soup along with the cream, lemon juice, and salt and pepper to taste. Heat through; do not allow to boil. Garnish lightly with daub of whipped sour cream or yogurt.

Hint: Saffron, a rich and expensive aromatic spice, has a slightly bitter taste.

SAVORY SPINACH & POTATO SOUP

Winter

Yield: about 6 servings

4 cups vegetable stock
3 medium leeks, trimmed and sliced
3 medium onions, chopped
3 cups diced potatoes
6 ounces fresh spinach, chopped
2 tablespoons sour cream
freshly ground black pepper to taste

1. In a soup kettle or Dutch oven, combine the stock, leeks, and onion. Bring to a boil, then reduce to a simmer, cover lightly, and cook for about 5 minutes. Add potatoes, cover again and continue to cook for about 20 minutes, or until potatoes are fork tender.

2. In the container of a blender or food processor, purée the soup, in batches, until smooth. Return to the pot, stir in the spinach and sour cream, and heat through.

3. Turn off the heat, and adjust the salt and pepper to taste. Serve immediately.

SCALLION-POTATO SOUP

Winter

Yield: about 4 to 6 servings

2 tablespoons margarine
1 small yellow onion, chopped
1½ cups chopped scallions
1½ cups diced potatoes
2½ cups vegetable stock
1 cup light cream
½ cup evaporated milk
salt and pepper to taste
chopped chives for garnish

1. Melt the margarine in a soup kettle or large saucepan, and sauté the onion and scallion until the onion is translucent. Add the potatoes and stock, bring to a boil, then reduce to a simmer, cover lightly, and cook for about 20 minutes, or until the potatoes are very soft. Remove from heat.

2. In the container of a blender or food processor, purée the soup, in batches, until smooth. Return to the pan. Add the cream and milk, heat through. (Do not boil.) Remove from heat, and adjust the salt and pepper to taste. Serve in heated bowls, with a garnish of chopped chives.

Hint: This is a potato soup flavored with onions that leaves room to add other ingredients if you choose.

2 cups sliced zucchini (courgette)
1½ cups diced potatoes
1 medium yellow onion, chopped
4 cups vegetable stock
1 cup diced Brie cheese

1. In a saucepan or soup kettle, combine the zucchini, potatoes, onion, and stock. Bring to a boil, then reduce to a simmer, and cook, stirring occasionally, for about 15 minutes, or until the potatoes are fork tender. Remove from heat, add the cheese, and stir until just melted.
2. Purée in batches, using a blender or food processor until smooth. Return to the pan, heat through, and serve with a crusty bread on the side.

Hint: I tried this with several types of cheese. All were good, but Brie was the best.

1 cup dried black beans, soaked in water overnight
8 cups vegetable stock or unsweetened apple juice
1 large yellow onion, sliced
1 medium carrot, peeled and sliced
4 sprigs fresh parsley
2 medium cloves garlic, peeled and finely diced
1 teaspoon ground thyme
3 cups hot cooked rice
½ cup dry sherry
1 small red onion, chopped
salt and pepper to taste

SHERRY
BLACK-BEAN
SOUP WITH
RICE

Year-Round

Yield: about 8 to 10 servings

1. In a soup kettle or Dutch oven, combine the drained beans, stock, yellow onion, carrot, parsley, garlic and thyme. Bring to a boil, reduce to a low simmer, cover lightly, and cook, stirring occasionally, for about 4 hours or until the beans are tender.
2. In the container of a blender or food processor, purée the soup in batches until smooth. Return to the pot, and bring to a boil. Then reduce to a simmer, cover lightly, and cook for about 30 minutes. Add the rice, sherry, and red onion.
3. Turn off the heat, and adjust the salt and pepper to taste. Serve immediately.

SIMPLE SUMMER VEGETABLE SOUP

Summer

Yield: about 6 to 8 servings

2 tablespoons margarine
1 medium yellow onion, chopped
2 large carrots, peeled and sliced
2 celery stalks, sliced
8 cups vegetable stock
2 large fresh ripe tomatoes, peeled, seeded, and chopped
2 medium zucchini, quartered and sliced
½ cup string beans
½ cup green peas
1 cup chopped fresh spinach
salt and pepper to taste

1. Melt the margarine in a soup kettle or Dutch oven and sauté the onion, carrots, and celery together, until the onion is tender.
2. Wash and cut the fresh spinach into strips; then set aside. Add the stock and tomatoes, zucchini, beans, and peas. Return to a boil, reduce to a simmer, and cook for an additional 15 minutes, or until the vegetables are tender.
3. Add the spinach; heat through. Adjust the salt and pepper to taste and serve immediately.

AUSTRIAN SPINACH-YOGURT SOUP

Summer

Yield: about 4 servings

1 medium onion, finely chopped
1 tablespoon margarine
2 teaspoons all-purpose flour
¼ teaspoon crushed dried tarragon
pinch of nutmeg
pinch of cayenne
15 ounces frozen chopped spinach, thawed
2 cups vegetable stock
¾ cup yogurt
lemon slices for garnish

1. Melt the margarine in a soup kettle or Dutch oven and sauté onion until translucent. Sprinkle on the flour, stirring until incorporated. Add the tarragon, nutmeg, cayenne, spinach, and stock. Bring to a boil, then reduce to a simmer, and cook for about 15 minutes.
2. In the container of a blender, purée the mix in batches, until smooth.
3. Return to the pot, and using a wire whisk, beat in the yogurt until smooth. Heat through; do not allow to boil. Adjust the salt and pepper to taste, and serve immediately, with lemon slices on each bowl.

2½ cups vegetable stock or water
10-ounce package creamed spinach, drained
¼ cup quick-cooking barley
⅛ teaspoon ground nutmeg
salt and pepper to taste

1. In a soup kettle or Dutch oven combine the stock and spinach. Bring to a boil, stir in the barley, and nutmeg; reduce to a simmer. Cover lightly, and cook, stirring frequently, until the barley is tender.

2. Turn off the heat, adjust the salt and pepper to taste, and set aside for about 5 minutes. Serve immediately.

1 tablespoon safflower oil
1 large yellow onion, minced
1 large potato, peeled and diced
1 large sweet potato, peeled and cut into 1-inch cubes
6 cups vegetable stock
1 teaspoon crushed dried dill weed
⅛ teaspoon cayenne pepper
1 cup frozen peas, thawed
1 cup sliced Romaine leaves, packed
salt and pepper to taste

1. Heat oil in soup kettle or Dutch oven and sauté the onion until lightly browned. Add the white potato and sweet potato. Continue to sauté for about 1 minute. Add 4 cups of the stock, dill weed, and cayenne. Bring to boil, reduce to a simmer, cover lightly, and continue to cook for about 20 minutes. Add the peas and lettuce. Cover and continue to cook until the peas are cooked and the potatoes are fork tender.

2. In the container of a blender or food processor, purée the soup in batches until smooth.

3. Return to the pot, add the remaining stock, and cook until heated through.

4. Turn off the heat, and adjust the salt and pepper to taste. Serve immediately.

Hint: For greener color, add more peas.

JERUSALEM ARTICHOKE & CARROT SOUP

Summer

Yield: about 4 to 6 servings

1 tablespoon butter or margarine
1 medium yellow onion, chopped
1 medium (about 4 ounces) Jerusalem artichoke, peeled and chopped
1½ cups chopped carrots
1 tablespoon minced celery
3 cups vegetable stock
½ cup milk
¼ cup grated carrots
salt and pepper to taste
heavy cream for garnish

1. Melt the butter in a saucepan or soup kettle, and sauté the onion, until translucent. Add the Jerusalem artichoke, chopped carrots, and celery, and stir while simmering, for about 3 to 4 minutes. Add the stock, and bring to a boil. Then reduce to a simmer, cover and cook, stirring occasionally, for about 20 minutes, or until the Jerusalem artichokes are tender. Remove from heat, and cool slightly.
2. When ready, purée, in portions, in a blender or food processor until smooth. Return the mixture to a clean saucepan, and add the grated carrots and milk. Adjust the salt and pepper to taste, heat through, and serve with a swirl of heavy cream.

Hint: If you mince the Jerusalem artichoke, it will cook faster and be easier to purée. Jerusalem artichokes, not really artichokes, are also known as sunchokes.

SWEET BEAN SOUP

Summer

Yield: about 6 servings

2 tablespoons margarine
2 medium yellow onions, chopped
1 medium clove garlic, peeled and minced
3 medium carrots, peeled and sliced
28-ounce can baked beans in brown sugar
11.5-ounce can V-8 vegetable juice
1 large Granny Smith apple, pared and diced
1 teaspoon Worcestershire sauce
shredded colby cheese

1. Melt the margarine in a soup kettle or Dutch oven, and sauté the onions and garlic, until the onions are lightly browned. Add the carrots, beans, V-8 juice, apple, and Worcestershire sauce. Bring to a boil, then reduce to a simmer, cover lightly, and cook for about 5 minutes.
2. Remove from heat, adjust the salt and pepper to taste, and serve immediately, with shredded cheese on the side.

1½ pounds sweet potatoes, peeled and diced
water to cover
1 tablespoon butter or margarine
3 medium yellow onions, thinly sliced
two 15.25-ounce cans cream-style corn
½ cup milk
¾ cup heavy cream
salt and pepper to taste

1. Place the sweet potatoes in a second saucepan, cover with water, and bring to a boil. Then reduce to a simmer, and cook, stirring occasionally, for about 20 minutes or until fork tender. Drain the sweet potatoes.
2. Melt the butter in another saucepan or a soup kettle, and sauté the onion until translucent. Add the corn and milk, and heat through. Remove from heat, Stir in the cream and sweet potatoes. Adjust the salt and pepper to taste, and serve immediately with fresh chives as a garnish.

Hint: Use either pale-skinned or dark-skinned sweet potatoes. There is a difference in taste.

1 large butternut squash, peeled and cut into 1-inch cubes
1½ cups sliced yellow onion
1½ cups chopped McIntosh apples
1 cup chopped carrots
2 teaspoons minced fresh ginger
5 cups water
salt and pepper to taste (optional)

1. In a soup kettle or Dutch oven, combine the squash, onion, apples, carrots, ginger, and water. Bring to a boil. Then reduce to a simmer, cover lightly, and cook for about 40 minutes, or until the squash is very tender.
2. Turn off the heat, and in the container of a blender or food processor, purée the soup in batches until smooth.
3. Return to heat, adjust the salt and pepper to taste, and serve immediately.

Hint: A touch of honey will add more sweetness.

THICK VEGETABLE SOUP

Winter

Yield: about 10 to 12 servings

1 tablespoon olive oil
1 cup chopped yellow onion
1 tablespoon minced garlic
16-ounce can crushed tomatoes
2 cups zucchini, cut into ½-inch cubes
3 medium carrots, peeled and cut into ¼-inch cubes
1 cup white turnips, peeled and cut into ¼-inch cubes
1 cup chopped celery
1 pound dried navy beans, soaked overnight
10 cups vegetable stock
¼ cup minced fresh basil leaves
salt and pepper to taste

1. Heat the oil in a soup kettle or Dutch oven and sauté the onion and garlic together until the onion is tender. Add the tomatoes, zucchini, carrots, turnips, and celery. Continue to cook, stirring frequently, for about 10 minutes, or until the turnips and carrots are fork tender.
2. Drain the beans, and add them to the vegetables along with the stock. Bring to a boil. Then reduce to a simmer, cover lightly, and cook, stirring occasionally, for about 60 minutes, or until the beans are very tender.
3. Add the basil, heat through, and turn off the heat. Adjust the salt and pepper to taste.
4. Serve immediately, alone or as part of a menu, with a garnish of choice on the side.

2 tablespoons butter or margarine
1 medium yellow onion, minced
1 celery stalk and leaves, chopped
½ cup sliced carrots
two 16-ounce cans crushed tomatoes
1 tablespoon tomato purée
1 tablespoon tomato sauce
1 tablespoon Worcestershire sauce
2 tablespoons fresh tarragon
3½ cups vegetable stock
granulated sugar to taste

THIN TOMATO SOUP

Spring
Yield: about 4 to 6 servings

1. Melt the butter in a saucepan or soup kettle, and sauté the onion, celery, and carrots together until the onions are translucent. Add the crushed tomatoes, tomato purée, tomato sauce, Worcestershire sauce, tarragon, and stock. Bring to a boil, then reduce to a simmer, cover lightly, and cook, stirring occasionally, for about 15 to 20 minutes. And then stir in the sugar.
2. Remove from heat, and purée in batches, using a blender or food processor, until very smooth. Pass through a fine sieve, and return to the pan.
3. Heat through, adjust the salt and pepper to taste, and serve immediately, with chopped celery greens as a garnish.

Hint: Substitute red for yellow onions if you wish.

2 tablespoons virgin olive oil
1 medium red onion, chopped
1 teaspoon ground coriander
¾ teaspoon ground turmeric
¾ teaspoon ground cumin
light pinch curry powder
pinch ground cloves
4 cups vegetable stock
16-ounce can chopped tomatoes
12-ounce package dried red lentils, rinsed and drained

INDIAN TOMATO LENTIL SOUP

Summer
Yield: about 6 to 8 servings

1. Heat the oil in a saucepan or soup kettle, and sauté the onion, until translucent. Add the coriander, turmeric, cumin, curry powder, cloves, stock, tomatoes, and lentils. Bring to a boil. Then reduce to a simmer, cover lightly, and cook, stirring for about 20 to 30 minutes, or until the lentils are very tender.
2. Remove from heat, and purée in batches, using a blender or food processor. Return to the saucepan, heat through, and serve as desired.

TOMATO-ONION SOUP WITH RIGATONI

Autumn

Yield: about 4 servings

1 cup water

1 large yellow onion, chopped

⅛ teaspoon garlic powder

28-ounce can diced tomatoes

1 tablespoon crushed dried parsley

1 cup rigatoni pasta

½ teaspoon crushed dried thyme

1 bay leaf

½ teaspoon crushed dried basil

1 tablespoon soy sauce

1 tablespoon honey

1. In a soup kettle or Dutch oven, combine the water, onion, and garlic powder. Bring to a boil, then reduce to a simmer, cover lightly, and cook for about 15 minutes.
2. Add the tomatoes, parsley, rigatoni, thyme, bay leaf, and basil. Return to a boil. Reduce to a simmer, cover lightly, and cook, stirring occasionally, for about 30 minutes, or until the rigatoni is al dente.
3. Add the soy sauce and honey, heat through. Discard the bay leaf, and serve immediately, with crusty bread on the side.

VILLA DE ESTES TORTELLINI SOUP

Spring

Yield: about 8 servings

1 tablespoon olive oil

¼ cup minced yellow onion

1 cup sliced mushrooms

1 medium clove garlic, peeled and minced

14.5-ounce can vegetable stock

2 cups water

9 ounces fresh cheese tortellini

1 cup frozen peas, thawed

2 tablespoons snipped parsley

1. Heat the oil in a soup kettle or Dutch oven, and sauté the onion, mushrooms, and garlic together until the onion is tender. Add the stock and water, and bring to a boil. Add the tortellini and peas, and return to a boil. Continue to cook for about 15 minutes, or until the tortellini is al dente.
2. Turn off the heat, stir in the parsley, and adjust the salt and pepper to taste. Serve immediately, with hot crusty bread.

2 cups dried white beans, soaked overnight

½ cup olive oil

2 cloves garlic, peeled and finely chopped

1 small onion, thinly sliced

2 celery stalks, diced

1 carrot, diced

2 sprigs fresh rosemary, finely chopped

5 teaspoons tomato sauce

½ head savory cabbage, shredded

2 to 3 leeks, chopped

3 zucchini, diced

finely chopped basil to taste

2 sprigs parsley, finely chopped

⅛ teaspoon ground cloves

⅔ cup cooked rice

2 tablespoons margarine

TOUGH GUYS' VEGETABLE SOUP

Year-Round

Yield: about 6 servings

1. In a soup kettle or Dutch oven, cook the beans and soaking water, cover lightly, stirring occasionally, for about 2 hours, or until tender.
2. Drain and reserve the liquid.
3. In the container of a blender or food processor, purée half the beans, in batches, until smooth.
4. Heat the oil in the same pot, and sauté the onion, garlic, celery, carrot, and rosemary until the onions start to color. Stir in the tomato sauce, and add the cabbage, leeks, zucchini, basil, parsley, and cloves, puréed beans, reserved beans, and bean cooking liquid. If mixture is too thick, add water, ¼ cup at a time. Cover lightly, and cook over a very low heat for about 30 minutes.
5. Stir the margarine into the rice and add to the soup mixture.
6. Turn off the heat, and adjust the salt and pepper to taste. Serve immediately.

TWIN SISTERS VEGETABLE SOUP

Year-Round

Yield: about 6 to 8 servings

2 tablespoons canola oil
1 medium red onion, chopped
2 small cloves garlic, peeled and minced
2 teaspoons crushed dried oregano
2 medium potatoes, peeled and diced
1 small zucchini, peeled and diced
1 large yellow squash, diced
3 stalks celery, chopped
2 large carrots, trimmed and chopped
2 bay leaves
16-ounce can crushed tomatoes
16-ounce can kidney beans, rinsed and drained

1. Heat the oil in a soup kettle or Dutch oven and sauté the onion, garlic, and oregano together until the onion is tender. Add the potatoes, zucchini, squash, celery, carrots, tomatoes, and bay leaves. Add just enough water to cover the vegetables. Bring to a boil, then reduce to a simmer, cover lightly, and cook for about 20 minutes, or until the vegetables are fork tender. Add the beans, and continue to cook for about 20 minutes longer.

2. Remove from heat, adjust the salt and pepper to taste, remove the bay leaves, and cool to room temperature. Cover tightly and refrigerate for at least 8 hours.

3. When ready, return the soup to the heat, and bring to a boil. Serve immediately.

1 tablespoon extra virgin olive oil
1 medium yellow onion, chopped
1 stalk celery, minced
1 large carrot, peeled and sliced
1 medium clove garlic, peeled and minced
2 tablespoons chili powder
½ teaspoon ground cumin
¼ teaspoon crushed dried oregano
½ teaspoon bottled hot sauce or to taste
1 cup water
1 cup lentils, rinsed and sorted
16-ounce can crushed tomatoes
10-ounce can cannellini beans

1. Heat the oil in a soup kettle or large saucepan, and sauté the onion, celery, carrots and garlic together until the onion is translucent.
2. Meanwhile, in a bowl, blend the chili powder, cumin, oregano and hot sauce, and stir into the hot mixture.
3. Add the water, and bring to a boil. Add the lentils and return to a boil. Reduce to a simmer, cover lightly, and cook, stirring occasionally, for about 15 to 17 minutes. Add the tomatoes and beans, cover again, and continue to cook for about 10 minutes longer, or until the lentils and beans are very tender.
4. Remove from heat and ladle into heated bowls. Serve with hot flour tortillas on the side.

Hint: Cannellini beans are sometimes called white Italian kidney beans.

VEGAN LENTIL SOUP

Year-Round

Yield: about 6 to 8 servings

2 tablespoons extra virgin olive oil
1 large red onion, thinly sliced
1 medium clove garlic, peeled and minced
¾ cup red lentils, rinsed and sorted
2 cups vegetable stock
16-ounce can crushed tomatoes
2 teaspoons tomato paste
2 tablespoons fresh French thyme
fresh lemon juice to taste

1. Heat the oil in a saucepan or soup kettle, and sauté the onion and garlic together until the onion is translucent. Add the lentils, and cook, stirring constantly, until coated. Add the stock, bring to a boil, and cook, stirring and removing any scum that may accumulate, for about 5 minutes. Add the tomatoes, tomato sauce, and about half the thyme.

2. Return to a boil, reduce to a simmer, cover lightly, and cook for about 20 minutes or until the lentils are tender. Add the lemon juice, adjust the salt and pepper to taste, garnish with the remaining thyme, and serve immediately.

VEGETABLE CELEBRATION SOUP

Summer

Yield: about 14 servings

1 tablespoon canola oil
2 medium yellow onions, peeled and minced
4 large carrots, peeled and diced
2 large fennel bulbs, trimmed and diced
10 cups vegetable stock or water
1 teaspoon crushed dried tarragon
1 teaspoon crushed dried thyme
1 large red bell pepper, seeded and diced
2 medium zucchini, peeled and diced
12 large fresh mushrooms, quartered
salt and pepper to taste
grated Parmesan cheese for garnish

1. Heat the oil in a soup kettle or Dutch oven, and sauté the onions until tender. Add the carrots, fennel, stock, tarragon, and thyme. Bring to a boil, then reduce to a simmer, cover and cook, stirring occasionally, for about 20 minutes, or until the vegetables are tender. Add the red pepper, zucchini, and mushrooms. Cover again, and continue to cook for an additional 10 minutes.

2. Turn off the heat, and adjust the salt and pepper to taste. Serve immediately, with a garnish of grated cheese.

2 teaspoons olive oil
½ cup chopped yellow onion
3 medium cloves garlic, peeled and minced
1 quart water or vegetable stock
3 packets Herb Ox instant vegetable bouillon granules
2 medium potatoes, peeled and diced
16-ounce can diced tomatoes
½ cup diced carrot
1 bay leaf
16-ounce can garbanzo beans (chickpeas), drained
1 cup cooked chopped kale
1 tablespoon minced fresh parsley
½ teaspoon crushed dried oregano
salt and pepper to taste

VEGETABLE SOUP WITH GARBANZO BEANS

Summer

Yield: about 4 servings

1. Heat the oil in a soup kettle or Dutch oven, and sauté the onion and garlic until the onion is translucent. Add the water and stock granules, stirring until dissolved. Bring to a boil, then reduce to a simmer, add the potatoes, tomatoes, carrot, and bay leaf; cover lightly, and simmer until vegetables are crisp and tender, about 30 minutes.

2. Add the chickpeas, kale, parsley, and oregano. Cook, stirring occasionally, for about 5 minutes. Remove from heat, and adjust the salt and pepper to taste. Serve immediately.

VEGETABLE SOUP WITH LEMON & MINT

Summer

Yield: about 6 servings

5 cups vegetable stock
2 large yellow onions, finely chopped
1 celery stalk and leaves, finely chopped
2 bay leaves
⅔ cup rice
two 10-ounce packages frozen mixed vegetables, thawed
2 tablespoons fresh lemon juice
salt and pepper to taste
10 mint leaves, finely chopped

1. In a soup kettle or Dutch oven, combine the stock, onions, celery, and bay leaves. Bring to a boil. Remove from heat, discard the bay leaves, and reserve the stock. Purée the vegetables (not the stock) in batches, in a blender or food processor. Set aside.
2. Bring the same stock to a boil, add the rice, and cook, uncovered, for about 10 minutes. Add the mixed vegetables, and continue to cook for about 10 minutes, or until the rice is tender.
3. Stir in the puréed vegetables and lemon juice. Bring to a boil, remove from heat, and adjust the salt and pepper to taste. Serve immediately, with the mint leaves as a garnish.

Hint: The underlying taste of lemon and the hint of mint are just enough to surprise us. Remember, lemon is acidic, and it will take much of the color out of the mixed vegetables.

VEGETABLE PASTA SOUP

Autumn

Yield: about 6 servings

2 cups vegetable stock or water
16-ounce can cut green beans, drained
6-ounce can tomato paste
1 cup uncooked small-shell macaroni
1 teaspoon crushed dried basil
salt and pepper to taste

1. In a soup kettle or Dutch oven, bring the stock to a boil. Reduce to a simmer, and add the beans, tomato paste, macaroni, and basil. Return to a boil, reduce to a simmer, cover lightly, and cook for about 15 to 20 minutes, or until the macaroni is al dente.
2. Turn off the heat, and adjust the salt and pepper to taste. Serve immediately.

4 cups vegetable stock
1 cup sour cream or unflavored yogurt
1 cup evaporated milk
1½ cups dried potato flakes
1½ cups chopped mushrooms
1½ cups dried mixed vegetables
salt and pepper to taste
chopped fresh parsley for garnish

VEGETABLE-POTATO SOUP

Winter

Yield: about 6 servings

1. In a soup kettle or Dutch oven, bring the stock to a boil, reduce to a simmer, and add the sour cream and milk. Add the potato flakes, return to a boil, reduce to a simmer, and cook, stirring until thickened.
2. Add the mushrooms and dried vegetables, return to a boil, reduce to a simmer, and cook for about 3 to 4 minutes.
3. Turn off the heat, and adjust the salt and pepper to taste. Serve immediately, with a garnish of parsley.

Hint: Here the potato flakes act as a thickening agent.

3½ cups vegetable stock
⅓ cup wild rice
2 large carrots, peeled and minced
1 medium white onion, minced
2 tablespoons finely minced green bell peppers
1 tablespoon minced fresh garlic
pinch crushed dried basil
1 tablespoon minced celery

WILD RICE & CARROT SOUP

Spring

Yield: about 4 to 6 servings

1. In a saucepan or soup kettle, bring the stock to a boil, add the rice, reduce to a simmer, cover lightly, and cook for about 10 minutes. Add the carrots, onion, peppers, garlic, basil, and celery, and continue to cook for about 20 minutes longer or until the carrots and rice are very tender.
2. Remove from heat, adjust the salt and pepper to taste and serve as desired.

Hint: A sprinkling of grated Parmesan or Romano cheese will complement the taste of this soup. Or serve with celery stuffed with pimento cream cheese.

WINTER VEGETABLE SOUP

Winter

Yield: about 6 servings

4 tablespoons margarine
2 cups diced leeks
1½ cups diced yellow onions
1 cup diced celery
1½ teaspoons crushed dried tarragon
½ teaspoon crushed dried thyme
5 cups vegetable stock
2½ cups diced potatoes
1½ cups sliced carrots
1 pound fresh spinach, chopped
1½ cups shredded cabbage
1 cup heavy cream
salt and pepper to taste

1. Melt the margarine in a soup kettle or Dutch oven and sauté the leeks, onion and celery together until the onion is tender. Add the tarragon, thyme, stock, potatoes and carrots. Bring to a boil, then reduce to a simmer, cover lightly, and cook, stirring occasionally, for about 20 minutes, or until the vegetables are fork tender.
2. Add half the spinach and half the cabbage. Continue to cook for about 2 minutes.
3. Turn off the heat, and in the container of a blender or food processor, purée the soup mixture in batches.
4. Return to the pot, add the remaining spinach, cabbage, and cream. Heat through, but do not allow to boil. Remove from heat, adjust the salt and pepper to taste, and serve immediately.

CHILLED SOUPS

Many soups in this section can be served hot or cold.
Chilled soups, while delightful on a summer day,
can be enjoyed year-round.

AFRICAN TOMATO & AVOCADO SOUP

Year-Round
Yield: about 2 to 4 servings

1 large avocado, mashed
1 tablespoon fresh lemon juice
three 16-ounce cans crushed tomatoes
2 tablespoons tomato paste
1 cup buttermilk or sour milk
1 tablespoon saffron or olive oil
2 tablespoons finely minced fresh parsley
salt and pepper to taste
hot pepper sauce to taste
1 cucumber, peeled, seeded, and diced for garnish
whipped sour cream, unflavored yogurt, or crème fraîche for garnish

1. Mash the avocado with the lemon juice.
2. In the container of a blender or food processor, combine the tomatoes, tomato paste, buttermilk, oil, and avocado. Process on HIGH until smooth. Pour into a bowl, add the avocado and lemon juice mixture, and then stir in the parsley. Adjust the seasoning and pepper sauce to taste.
3. Refrigerate for at least two hours before serving. When ready, remove from the refrigerator, and serve cold with cucumbers as a garnish and sour cream on the side.

AMERICAN-STYLE FRUIT SOUP

Summer
Yield: 6 to 8 servings

1 cup boiling water
3-ounce package watermelon-flavored gelatin
1 cup cold water or unsweetened apple juice
32-ounce can fruit cocktail
16-ounce jar citrus fruit salad
¼ cup fresh lime or lemon juice

1. Pour the boiling water into the container of a blender, replace the lid, and start the blender on LOW speed. Remove the lid, and slowly pour in the gelatin. Then add the water, and pour into a large bowl.
2. Add the fruit cocktail with syrup, fruit salad with juice, and lime juice. Cover tightly and refrigerate until thoroughly chilled.
3. When ready, ladle into chilled soup bowls, garnish with mint sprigs, and serve as an appetizer or as a dessert soup.

Hint: You may substitute pineapple or grapefruit juice for the water. You can try a variety of gelatins. Citrus fruit salad is found in the refrigerator section of most supermarkets.

1½ pounds fresh asparagus, tips and stalks separated
¼ cup margarine
1 cup leeks (white only), chopped
½ cup chopped yellow onion
½ cup chopped celery
1 small baking potato, peeled and diced
3½ cups vegetable stock
1 teaspoon fresh lemon juice
½ cup half-and-half
salt and pepper to taste
paprika to taste (optional)
whipped cream for garnish

1. Melt the margarine in a skillet, and sauté the asparagus tips (reserve the stalks), onion, leeks, celery, and potato until heated through, and then cover lightly, cooking over a low heat until the potatoes are soft, about 20 minutes.

2. In a soup kettle or Dutch oven, combine the stock and remaining asparagus stalks (without tips). Bring to a boil, then reduce to a simmer, cover lightly, and cook for about 10 minutes. Remove from heat, and strain through a fine sieve. Discard the stalks and return the liquid to the pot.

3. In the container of a blender or food processor, purée the vegetables from the skillet until smooth. Then stir into the stock, before adding the lemon juice, half-and-half, and adjusting the salt and pepper to taste. Cool to room temperature and refrigerate.

4. When ready to serve, and using a wire whisk, beat until smooth. Serve cold with whipped cream and paprika on the side.

AVOCADO & SPINACH SOUP

Summer

Yield: about 4 to 6 servings

2 tablespoons margarine
16-ounce package frozen chopped spinach, thawed
3 tablespoons all-purpose flour
2 cups soy milk
1½ cups vegetable stock
pinch of nutmeg
salt and pepper to taste
2 large avocados, finely chopped
1 cup quark or cottage cheese
1 small avocado, sliced and halved for garnish

1. Melt the butter in a saucepan and sauté the spinach over a low heat, stirring frequently for about 7 to 10 minutes. Sprinkle on the flour, and cook, stirring constantly, for about 1 minute, before adding the soy milk and stock. Bring to a boil, and add the nutmeg. Reduce to a simmer, and add the chopped avocados, and quark. Remove from heat, and in the container of a blender or food processor, purée the soup in batches, until smooth. Transfer to a bowl, cover tightly, and refrigerate for at least 4 hours.
2. When ready, adjust the salt and pepper to taste. Ladle into chilled soup bowls. Garnish with sliced avocado.

CHILLED APPLE-CINNAMON SOUP

Summer

Yield: about 4 servings

2 cups apple cider
1 tablespoon red-hot cinnamon candies
6 whole cloves
1 stick cinnamon
1 cup unsweetened applesauce
4 slices cinnamon toast, crust removed and cut into croutons

1. In a saucepan, combine the cider, candies, cloves, and cinnamon. Bring to a boil, then reduce to a simmer, cover lightly, and cook for about 10 to 15 minutes, or until the candy is completely dissolved. Remove from heat and strain, discarding the cloves and cinnamon. Return the liquid to the pan.
2. Add the applesauce, Cover tightly and refrigerate for at least 4 hours.
3. When ready, ladle into chilled bowls. Serve with a cinnamon toast cut into croutons.

1 pint fresh blueberries
1 cup fresh unsweetened orange juice
½ cup sour cream
1 tablespoon granulated sugar
1 tablespoon packed light brown sugar
¼ teaspoon ground nutmeg
1 tablespoon sour cream for garnish

1. In the container of a blender or food processor, purée blueberries, orange juice, ½ cup sour cream, granulated sugar, brown sugar, and nutmeg, until smooth. Pour into a large bowl, cover, and chill for at least an hour.
2. In a small bowl, and using a wire whisk, beat the remaining sour cream smooth. Then spoon into a pastry bag fitted with a fine round tip.
3. Pour the soup into chilled bowls, and press the sour cream from the pastry bag on the top of the soup, into a design.

½ cup half-and-half
1 cup diced potatoes, cooked until soft
3 cups diced cantaloupe
¼ cup dry sherry or white port wine
ground nutmeg for garnish
lime slice for garnish

1. In the container of a blender or food processor, combine the half-and-half, potato, and cantaloupe. Process on HIGH until smooth. Stir in the sherry, and chill for at least one hour before serving.
2. When ready, ladle into chilled soup bowls, sprinkle lightly with nutmeg, garnish with a slice of lime, and serve immediately.

Hint: Potatoes are used as a thickening agent. There are those who like to add salt to this dish. If so, salt to taste.

CHILLED CANTALOUPE SOUP

Summer

Yield: about 6 servings

1 large ripe cantaloupe, cubed
orange juice to cover
2 tablespoons fresh lemon juice
pinch of ground cinnamon
pinch of curry powder
pinch of turmeric powder
fresh mint leaves for garnish

1. Put the cantaloupe and orange juice in a large saucepan, bring to a boil, and immediately remove from heat; cool slightly.
2. In the container of a blender or food processor, purée the cantaloupe mix until smooth. Add the lemon juice, cinnamon, curry powder, and turmeric. Pour into a bowl, and chill in the refrigerator for at least 2 hours. Serve in chilled bowls with a mint leaf on top for garnish.

Hint: The spices give cantaloupe a bite, but remember that too much of the curry can make this soup sour.

CHILLED RASPBERRY SOUP

Summer

Yield: about 4 servings

two 10-ounce packages frozen raspberries, thawed
2 cups burgundy wine
2½ cups water
3-inch stick cinnamon
2 teaspoons cornstarch or arrowroot
2 tablespoons water
1 cup heavy cream blended with 2 tablespoons powdered sugar

1. In a soup kettle, combine the raspberries, 2½ wine, water, and cinnamon. Bring to a boil. Then reduce to a simmer, cover lightly, and cook, stirring occasionally, for about 15 minutes. Remove from heat.
2. In the container of a blender or food processor, purée the soup, in batches, until smooth. Strain through a sieve, discarding any seeds, and return the mixture to the pan.
3. Dissolve the cornstarch in 2 tablespoons water. Stir in the cornstarch mixture, return to a boil, and cook, stirring frequently, for about 2 to 3 minutes, or until barely thickened. Remove from heat, cool a little, cover tightly, and refrigerate for at least 8 hours.
4. When ready, ladle into chilled bowls, and drizzle on the cream. Then, using a knife, make several swirls in the soup, and serve immediately.

Hint: After the liquid wine has been brought to a boil, no alcohol remains in the liquid. This makes the soup safe for children to eat.

1 tablespoon cornstarch
2 tablespoons cold water
12-ounce package fresh cranberries
3 cups water
1 cup granulated sugar
¼ cup packed light brown sugar
2 cinnamon sticks
2 allspice berries
2 whole cloves
4 black peppercorns
¼ cup heavy cream, whipped to soft peaks
¾ cup dry red wine or to taste

CHILLED CRANBERRY SOUP

Summer

Yield: about 4 to 5 servings

1. In a cup, blend the cornstarch and water. Set aside.
2. Thoroughly rinse the cranberries under running water, shaking to remove excess water.
3. In a soup kettle or Dutch oven, combine the 3 cups of water, two sugars, cinnamon, allspice, cloves, and peppercorns. Bring to a boil. Then reduce to a simmer, add the cranberries, and cook, stirring occasionally, for about 15 minutes, or until the berries are tender.
4. Stir in the cornstarch mixture, bring to a boil, and cook, stirring constantly, until thickened.
5. Turn off the heat, chill slightly, and then refrigerate until ready to serve.
6. When ready, stir in the whipped cream and wine, adjust the flavor for sweetness, and serve in well-chilled bowls.

Hint: This would be great at Thanksgiving.

CHILLED CREAM-OF-VEGETABLE SOUP

Summer

Yield: about 6 servings

3 parsley sprigs
1 bay leaf
½ teaspoon crushed dried thyme
2 whole cloves
1 small clove garlic, peeled and crushed
1 cup chopped celery leaves
1 medium carrot, trimmed and diced
1 small green bell pepper, stemmed, seeded, and diced
1 cup finely chopped spinach leaves
1 large white onion, chopped
4 cups vegetable stock
¼ cup rice
2 egg yolks
2 cups half-and-half
salt and pepper to taste
sour cream for garnish
minced parsley for garnish
minced chives for garnish
2 medium tomatoes, peeled and chopped for garnish

1. Tie the parsley, bay leaf, thyme, cloves, and garlic in a square of cheese cloth to make a spice bag.
2. In a soup kettle or Dutch oven, combine the celery leaves, carrot, green pepper, spinach, onion, stock, spice bag, and rice. Bring to a boil. Then reduce to a simmer, cover lightly, and cook, stirring occasionally, for about 30 minutes, or until the rice is tender. Discard herbs in the cheesecloth, and remove from heat.
3. In the container of a blender or food processor, purée the mixture in batches, processing until smooth. Return to the pot, and reheat.
4. In a small bowl, using a wire whisk, beat the egg yolks and several tablespoons of soup together until smooth. Then stir this back into the hot soup mix until incorporated. (Do not allow to boil.) Add the half-and-half, heat through, remove from heat, and adjust the salt and pepper to taste. Cool to room temperature. Chill in the refrigerator for about 1 hour.
5. When ready to serve, using a wire whisk, whip vigorously, and ladle into chilled soup bowls. Serve immediately with sour cream, chopped parsley, chives and tomatoes on the side.

1 large (about 12-ounce) cucumber, peeled and seeded
1 tablespoon granulated sugar
1 teaspoon salt
8-ounce carton unflavored yogurt
8-ounce can tomato juice
½ teaspoon minced garlic
2 cups vegetable stock
⅔ cup chopped fresh mint leaves (loosely packed)
8-ounce carton light cream
dash hot sauce
salt and pepper to taste
mint sprigs for garnish

1. Place the cucumbers in bowl, sprinkle with sugar, and refrigerate for at least 30 minutes.
2. In the container of a blender, combine the yogurt, tomato juice, garlic, stock, and mint. Process on LOW until smooth. Cover and refrigerate for about 30 minutes.
3. When the cucumbers are ready, rinse under cold running water, and press dry, between double layers of paper towels.
4. Place the yogurt mixture into a serving bowl, add the cucumbers, cream, hot sauce, and salt and pepper to taste. Cover tight, and refrigerate for at least 2 hours before serving in well-chilled bowls, with mint sprigs as a garnish.

Hint: Cucumbers should always be served cold.

CHILLED JUICE SOUP

Summer

Yield: about 4 to 6 servings

6 whole cloves
3 cups orange juice
2 cups pineapple juice
⅓ cup granulated sugar
3 tablespoons cornstarch
¾ cup fresh lemon juice

1. In a large saucepan, combine the cloves, orange juice, and pineapple juice. Bring to a boil, reduce to a simmer.
2. In a bowl, blend the sugar and cornstarch. Then stir in the lemon juice, blending until smooth.
3. Using a slotted spoon, remove the cloves from the hot soup and discard. Then stir the cornstarch blend into the hot mixture. Cook, stirring until thickened and clear.
4. Cover tightly, and refrigerate until ready to serve.
5. When ready, ladle into chilled soup bowls or cups, and serve immediately.

CHILLED ORANGE-CARROT SOUP

Summer

Yield: about 8 to 10 servings

3 tablespoons margarine
¾ teaspoon grated ginger
8 medium carrots, peeled and sliced paper-thin
¾ cup leeks (whites only), sliced
4 cups vegetable stock or unsweetened apple juice
2 cups unsweetened orange juice
1 large orange, halved and sliced
10 springs of mint

1. Melt the margarine in a soup kettle or Dutch oven, and sauté the ginger, carrots and leeks, until the leeks are tender. Stir in 3 cups of the stock, bring to a boil, then reduce to a simmer, cover lightly, and cook for about 20 minutes, or until the carrots are tender. Remove from heat and cool.
2. In the container of a blender or food processor, purée the carrot mixture, in batches, until smooth. Return to the pot.
3. Add the remaining stock and half the orange juice. Bring to a boil. Then reduce to a simmer, and add the remaining orange juice, 1 tablespoon at a time, stirring well after each addition until the consistency is thin.
4. Turn off the heat, and adjust the salt and pepper to taste. Chill in the refrigerator for at least 2 hours.
5. When ready, and using a wire whisk, vigorously beat the soup before ladling into chilled soup bowls. Garnish with orange slices and mint sprigs, and serve immediately.

2 pounds fresh green pea pods
½ cup margarine
8 green onions, sliced
2 quarts vegetable stock
2 tablespoons fresh tarragon leaves
16 leaves romaine lettuce
½ cup crème fraîche
salt and pepper to taste
granulated sugar to taste
chopped fresh pea pods for garnish

1. Under running water, snap the ends from the pea pods and remove the strings.
2. Melt the margarine in a soup kettle or Dutch oven, and sauté the pods and onions together, stirring frequently, until the onions are tender. Stir in the stock and tarragon, bring to a boil, then reduce to a simmer, cover lightly, and cook, stirring occasionally, for about 15 minutes. Add the romaine and continue to cook for about 5 minutes, or until the lettuce is completely wilted. Remove from heat.
3. In the container of a blender or food processor, purée the soup, in batches, until smooth. Strain through a fine sieve into a large bowl, stir in the crème fraîche, cover and chill in the refrigerator for at least 4 hours.
4. When ready, and using a wire whisk, vigorously beat the soup before adjusting the salt and pepper to taste. Then stir in the sugar. Ladle into chilled bowls, and serve with a garnish of chopped pea pods.

Hint: As vegetables go, the pea pod is considered sweet; be very careful when you add the sugar to taste.

CHILLED RED PEPPER SOUP

Year-Round

Yield: about 6 servings

1 tablespoon margarine
3 large red bell peppers, stemmed, seeded, and finely diced
1 medium yellow onion, chopped
1 medium clove garlic, peeled and minced
1 cup vegetable stock
½ teaspoon crushed dried thyme
hot pepper sauce to taste
1 cup half-and-half

1. Melt the margarine in a saucepan and sauté the peppers, onion, and garlic until the onions are translucent. Add the stock, thyme, and pepper sauce to taste. Bring to a boil, then reduce to a simmer, cover lightly, and cook for about 10 minutes, or until most of the liquid has been absorbed. Remove from heat.
2. In the container of a blender or food processor, purée the mixture until smooth. Pour into a large bowl, and using a wire whisk, vigorously beat in the half-and-half. Cover and refrigerate for at least 4 hours.
3. When ready, and using the wire whisk, vigorously beat the soup, adjust the salt and pepper to taste, and ladle into chilled bowls. Serve immediately.

COLD PAPAYA SOUP

Summer

Yield: about 4 servings

1 medium (6-inch) ripe papaya
sugar to taste
2 tablespoons fresh lime juice
water or unsweetened apple juice

1. Peel and seed the papaya; then cut into chunks. Reserve the seeds in the refrigerator.
2. In the container of a blender or food processor, purée the papaya in batches until very smooth. Pour into a bowl, and adjust the sweetness to taste. Stir in the lime juice. If the mixture is too thick, add water or apple juice, 1 teaspoonful at a time. This soup is supposed to be very thick.
3. Cover and chill in the refrigerator for at least 4 hours, and then serve in chilled fruit cups with a small spoonful of the reserved seeds in the center.

3 tablespoons margarine
1 tablespoon vegetable oil
1 medium yellow onion, finely chopped
1 medium leek (white only), finely chopped
1 medium carrot, peeled and finely chopped
1 medium celery stalk, finely chopped
2 tablespoons chopped fresh basil
two 16-ounce cans diced tomatoes
3 tablespoons tomato paste
2 tablespoons all-purpose flour
2½ cups vegetable stock
½ cup light cream
salt and pepper to taste
fresh basil leaves for garnish
¼ cup sour cream or unflavored yogurt for garnish

1. Heat the margarine and oil together in a medium saucepan, and sauté the onion, leek, carrot, celery, and basil until the onion is transparent. Add the tomatoes and tomato paste, and cook, stirring occasionally, for about 5 minutes. Stir in the flour until incorporated, and add the stock. Bring to a boil, then reduce to a simmer, cover lightly, and cook without stirring for about 20 minutes. Remove from heat.

2. In the container of a blender or food processor, purée the mixture in batches, until smooth. Strain and press through a fine sieve, and return the mixture to the pot. Bring to a boil, then reduce to a simmer, and cook for about 3 to 4 minutes.

3. Turn off the heat, stir in the cream, and adjust the salt and pepper to taste. Cool slightly. Then cover tightly and refrigerate for at least 4 hours.

4. To serve, using a wire whisk, stir the soup vigorously. Ladle into chilled bowls, and serve with a garnish of basil leaves and a dollop of sour cream.

Hint: Keep basil growing in your kitchen; it often comes in handy.

CURRIED CHEESE & FRUIT SOUP

Year-Round
Yield: about 2 to 3 cups

1 cup unsweetened apple juice
¼ cup shredded Gouda cheese
1 medium McIntosh apple, pared and chopped
3-ounce package cream cheese
1 tablespoon honey
2 teaspoons lime juice or lemon juice
¼ teaspoon curry powder
1 fresh pear, pared, cored, and cut into wedges
1 fresh beach plum, skinned, seeded, and cut into wedges

1. In a saucepan, combine the apple juice, and chopped apple. Bring to a boil, and stir in the cheese. Cook, stirring constantly, until the cheese has melted. Remove from heat.
2. In the container of a blender, purée the cheese mixture, in batches, until smooth. Then, pour half the mixture back into the container of the blender, and add the cream cheese, honey, lime juice, and curry powder. Process on HIGH until smooth. Pour all of the mixture into a bowl, cover tightly, and chill for at least 4 hours.
3. When ready, serve in chilled bowls, with the fruit wedges on top.

Hint: This is a sweet soup with just enough of a bite to make your guests come back for a second taste.

DANISH FRUGTSUPPE FRA KOLDING

Year-Round
Yield: about 6 to 8 servings

8 ounces mixed dried fruit
½ cup dried apple, sliced
2 quarts cold water or unsweetened apple juice
¼ cup currants
¼ cup seedless green raisins
2 cups tapioca
1 stick cinnamon
2 tablespoons granulated sugar
1 tablespoon grated lemon zest
½ cup heavy cream

1. Thoroughly wash and drain the mixed dried fruit. In a soup kettle or large saucepan, combine the mixed dried fruit, apple slices, and water. Cover tightly, and set aside in a cool place for at least 8 hours.
2. When ready, add the currants, raisins, tapioca, and cinnamon. Return to the stove, and bring to a boil. Reduce to a low simmer, cover lightly, and cook, stirring occasionally, for about 2 hours. Add the sugar and lemon zest; continue to cook until the sugar is dissolved. Remove from heat, and cool. Then refrigerate until well chilled.
3. When ready, serve in chilled bowls, with a daub of whipped heavy cream and a sprinkling of chopped almonds or pecans.

4 medium cloves garlic, peeled and minced
¼ cup fine bread crumbs
6 tablespoons red wine vinegar
6 tablespoons extra virgin olive oil
2 pounds ripe tomatoes, peeled, seeded, and finely diced
¾ cup cucumbers, peeled, seeded, and diced
2 medium yellow onions, thinly sliced
¼ cup diced red bell peppers
¼ cup diced yellow bell peppers
1 tablespoon fresh parsley
1 tablespoon fresh basil
1 tablespoon fresh marjoram
2 cups ice water
hot sauce to taste
salt and pepper to taste

GAZPACHO

Autumn

Yield: about 6 servings

1. In the container of a blender, combine the garlic, bread crumbs, vinegar, and oil. Process on LOW, until smooth. Transfer to a large mixing bowl.

2. Add the tomatoes, cucumbers, onion, red pepper, yellow pepper, parsley, basil, marjoram, ice water, hot sauce, and salt and pepper to taste.

3. In the container of a blender or food processor, purée about one-fourth of the mixture, in batches, until smooth, and then return to the mixing bowl. Cover tightly and refrigerate for about 2 hours, or until well chilled.

4. When ready, serve in a chilled bowl with croutons on the side.

NEW HAMPSHIRE CARROT & APRICOT SOUP

Summer

Yield: about 6 to 8 servings

8-ounce package dried apricots
4 cups water
1 medium white onion, chopped
3 medium carrots, peeled and sliced
1 teaspoon ground cinnamon
1 bay leaf
1½ cups vegetable stock
½ cup unsweetened apple juice
½ cup unflavored yogurt
1 tablespoon honey

1. The day before, put the apricots in a bowl and just cover with water. Set aside until needed.
2. When ready, in a saucepan or soup kettle, combine the apricots with their liquid, onion, carrots, cinnamon, bay leaf and stock. Bring to a boil, then reduce to a simmer. Cover lightly, and cook, stirring, for about 1 hour, adding more water if needed.
3. Remove from heat, discard the bay leaf, stir in the yogurt and honey, and purée in batches, using a blender or food processor. Chill lightly and serve at room temperature with warmed honey on the side for drizzling over the soup.

Serve with a crushed honey graham cracker garnish on top.

Hint: Some would think that this is a crazy combination for a soup, but it works. Carrots have a tendency to be sweet, and apricots can tend to be sour.

1 tablespoon orange zest
3 large very ripe mangoes, pared
1 large navel orange, peeled and cut across into ¼-inch slices
1½ cups buttermilk
1½ cups fresh orange juice
3 teaspoons honey or to taste, warmed
1 tablespoon lemon or lime juice
8 small fresh mint leaves (optional)

ORANGE-MANGO SOUP

Summer

Yield: about 4 servings

1. In the container of a bender or food processor, purée the orange zest and mango together until smooth. Strain through a fine sieve, pressing with the back of a spoon. Pour the mixture into a bowl, cover tightly, and refrigerate for at least 1 hour.
2. When chilled, stir the buttermilk, orange juice, and 2 teaspoons honey into the chilled mixture. (If it appears too thick, add more buttermilk.)
3. Cover tightly and once more chill in the refrigerator for about 2 days.
4. When ready, add more lemon juice and 1 teaspoon honey. Pour into a chilled serving bowl, and float a slice of orange on top. Serve immediately, alone or as part of a menu, with a garnish of mint leaves.

Hint: The orange zest may be fresh or dried. If you use dried orange zest, reduce the measure to 1 teaspoon.

2 large ripe avocados, chopped
1 small bunch rocket (arugula) leaves
3 tablespoons fresh lemon juice
1 small clove garlic, peeled and chopped
¾ cup light cream
1 cup ice cubes
1 tablespoon grated ginger root
salt and pepper to taste
5 tablespoons tomato salsa
water as desired

ROCKET SOUP WITH TOMATO SALSA

Summer

Yield: about 4 to 6 servings

1. In a bowl, combine all the ingredients except the water, and then purée in batches using a food processor or blender.
2. Spoon into chilled bowls, and serve immediately with brushetta and whole cloves garlic, cut in half, on the side.

Hint: Rocket is also known as arugula or roquette. It is available in specialty produce markets and sold in small bunches with roots still attached.

SWEET & SPICY CARROT SOUP

Spring
Yield: about 6 to 8 servings

1½ cups cold water
¼ teaspoon salt
16-ounce package frozen carrots
1½ cups orange juice
½ teaspoon nutmeg
1 cup vegetable stock
1 orange, sliced thin for garnish
mint sprigs for garnish

1. In a soup kettle or Dutch oven, combine the water, salt and carrots. Bring to a boil, then reduce to a simmer, cover lightly, and cook for about 8 to 10 minutes, or until the carrots are very tender. Turn off the heat.
2. In the container of a blender, purée the carrots and cooking liquid until smooth.
3. In a large bowl, combine the puréed carrots with the orange juice, nutmeg, and stock, blending well. Cover the bowl and refrigerate 2 hours or until well chilled. Serve cold with a garnish of a fresh orange slice and a mint sprig on each bowl.

TART TOMATO & RED ONION SOUP

Autumn
Yield: about 6 servings

4 large fresh ripe tomatoes, quartered
1 large red onion, diced
3 tablespoons minced fresh basil leaves
½ medium clove garlic, peeled and minced
1 teaspoon granulated sugar
2 teaspoons mustard powder or 1 teaspoon prepared mustard
2 tablespoons lemon juice
2 tablespoons red wine vinegar
¼ cup olive oil
2 cups tomato juice
1 cup ice water
1 cup sour cream
2 teaspoons crushed dried dill weed for garnish

1. In the container of a blender or food processor, purée the tomatoes, red onion, basil leaves, garlic, sugar, and mustard until smooth.
2. In a large bowl, and using a wire whisk, beat the lemon juice, vinegar, oil, tomato juice and water together. Add the puréed mixture, stirring until blended.
3. Cover tightly, and refrigerate until thoroughly chilled, and then serve immediately, with a garnish of sour cream and dill weed.

Hint: Red onions have so much flavor, I can't imagine using anything else.

¾ cup blanched almonds
2 cloves garlic, peeled
1 clove garlic, peeled and crushed
salt and pepper to taste
4 slices stale white bread, crusts removed
4 cups ice water
7 tablespoons canola oil
3 tablespoons white wine vinegar
2 tablespoons sherry wine vinegar
1 tablespoon butter or margarine
6 slices white bread, crusts removed and diced
1½ cups seedless green grapes

1. In a blender, combine the almonds, 2 cloves garlic, and salt and pepper to taste. Process on HIGH until smooth.

2. Place 4 slices of bread in a bowl, and add 1 cup ice water. Soak through, squeeze out the water, and put the bread in the blender with the mixture.

3. With the processor running on LOW, add 6 tablespoons of the canola oil, and 1 cup ice water. Add the vinegars and blend on HIGH speed until smooth. Add 1 cup of water, and process on HIGH for about 1 minute. Pour into a bowl, and add the remaining cup of water. Adjust the salt and pepper to taste, cover tightly, and refrigerate for at least 8 hours.

4. When ready, prepare the croutons in a skillet. Heat the butter, remaining oil, and crushed garlic. Cook, stirring constantly, for about 2 minutes. Add the bread cubes and cook, tossing, until toasted.

5. Ladle the cold soup into chilled bowls, and sprinkle the croutons and green grapes on top. Serve immediately.

DESSERT SOUPS

Not everyone is familiar with dessert soups. But they're a delightful addition to a menu, whether you're dining alone or with company.

APPLE RAISIN SOUP

Summer

Yield: about 3 to 4 servings

2 cups unsweetened apple juice or cider
2 large McIntosh apples, pared and diced
¼ cup seedless raisins
2-inch cinnamon stick
1 tablespoon packed light brown sugar
1 tablespoon brandy or rum

1. In a soup kettle or Dutch oven, combine the apple juice, apples, raisins, and cinnamon. Bring to a boil, then reduce to a simmer, cover, and simmer for about 15 minutes, or until the apples are fork tender.

2. Remove from heat, stir in the brown sugar and brandy, cover tightly, and chill until ready to serve. When ready, discard the cinnamon stick, and serve as desired.

Hint: Apples and raisins have been married for years. They've been used in everything from cookies to bread to poultry stuffing, so they're a natural for soup. Most supermarkets carry a non-alcoholic brandy or rum flavoring next to the vanilla extract.

BREAD & BEER SOUP

Year-Round

Yield: about 12 servings

16-ounce loaf whole-wheat bread
16-ounce loaf pumpernickel bread
8½ cups water
8½ cups dark beer or ale
salt to taste
¾ cup granulated sugar
2 sticks cinnamon
1 tablespoon grated lemon zest
whipped heavy cream

1. Arrange the bread in the bottom of a soup kettle or very large saucepan, and pour the water over the top. Cover tightly and set aside in a cool place for at least 8 hours.

2. When ready, place the kettle on the stove, and simmer gently, stirring, until the mixture is very thick. Stir in the beer, salt, sugar, cinnamon, and lemon zest. Bring to a boil and remove from heat. Serve in heated bowls with a large daub of whipped cream on top.

Hint: Cooking eliminates the alcohol, leaving only the flavor of the beer.

1 cup canned pitted tart red cherries, undrained
1½ cups water
½ cup granulated sugar
1 tablespoon quick-cooking tapioca
⅛ teaspoon ground cloves
½ cup dry red wine

1. In a 1½-quart saucepan, combine the cherries, water, sugar, tapioca, and cloves. Set aside for about 5 minutes to allow the tapioca to moisten.
2. Bring to a boil. Then reduce to a simmer, cover, and cook, stirring frequently, for about 10 minutes. Remove from heat, stir in the wine, cover tightly, and chill for at least 2 hours.
3. When ready, stir to blend ingredients, and serve chilled.

1⅓ cups dry whole wheat bread crumbs
3 cups cold water or unsweetened apple juice
1 cup blanched almonds
2 medium cloves garlic
5 tablespoons extra virgin olive oil
1½ tablespoons amaretto
salt and pepper to taste

1. Place the crumbs in a bowl, and add ⅔ cup of the water.
2. In the container of a blender, combine the almonds and garlic, process on HIGH until very smooth. Stir this mixture into the bread crumbs.
3. Place the mixture into the container of a food processor. With the motor running on a slow speed, add the oil and amaretto, and process until smooth. Add the remaining water; adjust the salt and pepper to taste.
4. Refrigerate for about 4 hours or overnight. When ready, serve in chilled bowls, with a garnish of fruit slices and vanilla wafer crackers on the side.

CHILLED CURRIED PEACH SOUP

Summer

Yield: about 1 quart

1½ cups diced fresh peaches
2 cups vegetable stock or unsweetened apple juice
2 tablespoons margarine
1 small yellow onion, chopped
¾ teaspoon curry powder
pinch turmeric
1 small bay leaf
2 tablespoons all-purpose flour
salt and pepper to taste
peach-flavored yogurt for garnish

1. In the container of a blender or food processor, purée the peaches until smooth.
2. Melt the margarine in a soup kettle or Dutch oven, and sauté the onion until tender. Add the curry powder, turmeric, and bay leaf. Cook, stirring constantly, for about 2 minutes.
3. Turn off the heat, sprinkle on the flour, and stir until incorporated and smooth.
4. Return to the heat. Pouring in a narrow stream and stirring constantly, blend in the stock and peaches. Bring to a boil, then reduce to a simmer, and cook for about 3 minutes.
5. Turn off the heat, discard the bay leaf, and adjust the salt and pepper to taste. Cool slightly before chilling in the refrigerator for at least 1 hour.
6. When ready, and using a wire whisk, vigorously beat the soup, and then ladle into chilled soup bowls. Serve immediately with the peach-flavored yogurt on the side.

6 ounces fresh red currants
6 ounces fresh black currants
6 ounces fresh cranberries
1½ cups dry white wine
½ cup granulated sugar
2-inch cinnamon stick
1 tablespoon grated orange zest
juice of 1 orange
1¼ cups water
1 tablespoon crème de cassis liqueur (optional)
⅔ cup sour cream
black currant leaves to decorate (optional)

CURRANT & CRANBERRY SOUP

Summer
Yield: about 4 to 6 servings

1. In a soup kettle or Dutch oven, combine the red and the black currants, cranberries, wine, sugar, cinnamon, orange peel, juice, and water. Bring to a boil, then reduce to a simmer, and cook, stirring occasionally, for about 15 minutes, or until the fruit is tender.
2. Remove from heat. Discard the cinnamon stick.
3. In the container of a blender or food processor, purée the mix, in batches, until smooth, and then press through a fine sieve to remove the seeds. Pour into a bowl, cover tightly, and refrigerate for at least 2 hours.
4. When ready, using a wire whisk, beat in the crème de cassis until light, and ladle into chilled bowls. Daub a spoonful of sour cream on the top, swirl, and garnish with black currant leaves.

Amaretto-Flavored Sour Cream

⅔ cup sour cream
1 tablespoon amaretto

Beat vigorously together and chill until needed. Sprinkle with finely chopped almonds. Use this instead of the daub of plain sour cream to top the soup.

Hint: Red currants and black currants are wonderful when cooked and blended with cranberries.

CHILLED RASPBERRY ORANGE SOUP

Summer

Yield: about 12 servings

1½ tablespoons unflavored gelatin
⅓ cup cold water
¾ cup hot water
three 10-ounce packages frozen raspberries, thawed
3½ cups sour cream
1⅓ cups orange juice
1⅓ cups half-and-half
1⅓ cups white port wine
⅓ cup grenadine or sweet red wine
2 tablespoons crème de noyaux liqueur
salt and white pepper to taste
mint for garnish
whole raspberries for garnish

1. In a saucepan, soak the gelatin in the cold water for about 5 minutes. Then stir in the hot water, and heat, stirring until the gelatin is dissolved.
2. In the container of a blender or food processor, purée the raspberries until smooth. Then press through a fine sieve into a large bowl.
3. In the same bowl, add the sour cream, orange juice, half-and-half, sherry, grenadine, and crème de noyaux. Using a wire whisk, vigorously beat until smooth.
4. Cover and chill in the refrigerator for at least 8 hours or overnight. When ready, using the wire whisk, beat the soup, adjust the salt and pepper to taste, and ladle into chilled bowls. Garnish with mint and raspberries, and serve immediately.

CHILLED RHUBARB SOUP

Summer

Yield: about 6 servings

1 pint fresh strawberries
3 cups sliced fresh rhubarb
1¼ cups orange juice
½ to 1 cup granulated sugar
sliced kiwifruit or strawberries for garnish

1. In a large saucepan, combine the strawberries, rhubarb and orange juice. Bring to a boil, then reduce to a simmer, cover tightly and cook for about 10 minutes.
2. Turn off the heat, stir in the sugar, and then purée in batches, in the container of a blender or food processor until smooth. Pour into a bowl, cover tightly and refrigerate for about 2 hours, or until completely chilled.
3. To serve, ladle into chilled bowls, garnish with the fruit slices, and serve with a sweet bread or cracker on the side.

2 pints fresh strawberries
½ teaspoon instant tapioca
1 cup fresh unsweetened orange juice
1 tablespoon fresh lemon juice
cinnamon to taste
allspice to taste
½ cup granulated sugar
1 teaspoon lemon zest
1 cup buttermilk
1 thinly sliced lime for garnish
additional sliced strawberries for garnish

CLASSIC STRAWBERRY SOUP

Spring

Yield: about 6 servings

1. In a bowl, combine the tapioca and orange juice, and set aside for about 5 minutes. In the container of a blender or food processor, purée the strawberries until smooth.
2. In a saucepan, combine strawberries, tapioca and orange juice mix, lemon juice, cinnamon, and allspice to taste. Bring to a boil, then reduce to a simmer, and cook, stirring constantly, until thickened.
3. Turn off the heat. Stir in the sugar. Cool slightly, cover tightly, and refrigerate for about 2 hours, or until completely chilled.
4. To serve, stir in the lemon zest and buttermilk, and then using a wire whisk, stir vigorously before adjusting the sweetness to taste. Ladle into well-chilled bowls, garnish as desired, and serve immediately.

Hint: Strawberry soup is an old standard and thought to be one of the first cold berry soups created.

CHOCOLATE MINT SOUP

Year-Round

Yield: about 4 to 6 servings

12-ounce bottle stout beer
4 tablespoons bittersweet cocoa powder
¾ cup granulated sugar
1 cup soy milk
2 tablespoons crème de menthe

1. Two hours before needed, pour the beer into a saucepan and set aside.
2. When ready, place the saucepan containing the beer over a medium heat, add the cocoa powder, sugar, and soy milk. Heat to a slow boil (bubbles will form around the edge of the pan), and cook, stirring until the sugar is completely dissolved.
3. Remove from heat, and transfer to the container of a blender. Process on HIGH until foamy. Chill in the refrigerator until needed.
4. When ready, add the crème de menthe, garnish with fresh berries, and a sprig of fresh mint, and serve.

The crème de menthe is not optional. Although liquid mint flavoring can be substituted, the soup will not taste as good.

CHOCOLATE SOUP WITH WHIPPED CREAM

Year-Round

Yield: about 6 to 8 servings

2 teaspoons all-purpose flour
2 tablespoons skim milk
5 ¾ cups milk
½ pound semisweet chocolate, grated
⅔ cup granulated sugar
4 egg yolks
chocolate liqueur to taste
1 cup heavy cream, whipped to soft peaks

1. In a cup, combine the flour and skim milk, blending until smooth. Set aside.
2. In a soup kettle or Dutch oven, combine the milk and chocolate, and stirring constantly, bring to a boil. Stir in the flour mixture and cook, stirring constantly, until thickened. Turn off the heat and stir in the sugar. While vigorously stirring with a wire whisk, add the egg yolks.
3. Return to the heat and heat through, but do not allow to boil.
4. Turn off the heat and stir in the liqueur to taste. Ladle into bowls, and serve immediately with a spoonful of whipped cream on the top.

2 pounds ripe peaches, pared and diced
3 whole cloves
3 allspice berries
3 cardamom pods
2 cups fresh orange juice
3 tablespoons fresh lime juice
3 to 4 tablespoons warmed honey
1 teaspoon ground cinnamon
1 teaspoon ground ginger
1 cup unflavored yogurt or sour cream
1 tablespoon diced candied ginger
sprigs fresh mint for garnish

CINNAMON PEACH SOUP

Summer
Yield: about 4 to 6 servings

1. Tie the cloves, allspice, and cardamom in a 4-inch square of cheese cloth.
2. In a soup kettle or Dutch oven, combine the peaches, spice bag, orange juice, lime juice, honey, cinnamon, and ginger. Simmer for about 5 to 10 minutes, or until the fruit is well softened.
3. Remove from heat, discard the spice bundle, and cool the soup slightly.
4. In the container of a blender or food processor, purée the soup in batches until smooth. Place in a bowl, cover tightly, and chill for at least 4 hours.
5. Just before serving, and using a wire whisk, beat in the yogurt and stir in the ginger. Adjust the salt and pepper to taste, garnish with mint sprigs, and serve immediately.

Hint: The blend of cinnamon and good, ripe peaches is heavenly.

JUST PEACHY DESSERT SOUP

Summer

Yield: about 6 servings

3 pounds fresh ripe peaches
½ cup granulated sugar
1 cup water or unsweetened apple juice
3 to 4 tablespoons sugar
¼ cup fresh lemon or lime juice
1 tablespoon honey or dark corn syrup
1 teaspoon fresh rosemary
2 tablespoons sour cream or unflavored yogurt
coarsely crushed graham crackers

1. Place the peaches in a large saucepan or soup kettle, cover with hot water, bring to a boil, then reduce to a simmer, and cook for about 7 to 10 minutes. Remove from heat, reserving about ½ cup of the liquid. Drain, discarding the liquid, and when cooled slightly, pare the peaches, half, and discard the pit. Set aside.

2. In a clean soup kettle or saucepan, combine the ½ cup sugar, and water, bring to boil, and cook, stirring constantly, until the sugar is completely dissolved. Add about 6 of the peach halves, reduce to a simmer, and cook for about 10 to 12 minutes. Remove from heat and cool.

3. In a small saucepan, combine the remaining peaches, 3 tablespoons of sugar, lemon juice, honey, and rosemary. Simmer, stirring frequently for about 8 to 10 minutes. Remove from heat. Then in the container of a blender or food processor, purée the mixture, in batches, until smooth. Add the sour cream.

4. Ladle into heated bowls, float the remaining peach halves on the top, cut side down. Drizzle with amaretto dressing, and garnish with coarsely crushed graham crackers.

Amaretto Dressing

   2 tablespoons peach-flavored yogurt
   2 tablespoons amaretto

Blend until smooth. Drizzle over the top of the peaches.

four 1-ounce squares semisweet chocolate, chopped
8 cups milk
1 tablespoon unsalted butter
1 to 2 tablespoons granulated sugar
2½ teaspoons rice flour blended with 2 tablespoons milk
1 tablespoon cold water

1. In a large saucepan, or soup kettle, combine the chocolate, 2 cups of the milk, and butter. Bring to a slow boil, stirring frequently, until the chocolate is melted and the mixture is very smooth.

2. Add the sugar, pouring in a narrow stream and stirring until dissolved. Stirring constantly, add the remaining milk and rice flour mix. Cook, stirring frequently, until thickened. (Do not allow to come to a full boil.) Remove from heat, and serve with hot snowballs floating on the top.

Hint: The snowballs are little egg-white dumplings.

Snowballs
Yield: about 6 to 8 servings
   2 large egg whites
   3 tablespoons powdered sugar
   boiling water

1. Place about 3 inches of water in a saucepan, and bring to a boil.

2. In a bowl, using a wire whisk or electric mixer, beat the egg whites stiff but not dry. Continue beating as you add the sugar. Using a spoon, form the mixture into 6 to 8 balls. Drop the balls into the hot water, and cook, turning with a spoon, until set firm (about 5 minutes). Transfer to a wire rack, cover with paper towels to drain, and then float the balls on the soup as soon as they're ready.

PUMPKIN SPICE SOUP

Autumn

Yield: about 6 to 8 servings

16-ounce can pumpkin purée
two 13-ounce cans evaporated skim milk
1 tablespoon molasses
½ cup light corn syrup
½ teaspoon pumpkin pie spice
salt and pepper to taste
nutmeg to taste for garnish

1. In a large bowl, and using an electric mixer, blend the pumpkin, milk, molasses, corn syrup, and spice, until smooth.
2. Cover tightly, and refrigerate for 4 hours prior to serving. When ready, adjust the salt and pepper to taste, and sprinkle with nutmeg, just before serving.

STONED CHERRY SOUP

Summer

Yield: about 4 cups

1 pound fresh cherries, stoned
2 cups water or unsweetened apple juice
1 cup red wine
¼ cup granulated sugar
½ teaspoon orange zest
1 teaspoon cornstarch or arrowroot
heavy whipped cream

1. In a soup kettle or Dutch oven, combine the cherries, water, wine, sugar and zest. Stir vigorously, cover, and set aside for about 2 hours.
2. When ready, remove ¼ cup of juice from the mixture, and blend with the cornstarch. Bring the remaining mixture to a boil, reduce to a simmer, and cook, stirring for about 10 minutes.
3. Stir in the arrowroot mixture, and cook for about 2 to 5 minutes, or until thickened. Remove from heat. Ladle into heated bowls, and garnish with daubs of whipped cream.

Hint: This soup may also be served chilled. In that case, remove from heat, cool slightly, and refrigerate for about 2 hours or until chilled through. Ladle into chilled bowls, and garnish with chopped mint leaves.

1 cup quick-cooking tapioca
6 cups warm water
½ cup seedless raisins
8 ounces pitted prunes
2 cups black currant jelly
½ teaspoon ground cinnamon or nutmeg
pinch ground cloves
2 tablespoons distilled vinegar

1. Place the tapioca and water in a soup kettle or saucepan, bring to a boil, and cook, stirring until the tapioca is clear.
2. Add the raisins, prunes, currant jelly, cinnamon, cloves, and vinegar. Bring to a boil, reduce to a slow simmer, and cook uncovered, stirring occasionally, for about 90 minutes. Add more water, 1 tablespoon at a time, if needed.
3. Remove from heat. Ladle into heated bowls. Serve immediately, alone or with a piece of sweet cake or biscuits on the side.

1 large (about 3 pounds) fresh cantaloupe
2 tablespoons butter or margarine
1 tablespoon granulated sugar
1 tablespoon grated lemon zest
3 cups milk or soy milk
salt and pepper to taste

ZUPPA MELLONE

Summer

Yield: about 6 servings

1. Remove the rind and seeds from the cantaloupe, and then using a sharp knife, dice into small pieces. Reserve about 3 tablespoons of the diced cantaloupe.
2. Melt the butter in a soup kettle or large saucepan, and sauté the remaining cantaloupe for about 2 to 3 minutes. Add the sugar and lemon zest, and continue to cook, stirring for about 2 minutes. Add the milk, bring a slow boil, reduce to a simmer, cover lightly, and cook without stirring for about 15 minutes. Remove from heat.
3. In the container of a blender or food processor, purée the soup, in batches, until smooth. Pour into large bowl, and refrigerate for at least 2 hours, or until chilled through. When ready, serve in chilled bowls, with a garnish of chopped maraschino cherries, and vanilla wafers on the side.

Hint: Most people don't know that melon also grows very well in a cold climate.

INDEX

ABOUT THE AUTHOR

Author Gregg R. Gillespie has created many cookbooks, including *Tasty Treats for Demanding Dogs* (Sterling, 2001) as well as thousands of recipes for his best-selling Black Dog & Leventhal Publishers series: *1001 Cookie Recipes* (1995), *1001 Chocolate Treats* (1996), *1001 Snacks* (1997), *1001 Muffins* (1998), *1001 Chicken Recipes* (1999), *1001 Four-Ingredient Recipes* (2000), *201 Brownies and Bars* (2000), and many more.

Mr. Gillespie has lived all over the United States and currently tends his soup pot in upstate New York. He travels all over the world, collecting recipes, modifying and testing them, and adding them to his extensive collection. He enjoys napping with his pups, dreaming up new recipes, and discovering new ways to prepare food.